Homo Religiosus:

Are humans naturally predisposed to religion and supernatural beliefs? If so, does this naturalness provide a moral foundation for religious freedom? This volume offers a cross-disciplinary approach to these questions, engaging in a range of contemporary debates at the intersection of religion, cognitive science, sociology, anthropology, political science, epistemology, and moral philosophy. The contributors to this original and important volume present individual, sometimes opposing, points of view on the naturalness of religion thesis and its implications for religious freedom. Topics include the epistemological foundations of religion, the relationship between religion and health, and a discussion of the philosophical foundations of religious freedom as a natural, universal right, drawing implications for the normative role of religion in public life. By challenging dominant intellectual paradigms, such as the secularization thesis and the Enlightenment view of religion, the volume opens the door to a powerful and provocative reconceptualization of religious freedom.

Timothy Samuel Shah is Research Professor of Government at Baylor University's Institute for Studies of Religion; Director for International Research at the Religious Freedom Research Project at Georgetown University's Berkley Center for Religion, Peace & World Affairs; and Senior Director of the South and Southeast Asia Action Team with the Religious Freedom Institute.

Jack Friedman is pursuing his PhD in political science at the University of Maryland. He is a former project manager at Baylor University's Institute for Studies of Religion, and a former research assistant for the Religious Freedom Research Project at Georgetown University's Berkley Center for Religion, Peace, and World Affairs. He is also co-editor of *Religious Freedom and Gay Rights: Emerging Conflicts in the United States and Europe* (2016).

CAMBRIDGE STUDIES IN RELIGION, PHILOSOPHY, AND SOCIETY

SERIES EDITORS

PAUL MOSER, *Loyola University Chicago*
CHAD MEISTER, *Bethel College*

This is a series of interdisciplinary texts devoted to major-level courses in religion, philosophy, and related fields. It includes original, current, and wide-spanning contributions by leading scholars from various disciplines that (a) focus on the central academic topics in religion and philosophy, (b) are seminal and up-to-date regarding recent developments in scholarship on the various key topics, and (c) incorporate, with needed precision and depth, the major differing perspectives and backgrounds – the central voices on the major religions and the religious, philosophical, and sociological viewpoints that cover the intellectual landscape today. Cambridge Studies in Religion, Philosophy, and Society is a direct response to this recent and widespread interest and need.

RECENT BOOKS IN THE SERIES

Roger Trigg
Religious Diversity: Philosophical and Political Dimensions

John Cottingham
Philosophy of Religion: Towards a More Humane Approach

William J. Wainwright
Reason, Revelation, and Devotion: Inference and Argument in Religion

Gordon Graham
Philosophy, Art, and Religion: Understanding Faith and Creativity

Keith Ward
The Christian Idea of God: A Philosophical Foundation for Faith

Homo Religiosus?

*Exploring the Roots of Religion and Religious
Freedom in Human Experience*

Edited by

TIMOTHY SAMUEL SHAH

Baylor University and Georgetown University

JACK FRIEDMAN

University of Maryland

CAMBRIDGE
UNIVERSITY PRESS

CAMBRIDGE
UNIVERSITY PRESS

University Printing House, Cambridge CB2 8BS, United Kingdom

One Liberty Plaza, 20th Floor, New York, NY 10006, USA

477 Williamstown Road, Port Melbourne, VIC 3207, Australia

314–321, 3rd Floor, Plot 3, Splendor Forum, Jasola District Centre,
New Delhi – 110025, India

79 Anson Road, #06–04/06, Singapore 079906

Cambridge University Press is part of the University of Cambridge.

It furthers the University's mission by disseminating knowledge in the pursuit of
education, learning, and research at the highest international levels of excellence.

www.cambridge.org
Information on this title: www.cambridge.org/9781108422352
DOI: 10.1017/9781108381536

First published 2018

Printed in the United Kingdom by Clays, St Ives plc

A catalogue record for this publication is available from the British Library.

ISBN 978-1-108-42235-2 Hardback
ISBN 978-1-108-43395-2 Paperback

The philosophers of the eighteenth century explained the gradual weakening of beliefs in an altogether simple fashion. Religious zeal, they said, will be extinguished as freedom and enlightenment increase. It is unfortunate that the facts do not accord with this theory ...

The short space of sixty years will never confine the whole imagination of man; the incomplete joys of this world will never suffice for his heart. Alone among all the beings, man shows a natural disgust for existence and an immense desire to exist; he scorns life and fears nothingness. These different instincts constantly drive his soul toward contemplation of another world, and it is religion that guides it there. Religion is therefore only a particular form of hope, and it is as natural to the human heart as hope itself. Only by a kind of aberration of the intellect and with the aid of a sort of moral violence exercised on their own nature do men stray from religious beliefs; an invincible inclination leads them back to them. Disbelief is an accident; faith alone is the permanent state of humanity.

In considering religions from a purely human point of view, one can therefore say that all religions draw from man himself an element of strength that can never fail them, because it depends on one of the constituent principles of human nature.

— Alexis de Tocqueville, *Democracy in America*, Vol. I, Part 2, Chapter 9

Man can hardly be defined, ..., as an animal who makes tools; ants and beavers and many other animals make tools, in the sense that they make an apparatus. Man can be defined as an animal that makes dogmas. As he piles doctrine on doctrine and conclusion on conclusion in the formation of some tremendous scheme of philosophy and religion, he is, in the only legitimate sense of which the expression is capable, becoming more and more human. When he drops one doctrine after another in a refined skepticism, when he declines to tie himself to a system, when he says that he has outgrown definitions, when he says that he disbelieves in finality, when, in his own imagination, he sits as God, holding no form of creed but contemplating all, then he is by that very process sinking slowly backwards into the vagueness of vagrant animals and the unconsciousness of the grass. Trees have no dogmas. Turnips are singularly broad-minded.

— Gilbert Keith Chesterton, *Heretics*, Chapter XX

He has made everything beautiful in its time: also he has put eternity in men's hearts, so that no man can find out the work that God does from the beginning to the end.

— Ecclesiastes 3: 11

Contents

Contributors

Justin L. Barrett is Professor of Psychology at Fuller Theological Seminary.

Linda K. George is Professor of Sociology, Psychology and Neurosciences, and Psychiatry and Behavioral Sciences at Duke University.

Jordan Kiper is a graduate student at the University of Connecticut.

Jeff Levin is University Professor of Epidemiology and Population Health at Baylor University.

Stephen Macedo is Professor of Politics and the University Center for Human Values at Princeton University.

Alvin Plantinga is John A. O'Brien Emeritus Professor of Philosophy at the University of Notre Dame.

Christian Smith is William R. Kenan, Jr. Professor of Sociology at the University of Notre Dame.

Ernest Sosa is Board of Governors Professor of Philosophy at Rutgers University.

Richard Sosis is James Barnett Professor of Humanistic Anthropology at the University of Connecticut.

Christopher Tollefsen is Distinguished Professor of Philosophy at the University of South Carolina.

Nicholas Wolterstorff is Noah Porter Professor Emeritus of Philosophical Theology at Yale University.

Phil Zuckerman is Professor of Sociology and Secular Studies at Pitzer College.

Introduction

Jack Friedman and Timothy Samuel Shah

I

This volume invites a renewed inquiry into an enduring question: are humans naturally religious? Do they possess a set of common characteristics transcending time, place, and culture that incline them towards religion? The answer, according to growing body of research in the cognitive and evolutionary sciences of religion, appears to be yes. "A general theme emerging from ... cognitive and evolutionary studies," cognitive scientists Justin Barrett and Robert Lanman posit, "is the *Naturalness of Religion Thesis*," by which they mean that:

> [r]eligious thought and action are common across human history and cultures because of their relationship with particular naturally occurring human cognitive systems. Religion springs naturally from the way ordinary human cognitive systems interact with ordinary human social and natural environments.[1]

Echoing this notion is cognitive scientist Paul Bloom, who likewise holds that "there are certain early emerging cognitive biases that make it natural to believe in Gods and spirits, in an afterlife, and in the divine creation of the universe."[2] Religion appears to be natural, therefore, insofar as religious belief and action are deeply embedded in human cognition, in the way people ordinarily think about and experience the world.

This does not mean that religious belief and religious observance are necessary or inevitable for all people, or that the human brain is ineluctably

---

[1] Justin L. Barrett and Jonathan Lanman, "The Science of Religious Beliefs," *Religion* 38 (2008): 110.

[2] Paul Bloom, "Religion is Natural," *Developmental Science* 10 (2007): 150.

"hard-wired" for religion. To appreciate this caveat, one need only observe the many people throughout the world who do not profess any religious belief at all, and the still more who do not regularly engage in religious practices. What the naturalness of religion thesis does suggest, however, is that the conscious and sustained rejection of religion and of the super-natural, wherever it might arise, may require an overriding mechanism – a cultural and intellectual scaffolding – that the acceptance of religion does not similarly require.[3] Accordingly, although religious beliefs and practices may not manifest in all people, the naturalness of religion thesis maintains that these phenomena still arise *naturally* – that is, they regularly and predictably emerge through the normal development of human cognitive systems, without necessarily relying on the presence of "artificial" cultural or intellectual support structures.

What does this mean in practice? Apart from merely satisfying a healthy sense of scientific curiosity, why does the naturalness of religion thesis *matter*? What, if any, are the ethical, political, or social implications of a presumptive "naturalness of religion?" Does it suggest anything consequential about human nature, the nature of religion, or the proper ordering of society?

Of the many possible angles from which to approach these questions, this volume pursues one in particular: how might the naturalness of religion bear on the proposition – now increasingly contested – that there is a natural or human right to religious freedom that transcends at least to some degree the confines of particular historical and cultural contexts?[4] The chapters that follow revolve around this central question.

---

[3] Justin L. Barrett, "The Relative Unnaturalness of Atheism: On Why Geertz and Markusson Are Both Right and Wrong," *Religion 40* (2010): 169–172.

[4] It is tempting and common to speak of a universal right to religious freedom, or to claim that all people everywhere enjoy a right to religious freedom. Speaking loosely, there is truth in these claims. Speaking strictly, however, Nicholas Wolterstorff is surely correct when he points out in this volume that it may be more accurate to speak of a natural right to religious freedom than a universal right to religious freedom. All people with certain ordinary natural capacities can exercise religion, and they therefore possess a natural right to religious freedom in view of the fact that they possess the natural capacities that make it possible for them to exercise religion. But of course there are people in whom these capacities are not operative, and therefore there are people who do not possess a right to religious freedom in any ordinary or relevant sense. As Wolterstorff explains, "the right to free exercise of one's religion is, strictly speaking, a permission-right rather than a claim-right. That is, it is the right to be permitted to do something rather than the right to be treated a certain way by others. Of course, corresponding to the permission-right to exercise one's religion freely is the claim-right, with respect to others, that they not interfere with one's exercise of one's religion." Nicholas Wolterstorff, "Why There Is a

In so doing, they grapple, directly or indirectly, with what we shall term the "anthropological case" for religious freedom. The anthropological case for religious freedom is the contention that the viability and strength of the argument for religious freedom as a natural or human right rests at least partly on the claim that our species of *Homo sapiens* is also in a strong sense *Homo religiosus*, to borrow a phrase of Mircea Eliade.[5] In other words, a case for the right to religious freedom can be derived in part from evidence that religion is in some sense not merely epiphenomenal or accidental, but a regular and predictable feature of human nature and human experience, taken as a whole.

A proper examination of this question requires, first, that we situate the idea of religion's naturalness in a broader historical and philosophical context: a task to which we now turn.

The Enlightenment Critique and Secularization Theory

Notwithstanding a growing body of supporting evidence in the cognitive and evolutionary sciences of religion, the naturalness of religion thesis remains an underdog of sorts. It runs counter to a predominant narrative in Western thought, according to which religion is an irrational – indeed, unnatural – quirk of the credulous human mind, sustained only through inculcation, socialization, and indoctrination. Far from being natural, intrinsic, or otherwise fundamental to human experience, religion therefore represents a profoundly unnatural, unnecessary, and undesirable condition. While this outlook has remained prevalent and thriving in the present day, thanks in part to a vociferous cohort of self-styled "brights" and "new atheists,"[6] its origins lie in the intellectual revolutions of the seventeenth and eighteenth centuries, otherwise known as the Enlightenment.

Natural Right to Religious Freedom," this volume, p. 214. Wolterstorff adds, "the bearers of the natural right to religious freedom are those human beings who are capable of functioning as persons. A human being in a permanent coma cannot exercise her religion; accordingly, the issue of whether she has the permission-right to do so freely does not arise." Wolterstorff, this volume, p. 218, n. 49.

[5] Mircea Eliade, *The Sacred and the Profane: The Nature of Religion*, trans. Willard R. Trask (New York: Harcourt, 1987 [1957]).

[6] See, for example, Richard Dawkins, *The God Delusion* (London: Bantam Press, 2006); Daniel Dennett, *Breaking the Spell: Religion as a Natural Phenomenon* (New York: Viking, 2006); Christopher Hitchens, *God is Not Great: How Religion Poisons Everything* (New York: Twelve, 2009); Sam Harris, *The End of Faith: Religion, Terror, and the Future of Reason* (New York: W. W. Norton & Co., 2004).

Central to the Enlightenment was a broad and incisive critique of religion, fueled by fresh memories of Europe's sanguinary Wars of Religion, the tyranny of the day's reigning theocracies, and the nascent but profound revelations of modern science. On the one hand, these converging factors gave rise to a fervent anticlericalism that opposed the unbridled political authority of religious institutions.[7] On the other hand, the Enlightenment engineered a major paradigm shift with respect to religion and its role vis-à-vis society. At the risk of oversimplification, one can nevertheless generalize that throughout most of Western history, religion and religious truth had been a taken-for-granted cornerstone – or canopy, to use a different metaphor – of individual, social, and political life.[8] But the Enlightenment paradigm upended this prevailing norm with the development of two mutually constituting but dialectically opposed ideas: "religion" and "modernity." Religion came to be defined as essentially irrational, superstitious, despotic, and regressive, in contradistinction to "modernity," which signified the domain of reason, science, freedom, peace, economic prosperity, and universal human progress. Religion came to embody a dystopian past, while modernity assumed the symbolism of an idealized and inevitable future. Where religion lingered in the so-called "modern" world, it did so as an anachronism, a vestige of humanity's primitive origins quivering in dynamic tension with a world that is and must be, by its very nature, hostile to religion's presence. With modernity and religion locked in mutual opposition, and with the arc of history trending inexorably towards modernity, the demise of religion appeared a foregone conclusion.

Perhaps no-one anticipated the demise of religion with more breathtaking confidence than the French philosophe Nicolas de Condorcet in his *Outlines of an Historical View of the Progress of the Human Mind* (1795). For Condorcet, modernity first dawned during the Renaissance, for it was then that "the sciences and philosophy threw off the yoke of authority" – by which he meant, of course, theological and ecclesiastical authority. And reason's complete global triumph is only a matter of time.

---

[7] The legacy of Enlightenment anticlericalism appears, paradigmatically, in French laïcité, but also in other models of secularism that seek to contain, or privatize, religion.

[8] See, for example, Peter L. Berger, *The Sacred Canopy: Elements of a Sociological Theory of Religion* (New York: Knopf, 1968); and Charles Taylor, *A Secular Age* (Cambridge: Harvard University Press, 2007).

[E]very thing seems to be preparing the speedy downfall of the religions of the East, which, partaking of the abjectness of their ministers, left almost exclusively to the people, and, in the majority of countries, considered by powerful men as political institutions only, no longer threaten to retain human reason in a state of hopeless bondage, and in the eternal shackles of infancy ... Then will arrive the moment in which the sun will observe in its course free nations only, acknowledging no other master than their reason; in which tyrants and slaves, priests and their stupid or hypocritical instruments, will no longer exist but in history and upon the stage; in which our only concern will be to lament their past victims and dupes, and, by the recollection of their horrid enormities, to exercise a vigilant circumspection, that we may be able instantly to recognise and effectually to stifle by the force of reason, the seeds of superstition and tyranny, should they ever presume again to make their appearance upon the earth.[9]

This assumption of religion's inevitable demise – in which "priests and their stupid or hypocritical instruments, will no longer exist but in history and upon the stage" – persisted among many Enlightenment thinkers as a taken-for-granted and almost subliminal doctrine, so effortless in its certitude that it scarcely needed explication. Indeed, it had become such an article of Enlightenment faith that Tocqueville, for example, could observe that the eighteenth-century philosophers brimmed with the simple confidence that "[r]eligious zeal ... will be extinguished as freedom and enlightenment increase."[10] In the early- to mid-twentieth century, this predictive assumption began to receive systematic attention from a new generation of social scientists who sought to elaborate and explain the precise mechanisms of religion's "inevitable" extinction through new social scientific theories and methodologies. Over the twentieth century, this effort generated a vibrant scholarly paradigm and school of thought that came to be known as secularization theory.

The "theory of secularization," in fact, refers not to one theory, but to a diverse array of theories, each of which postulates some type – and often very different types – of religious decline. Like the Enlightenment critique of religion, these theories generally presuppose a fundamental incompatibility between religion and modernity. But unlike the Enlightenment critique, in which religious decline was *implicit* in an overarching religion–modernity dialectic, secularization theory sought to offer a systematic description and explanation of religious decline in terms of identifiable

[9] Marquis de and Marie-Jean-Antoine-Nicolas Caritat Condorcet, *Outlines of an Historical View of the Progress of the Human Mind* (Philadelphia: Lang and Ultick, 1795).
[10] Alexis de Tocqueville, *Democracy in America*, ed. J. P. Mayer, trans. George Lawrence (New York: Harper & Row, 1988 [1835, 1840]).

social, political, economic, and psychological processes.[11] Some secularization theories predict that the advancement of science and technology undermines religion's core metaphysical claims, thereby rendering religious belief cognitively hopeless.[12] Some posit that economic development and improved material well-being lead to decreased religiosity.[13] In other cases, secularization theories pivot on the idea of *structural differentiation*, the theory that religion declines as society fragments into discrete compartments or spheres. And from the theory of structural differentiation, still others extrapolate secularization as religious *privatization*, according to which religion, confined to a single differentiated sphere, is forced to retreat from public life and take up residence on the margins of society.[14]

Despite these and other theoretical variations, secularization theory's common denominator has been an effort to outline the conditions, mechanisms, and parameters of a presupposed religious decline. What "decline" means may differ from theory to theory.[15] But most retain an unflagging assumption that some sort of decline is on the horizon, if not already here, drawing closer and closer in lockstep with secular modernity. The sociologist of religion Peter Berger gave this assumption paradigmatic expression when in 1968 he predicted – with a confidence that recalled Condorcet – that "by the 21st century, religious believers are likely to be found only in small sects, huddled together to resist a worldwide secular culture."[16]

Now well into the second decade of the twenty-first century, however, it is hard to see evidence of an irresistible, "worldwide secular culture," or the reduction of the world's believers into small, isolated sects. (To his credit, Berger long ago abandoned his commitment to secularization as a

---

[11] For an analytical overview and critique of secularization theories, see Timothy Samuel Shah, "Secular Militancy as an Obstacle to Peacebuilding," in *The Oxford Handbook of Religion, Conflict, and Peacebuilding*, eds. Atalia Omer, R. Scott Appleby, and David Little (New York and Oxford: Oxford University Press, 2015), 380–406.

[12] See Berger, *Sacred Canopy*.

[13] Pippa Norris and Ronald Inglehart, *Sacred and Secular: Religion and Politics Worldwide* (New York: Cambridge University Press, 2011).

[14] See Thomas Luckmann, *The Invisible Religion: The Problem of Religion in Modern Society* (New York: Macmillan, 1967).

[15] For instance, religious decline might refer to an erosion of influence or authority at the level of individuals, societies, or institutions. See Karel Dobbelaere, "Bryan Wilson's Contributions to the Study of Secularization," *Social Compass* 53 (2006): 141–146.

[16] Peter Berger, "A Bleak Outlook is Seen for Religion," *The New York Times*, February 25, 1968, p. 3.

description or prediction of modern global reality, as we note below.) To the contrary, for instance, a recent Pew study reports that 5.8 billion people – or 84 percent of the world's population – affiliate themselves with one religion or another.[17] Although some indicators of decreased religiosity have undoubtedly been documented in certain regions, such as in the nations of industrialized Europe and, more recently, in North America,[18] global religiosity remains decidedly high, and in some cases, resurgent. The rise of Pentecostal Evangelicalism in Latin America, Asia and Africa, of political Islam in North Africa and the Middle East, and of Hindu nationalism in India, offer just a few examples of socially and politically consequential religious resurgence that vex the traditional narrative of secularization.[19]

What this suggests is that history does not march to a uniform, linear beat of *secularization*. Rather, it moves dynamically and unpredictably to the protean rhythms of religious *transformation*, whereby religion is not necessarily in decline, but constantly in flux. In recent years, appreciation of this important nuance has prompted many erstwhile champions of secularization theory to lose faith in its explanatory potential.[20] Even Berger, though an influential secularization theorist in the 1960s, demonstrated uncommon scholarly humility in 1998 when he acknowledged that "the world today ... is as furiously religious as it ever was, and in some places more so than ever. This means that a whole body of literature

---

[17] Pew Research Center, "The Global Religious Landscape: A Report on the Size and Distribution of the World's Major Religious Groups as of 2010," December 2012, www.pewforum.org/files/2014/01/global-religion-full.pdf.

[18] For instance, see Pew Research Center, "America's Changing Religious Landscape: Christians Decline Sharply as Share of Population; Unaffiliated and Other Faiths Continue to Grow," May 12, 2015, http://assets.pewresearch.org/wp-content/uploads/sites/11/2015/05/RLS-08–26-full-report.pdf. The study found that religiously unaffiliated American adults – persons eighteen years or older who identify as atheist, agnostic or "noting in particular" – now make up 22.8 percent of the national population, a six-point increase since 2007.

[19] For one account of religion's highly public and politically consequential resurgence around the world, see Monica Duffy Toft, Daniel Philpott, and Timothy Samuel Shah, *God's Century: Resurgent Religion and Global Politics* (New York: W. W. Norton & Company, 2011).

[20] For instance, see Rodney Stark, "Secularization, R.I.P," *Sociology of Religion* 60 (1999): 249–273. Others are more apprehensive about a wholesale withdrawal from secularization theory. For example, see Jose Casanova, *Public Religions in the Modern World* (Chicago: University of Chicago Press, 1994). Casanova argues that secularization theory is actually comprised of three distinct theses: (1) decline in religious beliefs and practices, (2) religious privatization, and (3) the differentiation of spheres. He rejects theses (1) and (2), but maintains that thesis (3) is still tenable.

by historians and social scientists loosely labeled 'secularization theory' is essentially mistaken."[21]

Where does this leave us? The aim here is not to engage in polemics against secularization theory but to bring critical attention to the assumptions that undergird its theoretical infrastructure. And it is precisely these assumptions that scholarly exploration of the "natural-ness of religion" invites us to interrogate from a fresh perspective. Following the Enlightenment critique of religion, as we have seen, secularization theory presupposes that religion is inherently irrational, superstitious, and anti-modern. Just as important, however, is that secularization theory presupposes that religion is a contingent product of culture and society. On this assumption, religion enjoys no enduring connection to human nature or experience, much less human flourish-ing, but thrives only when a narrow set of artificial conditions and supports are in place. Remove these conditions and supports – think of Condorcet's "priests and their stupid or hypocritical instruments" – and religion will suffer a "speedy downfall" (Condorcet again). The implication is that religion is an inessential and indeed temporary facet of the human condition that is doomed in the face of the comprehensive and revolutionary transformations wrought by modernity. While reli-gion may have once seemed necessary, intrinsic, and *natural*, it becomes optional, extraneous, and *unnatural* when humanity shakes off the "shackles" of tradition, and human beings appear for the first time on the stage of history in their natural and pristine form as "unencumbered selves."[22]

If religion is not constitutive of "humanness," however, and if it is primed to evanesce in the face of an ever-approaching modernity, then we must wonder about what seems to be the stubborn persistence of religion in the modern world. What can explain that? What is more, how do we

---

[21] Peter L. Berger, "The Desecularization of the World: A Global Overview," in *The Desecularization of the World: Resurgent Religion and World Politics*, ed. Peter L. Berger (Washington: Eerdmans/Ethics and Public Policy Center, 1999), 2.

[22] The phrase is Michael Sandel's and is at the heart of his critique of John Rawls's *Theory of Justice* (Cambridge: Harvard University Press, 1971). To summarize, Sandel's critique is that Rawls' liberal theory of justice is based on a metaphysical view that human beings are essentially "unencumbered" – i.e., not essentially constituted by their religious and moral commitments, including their commitments to the good, but essentially separate from, and prior to, these commitments as individualist and instrumentalist choosers in a marketplace. See Michael J. Sandel, *Liberalism and the Limits of Justice*, 2nd ed. (Cambridge and New York: Cambridge University Press, 1988 [1982]).

square the enduring presence of religion, or some manifestation thereof, in all cultures throughout human history?[23]

Perhaps, as this volume explores, the answer lies in religion's naturalness. Could it be that religion has survived the advent of modernization because it arises, not by accident or from contingent circumstances that obtain one moment and disappear the next, but from capacities and dispositions that are intrinsic to human nature and persist, albeit in different forms, across time and space?

Naturalness of Religion and Religious Freedom

If religion is indeed natural, how – if at all – does this bear on the idea of a natural or human right to religious freedom? Does the naturalness of religion generate *ipso facto* a corresponding right to religious freedom; one that all people possess by virtue of their humanity?

At first glance, the notion that a natural or human right to religious freedom logically follows from religion's naturalness encounters the problem, most famously raised by philosopher David Hume,[24] of deriving an "ought" from an "is." Hume maintained that empirical observations are value-free, and therefore cannot, by themselves, generate prescriptive or moral claims, such as rights, duties, obligations, codes of conduct, or any similar ethical norms. Along this line of reasoning, "naturalness," as an empirical observation, merely describes how the world *is*; it does not prescribe how it *ought* to be. To assign value on the basis of naturalness would be to make an unjustified deductive leap. It would be, in Hume's estimation, to commit the logical fallacy of deriving an "ought" from an "is." Accordingly, the naturalness of religion cannot by itself generate a normative claim about a right to religious freedom. In order for people to have such a right, the Humean argument would insist, religion or the assertion of its naturalness must also be accompanied by some sort of normative principle – for instance, that religion is a basic human good, and goods should be safeguarded and promoted. But if this is the case, does religion derive its goodness from its naturalness? If not, then naturalness is irrelevant to the equation; some other factor must be responsible for the good of religion that

---

[23] For one excellent discussion of religion's remarkable persistence across human history, which also offers to explain this persistence, see Martin Riesebrodt, *The Promise of Salvation: A Theory of Religion* (Chicago: University of Chicago Press, 2010).

[24] David Hume, *A Treatise on Human Nature*, Book III, Section I, available at: www.gutenberg.org/files/4705/4705-h/4705-h.htm#link2H_4_0085.

generates the right to religious freedom. If so, then a further principle is needed to bridge the gap between naturalness and rights – for instance, that what is natural is ipso facto good, valuable, and therefore worth protecting. But such a principle is question-begging, for it supposes that religion derives its goodness from its naturalness, while defining naturalness as necessarily good. And the principle raises still more undercutting questions: what does it mean to be "natural?" Is immoral, but otherwise seemingly "natural," behavior – such as dishonesty, violence, or oppression – thereby sanctioned? And by the same token, are things that we value, but which do not appear particularly natural or easily sustained – such as absence of suffering, peace, or democracy – therefore unworthy of protection? From the Humean perspective, religion must be proven to have value for human beings and their societies, but such a value must necessarily be independent of any putative naturalness.

On the other hand, and without dispensing with the Humean argument, there may nonetheless be a compelling *prima facie* and practical case for deriving a right to religious freedom from religion's naturalness. What if religion were not simply natural but also *fundamental* and *intrinsic* in some way to human nature and experience? If religion were natural to human beings in this sense, religion would be at the core of human life: so much so that suppressing it – depriving human beings of their freedom to exercise religion – would necessarily run against the grain of human nature and therefore require extreme and sustained coercion. Such coercion would not only be extreme and probably violent in itself, but it would presumably elicit a violent and reactive backlash, all of which would perpetuate human suffering and stifle progress.[25] As cognitive scientists Roger Trigg and Justin Barrett point out, "one of the most important facts that CSR [cognitive science of religion] draws attention to is that religion is not a private and idiosyncratic phenomenon with no place on the public stage. It is there at the heart of human activity," which means that "religion cannot, and must not, be ignored in public life ... The more religion is privatized and thought to be beyond the scope of public, rational discussion, the more it will fester and break out in all kinds of unpredictable and undesirable ways."[26]

---

[25] For a powerful argument that secular schemes of national "liberation" have often invited a strong religious backlash, see the recent illuminating study by Michael Walzer, *The Paradox of Liberation: Secular Revolutions and Religious Counterrevolutions* (New Haven: Yale University Press, 2016).

[26] Roger Trigg and Justin Barrett, introduction to *The Roots of Religion: Exploring the Cognitive Science of Religion*, eds. Trigg and Barrett (Farnham: Ashgate Publishing, 2014), 10.

In other words, if there were a strong case that religion were natural to human experience in the robust sense of being tied to fundamental or basic features of our humanity, this would all by itself suggest a need to carve out greater freedom for religion and its free exercise in society. If religion really were "at the heart of human activity," presumably it should be restricted or excluded in society for only the gravest reasons. Likewise, if religion were natural in this strong sense, we should expect – as a matter of empirical fact – that religion *cannot* be suppressed, or eradicated, or dismissed as obsolescent without highly disruptive and deleterious consequences for individuals and for society as a whole.

On this last point, a case study of Bolshevik Russia proves instructive. Upon taking power in the Russian Revolution of 1917, Vladimir Lenin and his Bolshevik party undertook a systematic program of religious repression, persecution, and reeducation. Churches were forcibly closed, expropriated, or plundered; the ringing of church bells was forbidden; monks and priests were banished from their posts, deprived of the right to vote, and discouraged from wearing clerical garb in public; and those who defied Soviet authority were often sent to labor camps or simply shot.[27]

The Bolshevik's anti-religious campaign was unique in the history of religious persecution. Unlike most cases throughout history, it did not follow religious or sectarian lines; neither the perpetrators nor the victims belonged to any one religion or sect in particular. Instead, for the Bolshevik party the target was religion itself. Following Karl Marx, Lenin's Bolsheviks viewed religion as the pathological expression of human suffering – the "opiate of the masses" – engendered by capitalism. As such, not only was religion a dispensable human construct devoid of any enduring or inherent relation to humanity, it was an obstacle to overcome in the name of human progress and flourishing.

If the Marxist–Leninist rationale for persecuting religion rings familiar, it is because it is of the same pedigree as the Enlightenment critique of religion. If,

---

[27] Paul Froese, *The Plot to Kill God: Findings from the Soviet Experiment in Secularization* (Berkeley, CA: University of California Press, 2008). See also Sheila Fitzpatrick, *Stalin's Peasants: Resistance and Survival in the Russian Village After Collectivization* (New York: Oxford University Press, 1994): 33; and "Revelations from Russian Archives: Anti-religious Campaigns," Library of Congress, www.loc.gov/exhibits/archives/anti.ht ml. Other notable examples of "forced secularization" (i.e., attempts to eliminate, restrict or suppress religion through coercive, top-down measures) have occurred in Kemalist Turkey under Atatürk, Cambodia under the Khmer Rouge, Maoist China, and in Mexico with the anti-clerical constitutions of 1857 and especially 1917. On the Chinese case, see Fenggang Yang, *Religion in China: Survival and Revival Under Communist Rule* (New York: Oxford University Press, 2011).

as the Enlightenment critique suggests, religion embodies humanity's primitive appetite for irrational superstition, then religion is something to overcome in the name of human progress. If religion's demise is foretold in the prophecy of modernization, as secularization theory supposes, then religion can be safely disregarded until its final disappearance. And if religion is something retrograde to overcome as well as doomed to disappear in any case, it hardly seems worthy of legal or political protection. Indeed, efforts to accelerate its inevitable downfall would simply amount to being on the side of human progress or, as the now-popular saying goes, "the right side of history."

But just as antireligious ideologies could plausibly justify denials of religious freedom on the grounds that religion is untethered to human nature and inimical to human progress, perhaps evidence that religion emerges from core human capacities and fosters the flourishing of human nature can plausibly supply a powerful (though perhaps not sufficient) defense of religious freedom. For if religion is embedded in the basic mechanisms of human cognition, if it is an anthropological constant, and if it even seems closely tied to human well-being and proper functioning, then religious freedom may be justifiable as a defense not so much of the rights of religion as of the rights of humanity and of core dimensions of human experience. On this reading, religious freedom would be the right to be human, for to be human is, in part, to be *Homo religiosus*.

On Definitions

Before proceeding, a final point of clarification is in order. The contributors to this volume face the challenge, inherent in most careful analyses, of definition. As we have already seen, what we mean by "natural" has an unavoidable bearing on the import of the naturalness of religion thesis. Similarly, we must inquire into the nature of the thing that we are calling natural: what is religion? Is it a system of personal beliefs about the supernatural? The expression of these beliefs in a comprehensive way of life? Sacred rituals performed collectively in public or private? Or perhaps adherence to a sacred moral code? Unfortunately, there is no easy answer, no consensus definition to fall back on. Religion is, and will likely remain, what W. B. Gallie termed an "essentially contested concept" – one that is widely recognized and used, but whose meaning remains in perpetual dispute.[28]

---

[28] W. B. Gallie, *Philosophy and the Historical Understanding* (New York: Schocken Books, 1964): 157–192. Also see John Gray, "On Liberty, Liberalism and Essential Contestability," *British Journal of Political Science* 8, no. 4 (1978): 385–402.

Without a conclusive and generally recognized definition of religion to fall back on, is the present analysis of religion's naturalness rendered futile? Perhaps so, according to an increasing number of scholars of religion subscribing to an "anti-essentialist" school of thought. In the view of "anti-essentialists," any attempt to define religion will ultimately fail, because "religion" is an invented category, a cultural construct with no intelligible or stable referent corresponding in the empirical world. When we look across the world and across history, we find no self-contained, common phenomenon that an impartial spectator could safely identify as "religion." Rather, what we find is "a diverse, shifting, and multiform field of lived religious practice."[29] This field exhibits radical and incommensurable variation across time and place, because, in the end, "there is no transhistorical and transcultural essence of religion. What counts as religion and what does not in any given context is contestable and depends on who has the power and authority to define religion at any given time and place."[30]

The locus of that power to define, the "anti-essentialists" roundly surmise, is and was the modern Protestant West. There, "religion" arose from the collective consciousness of Western culture through a process of reification, which involved "mentally making religion into a thing, gradually coming to conceive it as an objective systematic entity."[31] But in the view of the "anti-essentialists," this artificial projection was not merely a passive intellectual fallacy; it was a positive bid by European hegemons to arrogate to themselves political power over religion. Religion, once diffused and embedded in everyday life, became an isolated, stand-alone entity distinct from other spheres of life and conceived mainly in terms of individuals' interior theological beliefs. Defined as both discrete and interior, "religion" could be newly identified, cordoned off from politics, and subjected to political subordination and control.[32]

---

[29] Elizabeth Shakman Hurd, *Beyond Religious Freedom: The New Global Politics of Religion* (Chicago: University of Chicago Press, 2015), 6.

[30] William T. Cavanaugh, *The Myth of Religious Violence: Secular Ideology and the Roots of Modern Conflict* (New York: Oxford University Press, 2009), 59.

[31] Wilfred Cantwell Smith, *The Meaning and End of Religion* (Minneapolis: Fortress Press, 1991), 51.

[32] For an attempt to characterize recent anti-essentialist critiques of religion and religious freedom along these lines, and also to offer a critical assessment, see Daniel Philpott and Timothy Samuel Shah, "In Defense of Religious Freedom: New Critics of a Beleaguered Human Right," *Journal of Law and Religion*, 31, no. 3 (November 2016): 380–395.

Taken to its logical conclusion, the "anti-essentialist" outlook precludes fruitful discussion of religion. If "religion" signifies nothing objectively real or enduring, if its meaning is historically dynamic and purely
socially constructed, then it is impossible to know what we are talking
about when we talk about religion. To invoke it in any sense is to impute
to it a non-existing essence, thereby manufacturing the very thing we wish
to apprehend in its denuded form. Further, if "religion" represents nothing more than a hegemonic project of the modern West, then its continued
use suggests something more insidious at work: a covert maneuver to
commandeer and exert political control.

Now, there is some well-founded reason for the "anti-essentialist"
angst. The signifier "religion" is an imperfect vehicle for communicating
an imperfectly understood empirical phenomenon. But the problem the
anti-essentialists fixate on is hardly unique to religion. As Nicholas
Wolterstorff points out in his contribution to this volume, all terms and
concepts are conditioned by the history of their use. Like religion, the
concept "democracy," to take one example, was forged within a specific
cultural milieu, shaped by historical contingencies, and lacks an agreed
upon definition. But surely this does not mean we cannot engage in
productive discussions about democracy, nor does it require that we jettison the concept itself or refer to it only in scare quotes.

Aware that religion, like many other words and concepts, is inherently
ambiguous, this volume nevertheless maintains an outlook rooted in
"critical realism." As helpfully articulated by sociologist Christian Smith
in this volume, a critical-realist approach to religion recognizes that the
concept "religion" does in fact correspond to a confluence of phenomena
that really exist in the world, even if these phenomena can never be
perfectly disentangled from other phenomena. Following the late
University of Chicago religion scholar Martin Riesebrodt, Smith proposes
the following definitional approach:

Riesebrodt defines religion as, "a complex of practices that are based on the
premise of the existence of superhuman powers, whether personal or
impersonal, that are generally invisible." People are religious, according to
Riesebrodt, in order to tap those superhuman powers to help them avert and
solve problems they confront – from getting hurt or sick to suffering a bad
existence after death. In his approach, Riesebrodt asks us to focus on religious
"liturgical" practices rather than abstract belief systems, which avoids a number
of problems in other definitions. This substantive (not functional) definition of
religion provides traction for identifying when religion is present or absent,
stronger or weaker in human life. At the same time, however, it does not focus
us on the centrality of religious beliefs, but on religious practices. That deftly

sidesteps the misguided thrust of recent radical-constructionist accounts of religion that liquidate the subject.[33]

Though religion is always intertwined with other phenomena, it *can* be singled out for analysis, if always inadequately. Though efforts to define religion are often vulnerable to political manipulation, it *can* be identified in ways that are not wholly governed by ulterior motives to control and dominate.

The first step is to ask, what are some qualities that characterize this really existing thing called "religion?" In accordance with the focus on religious practices Christian Smith articulates above, following Riesebrodt, a major theme of this volume is that religion is not simply a set of personal beliefs about the divine or a matter of engaging in purely private religious practices. As Nicholas Wolterstorff argues in this volume, religion involves both a religious "temperament" – a belief in a transcendent realm that orders and explains existence – and the expression of that "temperament" in a way of life. This means that, in addition to a private dimension of personal belief, religion is also characterized by a public dimension in which people, consciously or unconsciously, translate their beliefs into a wide variety of everyday activities that are necessarily also social, political, cultural, economic, etc.

What difference does an awareness of this public dimension make? Why does defining religion as such matter at all? Apart from the well-founded desire for conceptual clarity, it matters because any conception of religious freedom necessarily depends on what we mean by "religion." To define religion is to demarcate the boundaries of freedom; it is to determine which pursuits, values, practices, and social spaces are entitled to protection. On one hand, if "religion" is simply a matter of personal belief and private worship, then "religious freedom" is merely the right to form beliefs and express them privately in one's home or place of worship. To be sure, this private dimension is crucial to any robust definition of religious freedom. On the other hand, if Trigg and Barrett are correct in claiming that religion involves a public dimension, in part by virtue of its natural foundations in human cognition, a dimension in which religious faith invariably enters public life and informs a comprehensive way of life, then religious freedom necessarily includes the right to exercise one's religion in public life, including political and economic life. Failure to recognize this public dimension renders a vast swath of vital religious activity wholly unprotected.

---

[33] Christian Smith, this volume, p. 43.

II

This volume is the product of a seminar series hosted by the Religious Freedom Project at Georgetown University's Berkley Center for Religion, Peace, and World Affairs between 2010 and 2013. Under the leadership of Director Thomas F. Farr and Director for International Research Timothy Shah, this Project was, and its successor, the Religious Freedom Research Project, remains, the only university-based program in the world devoted exclusively to interdisciplinary inquiry about religious freedom – what it is and how it is related to the well-being of individuals and societies everywhere. It has been generously supported by the John Templeton Foundation and enjoys a close partnership with the Institute for Studies of Religion at Baylor University.[34]

The seminar series hosted by the Religious Freedom Project brought together some of the world's most eminent scholars from a wide range of disciplines to discuss the overarching theme of "Religion as Intrinsic to Human Experience" and what bearing, if any, this theme has on the nature, universality, and status of religious freedom. Each of the five seminars began with an "anchor scholar" who presented an original essay, followed by a response from another expert in the relevant field. The structure of this volume reflects the structure of the seminar series: the articles are paired in a presentation–response format.

The first four chapters examine the naturalness of religion from the perspective of sociology, cognitive science, and evolutionary science. In the first article, "Are Human Beings Naturally Religious?" sociologist Christian Smith cautions that this question invariably depends on what we mean by "natural." If "natural" refers to an innate and irrepressible drive guaranteeing that all people are bound to become religious in some obvious and conventional sense, then religion is not natural. After all, Smith points out, many people live quite happily without religion. Similarly, if by "natural" we mean all human cultures have a functional

---

[34] The seminar series that generated the papers and debates featured in this volume was sponsored by the Religious Freedom Project, which operated from 2011 to 2016 thanks to generous funding by the Templeton Foundation and Baylor University. A successor organization, the Religious Freedom Research Project (RFRP), continues to carry out programs of research and public education on religious freedom. In particular, the RFRP brings together leading scholars and policymakers to examine and debate the evolution of international religious freedom policy and the contributions of religious liberty to the global common good. The RFRP is made possible by a partnership with Baylor University's Institute for Studies of Religion and the generous support of the Bradley Foundation.

need for making religion a "centrally defining feature of society," then religion is not natural in this sense either, for societies vary in how religion figures into their way of life. However, Smith proposes that religion *is* natural in the sense that all people possess "a complex set of innate features, capacities, powers, limitations, and tendencies that capacitate them to be religious (i.e., to think, perceive, feel, imagine, desire, and act religiously), and that, under the right conditions, tend to predispose and direct them toward religion."

According to Smith, these features, capacities, powers, limitations, and tendencies are constitutive of the human condition, which is itself characterized by four components that collectively incline people towards religion. First, the human condition is one of epistemological uncertainty. We lack access to foundational and indubitable truths because all knowledge is built on propositions, or chains of propositions, that must eventually take something as given. This makes humans fundamentally believing – not knowing – animals. Second, humans gravitate towards religion because they possess the capacity and desire to solve problems, especially ones that cannot be answered in finite, immanent terms. Third, humans desire to answer important "Life Questions" for which religion has historically been a primary source of answers. And fourth, humans are drawn to religion by what Charles Taylor has called the moral condition of unavoidably operating with reference to strong normative commitments, ones that are not culturally relative or based on personal preference.[35]

Shifting to religious freedom, Smith argues that insofar as religion is natural, and hence fundamental to human experience, governments professing a commitment to the values of liberty, equality, and human flourishing must therefore be prepared to protect religious freedom. To restrict religious freedom would be to suppress the basic capacities that make us human. What's more, because religion is such a fundamental aspect of the human condition, attempts to suppress, control, or eliminate it are bound to require highly coercive and violent measures. The preservation of religious freedom, then, is a practical necessity as a precondition for peace and social justice.

In "Are Human Beings Naturally Religious? A Response to Christian Smith," sociologist Phil Zuckerman concedes Smith's point that humans

---

[35] See Charles Taylor's *Sources of the Self: The Making of the Modern Identity* (Cambridge: Harvard university Press, 1989) and his *The Ethics of Authenticity* (Cambridge: Harvard University Press, 2008 [1991]).

exhibit an innate capacity for religion, which, under the right conditions, compels them towards religion. But he emphasizes that humans also display natural capacities and tendencies to be nonreligious. And if both capacities and tendencies are natural, then "naturalness" is emptied of the conceptual substance necessary to say anything meaningful and useful about anything. For, under the right conditions, Zuckerman observes, people are predisposed to do just about anything. Under the right conditions, "people can be directed towards genocide, organ-donating, communism, graffiti-spraying . . . Thus, to say that 'under the right conditions' people tend to be religious, isn't saying anything much at all." Accordingly, Zuckerman finds religion's naturalness (or lack thereof) to be immaterial to the question of religious freedom. Religious freedom should not be based on religion's naturalness but on the concern for *human* freedom more generally.

The third contribution is by Justin Barrett, a leading authority on the cognitive science of religion. In "On the Naturalness of Religion and Religious Freedom," he articulates and defends the naturalness of religion thesis from his extensive research in the cognitive sciences: "because of the nature of human minds, religious expression in beliefs and practices is nearly inevitable in most people." To support this claim, Barrett draws on budding research from the cognitive science of religion in particular, which suggests that religious behavior is embedded in several basic features of human cognition. First, human minds are predisposed to detect intentional agents in their environments even when they are not visibly present. Second, once an agent is detected, human minds are inclined to draw inferences about the motivations and internal experiences of those agents. Third, human minds are conditioned to seek purpose and meaning in the natural world. When combined, these three modes of cognition generate religious reasoning about supernatural entities, such as gods and spirits, and about the natural world, to which human beings naturally impute teleological order and design.

Religion is natural, therefore, because it arises easily and predictably from basic human cognitive systems. In other words, it is our natural cognitive systems – as they interact with our surroundings – that predispose us towards religious ideas and behaviors. In calling religion "natural" in this way, however, Barrett takes care to point out that he does not advocate the view that religion is unalterable or "hard-wired' into the human brain. Religion is natural in that it is characterized by "ease, automaticity and fluency" – that is, basic religious beliefs and behaviors require little conscious attention or effort.

Barrett makes a further distinction between two types of naturalness. When behaviors require significant practice, cultivation, or expertise to reach the point of "ease, automaticity and fluency," they are forms of *practiced* naturalness. However, when they arise as part of normal human development, requiring little or no practice, they represent *maturational naturalness*. The central thrust of Barrett's chapter is that religion is maturationally natural, arising from within normal cognitive faculties, which include our hypersensitive tendency to perceive intentional agents, to reason about what other agents are experiencing, and to seek purpose in the natural world. Importantly, these faculties are embedded in our normal cognitive functioning; they are not "add-ons to human nature or systems that we can simply turn off." The implication is that, contrary to claims that religion constitutes pathogenic or defective behavior, human cognitive systems are properly functioning when they generate religious beliefs and religious forms of engagement with our surroundings. Likewise, contrary to the assertion that religion requires an elaborate cultural scaffolding to support it, this suggests that religiosity is anchored in unmediated human experience.

On the subject of religious freedom, Barrett limits his focus to the practical consequences of coercively suppressing religion. He cites "adaptationist" evolutionary accounts of religion, which theorize that religion is adaptive because, for instance, it promotes cooperation and sociability. If religion has an important and adaptive social function, as adaptationist theories maintain, then it follows that inhibiting religious beliefs and practices will have deleterious effects on society, as examples of religious repression in places such as Soviet Russia and Maoist China arguably show.

If Barrett's interests lie in the cognitive mechanisms that make religious beliefs and practices nearly inevitable in most people, the authors of the next essay are interested in the evolutionary mechanisms responsible for religion's prominence in human culture. Responding to Barrett in "Sacred Versus Secular Values: Cognitive and Evolutionary Sciences of Religion and Their Implications for Religious Freedom," evolutionary anthropologists Richard Sosis and Jordan Kiper propose signaling theory as the best explanation for why and how religious beliefs and practices emerged and persisted in human history. Signaling theory hypothesizes that because religious activities often involve exacting and costly work, participating in them functions as a reliable indicator of trustworthiness and group commitment. Since trustworthiness and group commitment create the advantageous qualities of solidarity and cooperativeness within a community, religion has an adaptive value.

Viewing religion through the lens of signaling theory leads Sosis and Kiper to conclude, contrary to Barrett, that religion is most likely a case of *practiced* rather than *maturational* naturalness. In a way that is akin to Riesebrodt's practice-centered definition of religion, Sosis and Kiper understand religion primarily as a complex system of ritual practices that signal group commitment. As such, however, they conclude that religion does not naturally arise with ease, fluency and automaticity. Instead, it must be cultivated through continuous performances and sustained cultural norms. Furthermore, Sosis and Kiper conclude that whether religion is an instance of maturational or practiced naturalness does not bear on the right to religious freedom. "[R]eligious freedom may be a fundamental political right that deserves legal protection, but the justification and the level of such protections cannot be derived from the naturalness of religion alone," they write. Deriving religious freedom from its supposed naturalness would confuse scientific description with normative prescription – two realms that do not overlap, in their view, in part because of their insistence on a Humean distinction between fact and value, description and prescription. At the same time, Sosis and Kiper emphasize that their research provides an indirect argument for religious freedom insofar as it "highlight[s] the potentially negative unintended consequences of manipulating or interfering with religious systems from the outside."[36]

The fifth and sixth chapters turn to the theme of religion and its relationship to human rationality. In "Theism, Naturalism, and Rationality," philosopher of religion Alvin Plantinga explores the epistemological foundations of religious belief, on one hand, and materialistic naturalism, on the other. First, he argues that religious belief – here, belief in an omniscient, omnipotent, omnibenevolent God who created the world – is rational, but only if it is true. That is, the rationality of religious belief is predicated on the existence of a God who intentionally equipped humans with the capacity to perceive Him. Second, Plantinga pursues the stronger claim that belief in God is foundational to rationality – or, more precisely, that theism is a precondition for our confidence that our epistemic powers are reliable, while naturalism (which is necessarily atheistic) is incompatible with a rational confidence in our epistemic competence.

---

[36] Sosis and Kiper, "Sacred Versus Secular Values: Cognitive and Evolutionary Sciences of Religion and Their Implications for Religious Freedom," this volume, p. 90.

He advances this two-pronged argument primarily by way of showing that atheistic naturalism, which denies the existence of God or anything like God and presumes that human beings emerged through blind evolutionary processes, is self-defeating. If, as naturalism maintains, humans evolved via unguided natural selection, and if natural selection favors adaptive behaviors and beliefs irrespective of their truth content (which he suggests is the case), then it follows that humans would have evolved to have adaptive – but not necessarily true – beliefs. If naturalism were true, the naturalist cannot have confidence in the reliability of her beliefs, including her belief in naturalism. And to argue in defense of the naturalistic worldview would be to rely on the very thing under question, namely the reliability of one's capacity to reason. This strong argument for the disjunction of rationality and naturalism and the conjunction of rationality and theistic religion provides an unusual and compelling argument for religious freedom. "Protecting the right to religious *belief*, therefore, simply amounts to a recognition of the human condition, a condition in which human rationality coheres best with a 'supernaturalist metaphysics' and a religiously grounded account of human cognition."[37]

In "Alvin Plantinga on Theism, Naturalism, and Rationality," philosopher Ernest Sosa raises several objections to Plantinga's argument. First, Sosa highlights an inconsistency that tends to arise for theists confronted with the argument from evil. The argument from evil holds that the presence of evil in the world undermines the existence of an omnibenevolent, omnipotent, omniscient God. A typical theistic rejoinder to the argument from evil is that humans simply cannot comprehend God's mysterious ways. But by the same token, Sosa contends, theists cannot claim to know that God created humans with reliable cognitive faculties. It would, of course, be logically inconsistent to claim ignorance on the problem of evil while expressing confidence in God's epistemic benevolence.

Next, Sosa objects to Plantinga's depiction of naturalism as the outlook that all phenomena are reducible to the activity of rote physical processes. This characterization is overly narrow, Sosa maintains, for "not all

---

[37] For other statements of Plantinga's argument that belief in naturalism is incompatible with a rational confidence in the reliability of our epistemic powers, see Alvin Plantinga, *Warrant and Proper Function* (Oxford: Oxford University Press, 1993), particularly at p. 237, and Alvin Plantinga, *Where the Conflict Really Lies: Science, Religion, and Naturalism* (New York: Oxford University Press, 2012).

naturalists are so radically reductive as Plantinga's materialist is supposed to be." In the final thrust of the article, Sosa challenges Plantinga's assertion that the naturalist has an "undefeated defeater" for the claim that brute evolutionary forces produce reliable beliefs. Naturalism is only self-defeating, Sosa reminds us, if it has no recourse to establish the reliability of knowledge under naturalist conditions other than on the basis of its own tainted logic. "We do have another basis, however, beyond anything we may believe about the etiology of our faculties." That basis, he suggests, is the faculties themselves, which we tacitly accept and rely on for reliable information in everyday situations.

From here, the volume shifts to the theme of religion and health. Does religion promote well-being? Does it help maintain healthy populations? Is it a necessary condition for human flourishing? If so, if religion is indeed central to health, what are the implications for religious freedom? Does it generate or strengthen an obligation of governments to guarantee religious freedom for all people?

"Research on Religion and Health: Time to Be Born Again?" by sociologist Linda K. George, offers an illuminating appraisal of religion and health science to date. In it, George argues the field has become stagnant. Though religion–health science has demonstrated positive links between religion and mental and physical health, it has failed to explain these associational links in terms of a compelling, comprehensive theory. Instead, it has approached these links through a tunnel vision fixed on several standard causal mechanisms, such as that religious participation fosters social support systems, promotes healthy behaviors, and provides psychological resources – none of which, she contends, have advanced our understanding of the religion–health relationship appreciably. Future research should aim to broach new theoretical questions around these causal links, including: Does engagement in multiple dimensions of religious participation yield greater health benefits than engagement in one or two? How does the experience of having a close personal relationship with God – a surprisingly unexplored dimension of religious participation – bear on health outcomes? And to what extent might religious contexts (i.e., social, cultural, and geographic settings) promote health over and above personal religious involvement? In addition to formulating new questions, George recommends that future research develop and employ new methodological strategies. Specifically, future research should shift from examining micro-level causal mechanisms, to exploring meta-theories capable of accounting for society-wide belief structures and systems of meaning. She suspects that the religion–health relationship will ultimately lie in the comprehensive worldview and system of meaning religion often provides – imparting coherence and purpose to people's lives – rather than any particular religious belief or practice. "As articulated throughout this volume, there are many reasons to sustain, protect, and celebrate religious freedom," George notes in the conclusion of her essay. "Although imperfectly understood, the well-documented links between religion and human health are surely one of those reasons."[38]

Building on George's appraisal, epidemiologist Jeff Levin proposes new directions for research on religion and health in "Religion, Health, and Happiness: An Epidemiologist's Perspective." Levin reiterates George's observation that religion, viewed from a wide lens and across populations, is associated with salutary health outcomes. But this association remains poorly understood due to a lack of properly conceived and applied conceptual, theoretical, and methodological questions. Levin confronts this problem from an epidemiological lens, which begins by clarifying concepts such as "religion" and "health" and then moves on to exploring theoretical questions about how or why religion affects health. Here, Levin advises two methodological adjustments. First, he urges the design of longitudinal studies able to track religion–health impacts on individuals over time and across populations. Second, he advocates studies that are capable of evaluating policy-relevant questions. Such questions include, among others, whether religion improves well-being by mitigating the risks or health consequences of "deviant" behavior, whether religion is a necessary or sufficient condition of a good life, and whether religious institutions can function as effective conduits for the promotion of democratic values and global security.

While the chapters by George and Levin are designed to raise more questions than definitive answers, and while an adequate understanding of the associations between religion and health requires further research into underlying causal mechanisms and pathways, we can in the meantime begin to consider tentative implications for religious freedom. If religion plays a distinctive role in promoting mental and physical health and is therefore conducive to human well-being, then we may have yet another reason to believe that religion is not only natural in the sense of persistent and widely present in human experience but also natural in the sense of *good* for human nature and conducive to human fulfillment. Insofar as governments are charged with promoting the public good, the positive

[38] George, this volume, p. 176.

relationship between religion and health offers a promising line of justification for a right to religious freedom.

However, this line of justification also raises further questions. If religion is a *good* or a source of good, is this by itself sufficient to generate a *right* to religious freedom? Can a good *ipso facto* generate a corresponding right? Taking another step back, what is the relationship between the *good* of religion and the *right* to religious freedom? And to address that question, we must take another step back and ask: what is the most philosophically defensible account of the basis for rights in the first place?

The final three chapters address these lingering questions in a discussion of the nature of the right to religious freedom, its philosophical grounding, and its practical meaning. In "Why There Is a Natural Right to Religious Freedom," philosopher Nicholas Wolterstorff argues that religious freedom is indeed a universal *right*, but not primarily because religion is a human *good*. It would be a great *good*, he points out, if an art museum gave him a prized Rembrandt painting, but it doesn't therefore follow that he has a right to this luxury. I have a right to X when I have a strong moral claim or entitlement to X, such that I would be wronged if I were denied X. Few of us would claim that we have a strong moral entitlement to a Rembrandt painting, as great a good as it might be in our lives, or that we're being wronged if we don't possess one. On the other hand, many of us would claim that we have a strong claim and entitlement to religious freedom, and that we would be gravely wronged if that right were denied or disrespected. All this suggests that we don't have a right to a Rembrandt painting, that we do have a right to religious freedom, and that something being a great good (such as a Rembrandt painting) can't be sufficient to generate or justify a right.

What, then, is the basis of the kind of strong moral claim or entitlement that constitutes a natural right? What kind of right does it yield? Wolterstorff argues that our right to religious freedom is *natural*, meaning that it arises from the essential, or natural, features of human experience. Unlike political or legal rights, which exist only in the context of conferring political institutions or laws, natural rights may be ignored or violated, but they cannot be taken away, because they spring from an enduring source, such as human nature, independent of particular historical contingencies.

Inasmuch as the right to religious freedom arises naturally – that is, from human nature – the existence and contours of this right will fundamentally depend on our understanding of human nature – on what is deemed natural, intrinsic, or essential to being human. Wolterstorff thus builds his case for the natural right to religious freedom by way of introducing a conception of the human person as possessing a special worth, or "dignity," that stems from several basic human capacities. Whereas philosophical accounts of human dignity typically place emphasis on the capacity for rational and normative agency, the ability to use reason to determine one's actions and moral choices, Wolterstorff concludes that mere rationality provides an insufficient basis for grounding human dignity. If the capacity for rational agency is what gives humans dignity, he observes, people with an undeveloped sense of rational agency, such as children or the mentally impaired, would lack dignity. Without rejecting the relevance of rational and normative agency wholesale, Wolterstorff identifies two other natural capacities and suggests both that they are important sources of human dignity and "directly relevant to the natural right to free exercise of one's religion." The first is "the capacity to interpret reality and one's place therein." Although how we interpret reality is variable, the capacity itself is amazing. The second is the capacity to form a "valorized identity." People assign importance to various facets of their lives – their beliefs, commitments, plans of action, memories, persons, animals, objects, etc. – thereby creating a web and hierarchy of normative priorities. All human action begins with, and functions in relation to, this network of values. Christian Smith in this volume refers to this fact as the human "moral condition" of "unavoidably operating in relation to moral beliefs." Try as we might, we cannot escape the normative commitments that layer our conscious and unconscious decisions.

Taken together, Wolterstorff argues that these capacities endow human beings with a powerful and intrinsic value – a dignity – that demands respect. Respecting human dignity is not simply a matter of sustaining biological life; it is a matter of sustaining a specific kind of life, a life worthy of dignified beings. And central to a life of dignity is the free exercise of basic human capacities. Conversely, to experience the deliberate stifling or blockage of one's basic capacities is to suffer a kind of dehumanization.

How exactly does the right to religious freedom emerge from these two extraordinary human capacities? The answer hinges on Wolterstorff's conceptualization of religion, which consists, first, of a belief in the presence of an all-encompassing transcendent order responsible for the creation of the universe and our place, purpose, and value therein; and second, the expression of this belief in a comprehensive way of life. Formulated as such, the free exercise of religion is vital to the

capacity for transcendent interpretation and valorized identity formation. To the extent that people have a right to exercise these capacities,
then, people have a right to religious freedom. In short, we have a right to
religious freedom because our capacity to be religious is intimately
related to our dignity as humans.

In his final analysis, Wolterstorff turns his attention from the philosophical foundations of religious freedom as a natural right to the limits
justifiably imposed on religious liberty by liberal democratic societies.
Wolterstorff observes that the political philosophy of liberalism typically
revolves around the idea that religion must "shape-up" in specific ways in
order to conform to the norms and values of liberal democracy. It is true,
Wolterstorff grants, that religion must behave according to a set of governing democratic rules. But the problem is that the rules and boundaries
regulating the relationship between religion and the state are often tilted in
favor of the state, to the detriment of religious citizens. Wolterstorff
ascribes this bias to the legacy of liberalism, which traditionally insists
that religion must assume a privatized role vis-à-vis the state and society –
that, in other words, religious citizens and their institutions should not
interfere in the public affairs of government and politics.

Though Wolterstorff deals with several variants of the idea that religion should "shape up," his critique of political philosopher John Rawls
merits special attention. Rawls argued that in deliberation over important
political issues, citizens and public officials should refrain from invoking
purely religious reasons in support of their positions. Instead, they should
make an effort to justify their views with reasons and evidence that are
"public" in nature – that is, reasons whose cogency is widely accessible,
depending not on particular metaphysical or moral doctrines, but on
widely shared principles and modes of reasoning.[39] In effect, Rawls's
notion of public reason circumscribes the types of arguments that religious
persons can and should make in public.[40] This restriction is necessary,
Rawls judged, because religious reasons are essentially incapable of being

---

[39] See John Rawls, *Political Liberalism* (New York: Columbia University Press, 1993). Also
see John Rawls, "The Idea of Public Reason Revisited," *The University of Chicago Law
Review* 64 (1997): 765–807.

[40] Not coercively through laws and policies, however. In "The Idea of Public Reason
Revisited," Rawls stresses that the idea of public reason expresses a moral duty, not a
legal one. He points out that, were public reason to contain a legal duty, it would be
incompatible with freedom of speech. See Rawls, "The Idea of Public Reason Revisited,"
769.

a broadly acceptable basis on which to exercise public authority over the diverse members of a political community.

Wolterstorff contends that Rawls's idea of public reason imposes an impractical and unjustified restriction on religious freedom. Some religious individuals, he points out, orient their lives wholly in terms of their religion. Whether taught to rely on religious reason as a matter of ethical principle or as a matter of fidelity to God, they know no way to reason about matters of justice and their obligations to their fellow citizens outside of the teachings of their religious faith. For these people, the requirements of public reason may be too great a demand. They may simply not be capable of articulating their political positions in "public" terms as Rawls would like, or they may be able to do so only with undue strain. In either case, Wolterstorff maintains, public reason imposes a unilateral burden on religious individuals to act against their consciences by conforming to secular norms – a kind of burden that public reason does not impose on nonreligious individuals. Pressing the natural right to religious freedom to its logical conclusion, Wolterstorff argues that this right requires, among other things, that deeply religious individuals enjoy the freedom to bring their religious reasons to bear on matters of public import.

The next chapter, "Religious Liberty, Human Dignity, and Human Goods" by philosopher Christopher Tollefsen, contrasts Wolterstorff's right- and dignity-based account of religious freedom with an alternative, goods-based approach. Recall that Wolterstorff argues that a right (in this case, religious liberty) cannot be derived solely from a good (in this case, religion). In order to establish a right to religious freedom, something else must be introduced to the equation. This "something else" is human dignity, grounded in several unique human capacities. Although religion, exercised via these capacities, may entail the actualization of a great good, Wolterstorff concludes that we have a *right* to religious freedom primarily because the free exercise of religion is closely tied to human capacities central to human dignity.

Like Wolterstorff, Tollefsen thinks that we have a natural right to religious freedom, and agrees that human dignity plays a role in characterizing and grounding this right. But unlike Wolterstorff, he thinks that this right follows primarily from the *good* of religion. Human dignity, Tollefsen contends, lacks meaning and substance unless it is ordered to an account of those basic human goods that orient and motivate human reasoning and choosing. Religion is one such basic good because it provides "intelligible reason for action by promising something desirable."

Moreover, religion is a *basic* good because it is desired for its own sake, not for some other good. And it is a *common* good because its goodness provides reasons for action that multiple agents can share and act on cooperatively.

To appreciate how Tollefsen's characterization of religion as a *basic common good* bears on the question of rights, we should consider the broader philosophical context in which Tollefsen reasons. As a proponent of the "new natural law theory,"[41] Tollefsen views human action as fundamentally motivated by, and directed towards, the pursuit of basic goods whose attainment enables human flourishing. Hence the protection of goods, especially basic ones like religion, is a fundamental precondition of human well-being. People have a right to religious freedom first and foremost because religion, as a basic good, is indispensable to human flourishing.

Although this goods-based account does not rely on a notion of human dignity, Tollefsen stresses that the two are not incompatible. In fact, human dignity, defined as the excellence of beings with the capacity for reasoned choice, is central to the pursuit of goods. To pursue and participate in the basic goods, one must have the capacity to freely *choose* which goods to pursue, and in what way. Human dignity and human goods are thus closely conjoined in Tollefsen's account. He cautions, however, that human dignity lacks normative force when it is not coupled with a corresponding account of human goods. This problem manifests in at least two ways.

On the one hand, if, as is often the case, human dignity is understood simply as the capacity to be self-determining, the injunction to protect dignity may indirectly lend credence to actions that are actually antithetical to basic goods. Taking assisted suicide, for example – an issue that is often framed and justified in terms of human dignity as self-determination – Tollefsen notes that the decision to end one's own life runs counter to the good of protecting life. If life is a basic good, and if basic goods are inextricable to human dignity, then the choice to die not only defies the moral obligation to protect the good of life, but it violates human dignity itself. On the other hand, though Wolterstorff does not reduce human dignity to the mere capacity for reasoned choice, or self-determination, Tollefsen maintains that Wolterstorff's account nevertheless succumbs to a different fallacy,

---

[41] See Christopher Tollefsen, "New Natural Law Theory," *LYCEUM* vol. X, no. 1 (2008), available at: http://lyceumphilosophy.com/10-1/Lyceum-10-1-Tollefsen.pdf.

that of failing to order human capacities to the goods to which they are naturally oriented. As a result, the correlative rights produced under Wolterstorff's account of dignity are better equipped to protect bare capacities than they are to protect basic goods – a crucial problem if the point of rights is to protect basic goods, as Tollefsen claims.

The volume's final article, "Public Reason and Democratic Values: A Reply to Nicholas Wolterstorff" by political philosopher Stephen Macedo, registers a critique of Wolterstorff's objection to the Rawlsian-style project of getting religion to "shape up." Does Rawls's demand for religious "shaping up" – that religious individuals offer only "public" reasons for their political positions – impose on those individuals an unjustifiable burden, as Wolterstorff alleges? Moreover, is Wolterstorff on solid ground when he suggests that such a demand is also unrealistic in practice, as many people are either not in the habit of conforming to this particular demand, or are simply unable on principle or in good conscience to translate their deeply held religious beliefs into "public," secular language? Macedo demurs on both normative and descriptive grounds. The idea of public reason, he argues, reflects an important obligation of democratic citizenship, one that, in fact, is already prevalent and ingrained in American political culture. This is the obligation of citizens living in a pluralistic society to find "common ground" when determining basic and mutually binding rights, laws, and policies. When making important political decisions, in other words, people should try to justify their positions using "public" reasons and evidence that members of all faiths (or no faith) could share, not ones based on particular religious doctrine. The failure or refusal to offer publicly accessible justifications for one's political positions, Macedo concludes, is a clear violation of this obligation.

As it happens, however, most American citizens, even avowedly religious ones, already subscribe to the practice of public reasoning, Macedo points out. Studies of conservative Christian activists and advocacy organizations demonstrate that the religious often go to great lengths to formulate philosophical arguments not grounded in sacred scripture. Similarly, Macedo cites the debate over gay rights in America, which has shifted from a framework of overtly religious claims to more secular claims that invoke matters of public interest, such as procreation and the well-being of children. According to Macedo, this shift is, at least in part, a practical and necessary response to the fact of religious diversity. Because people disagree about religion in fundamental and intractable ways, purely religious arguments will often fail to win broad support.

Only by framing arguments in terms that adherents of multiple faiths could endorse is it possible for such arguments to prevail.

III

So is religion a feature of human nature and experience, and if it is, does religion's naturalness help to ground and shape a defensible account of religious freedom as a natural or human right? The questions are of both practical and theoretical importance for at least two reasons.

The first reason is that religious freedom is in global crisis. According to the Pew Research Center, roughly 5.5 billion people, or 77 percent of the world's population, were living with "high" or "very high" restrictions on religion in 2013.[42] And this crisis is not abating. Though restrictions stemming from governments and "social hostilities"[43] declined modestly from 2012 to 2013, social hostilities have experienced a steady rise, from afflicting 45 percent of the global population in 2007 to 73 percent in 2013. Government restrictions have likewise trended up from 58 percent in 2007 to 63 percent in 2013. Taken together, the share of the global population living with "high" or "very high" restrictions on religion, whether government restrictions or those stemming from social hostilities, has increased from 68 percent in 2007 to 77 percent in 2013.[44]

Moreover, contrary to what one might expect, these increases are not limited to non-Western parts of the world. For instance, from 2011 to 2012, Europe was one of the few regions to experience a rise in government religious restrictions.[45] Between 2007 and 2013, government restrictions in Europe rose from a median score of 1.6 to 2.5,[46] and social hostilities rose from a median score of 1.2 to 2.3, well above the world

---

[42] Pew Research Center, "Latest Trends in Religious Restrictions and Hostilities: Overall Decline in Social Hostilities in 2013, though Harassment of Jews Worldwide Reached a Seven-Year High," February 26, 2015, p. 4, www.pewforum.org/files/2015/02/Restricti ons2015_fullReport.pdf. For 2007 figures of government restrictions and social hostilities, see Pew Research Center, "Religious Hostilities Reach Six-Year High," January 14, 2014, p. 7, www.pewforum.org/files/2014/01/RestrictionsV-full-report.pdf.

[43] Pew defines as social hostilities as "acts of religious hostility by private individuals, organizations, or groups in society." Pew Research Center, "Religious Hostilities Reach Six-Year High," 10.

[44] Pew Research Center, "Latest Trends in Religious Restrictions and Hostilities," 4. For 2007 figures of government restrictions and social hostilities, see Pew Research Center, "Religious Hostilities Reach Six-Year High," 7.

[45] Pew Research Center, "Religious Hostilities Reach Six-Year High," 26.

[46] Pew Research Center, "Latest Trends in Religious Restrictions and Hostilities," 22.

average of 1.6 (and, notably, higher than every other region except the Middle East and North Africa).[47]

A separate study on government involvement in religion (GIR) conducted by political scientist Jonathan Fox draws similar conclusions.[48] Assessing the prevalence of two models of religious freedom – "free exercise" and "equality" – across the globe, Fox finds that robust religious freedom is exceedingly rare, even within Western liberal democracies. When held to the "free exercise" model, which assesses the ability to practice one's religion freely and maintain religious institutions, only 14 percent of countries register as religiously free, and only 18 percent of Western democracies. Countries fared even worse when held to the "equality" model, which measures the extent to which all religious individuals and groups in a society are treated "equally" (i.e., not systematically favored or discriminated against) by the state. By this standard, only 5 percent of all countries are religiously free, including no Western democracies. Even when relaxing the criteria to allow for minor infractions, still only 37 percent of all countries, and 48 percent of Western democracies, satisfied the "free exercise" standard of religious freedom. Likewise, only 17 percent of all countries, and 11 percent of Western democracies, met the "equality" standard.[49] With this global crisis of religious freedom comes an increasing urgency to explore whether a case for religious freedom can be grounded in the universal language of human nature and human experience.

Affirming religious freedom as a right is imperative for a second reason. A new front has opened in the global crisis of religious freedom, this time waged not on the ground, as it were, but in the halls of Western academia, where a new cadre of religious freedom critics has emerged. The intellectual point of departure of these "new critics" is a postmodern suspicion of universal truth claims and a postcolonial sensitivity to cultural imperialism, which guides them to the "anti-essentialist" conclusion that like religion, religious freedom is a Western construct, invented and propagated as a means of exerting political manipulation. By historicizing religious freedom in terms of a genealogical origin in a particular culture at a particular time, the new critics conclude, "far from being a universally valid principle, religious freedom is the product – and the agenda – of one culture in one historical period: the modern

---

[47] Ibid., 24.   [48] See "The Religion and State Project," www.thearda.com/ras/.
[49] Jonathan Fox, "Religious Freedom in Theory and Practice," *Human Rights Review* 16 (2015): 1–22.

West."[50] There, the new critics' story goes, the concept "religious free-dom" was created by modern, centralizing European nation-states as a technology of control and domination. Implicit in this story is a norma-tive verdict, namely that religious freedom, as both an instrument of repression and the legacy of one particular culture, should not be advo-cated among people outside the West – people for whom the principle of religious freedom is bound to be conceptually and morally foreign. Doing so, the new critics say, amounts to cultural imperialism, offending non-Western people's dignity and native sense of morality.

The new critics' argument boils down to two pivotal but equally dubious claims, one normative and the other descriptive. The first claim is that religious freedom should not be foisted on non-Western societies. This thinking relies on notions of cultural relativism and assumes that a norm or value's sphere of validity is demarcated by the cultural and historical conditions in which it developed. The problem here, as with cultural relativism in general, is the conflation of cultural and historical particularity with normative validity. The new critics fail to recognize that the validity of moral norms and values does not hinge purely on the particular details and pathways of their historical emergence. For exam-ple, although there is now a consensus in the global community that slavery is an egregious wrong, formal proscriptions of the practice emerged locally and under culturally particular conditions. In fact, until relatively recently in human history, principled opposition to slavery was the exception rather than the rule. But does this mean that opposition to slavery has only local and contingent normative force and meaning, and that it is forever conjoined with the particular ideological, moral, and religious agendas of the earliest anti-slavery pioneers? The categorical evil of slavery, we can be sure, transcends geographic and temporal bound-aries. Likewise, though the principle of religious freedom is not ahistori-cal, its moral force may still be universal, extending to all peoples of all cultures.

The other claim pertains to the empirical details of religious freedom's historical emergence – namely that religious freedom was an isolated inven-tion of the modern West, developed for hegemonic political purposes. On the one hand, the new critics provide no evidence that modernizing states of early modern Europe developed and deployed the idea of religious freedom as a mechanism of political domination. Much to the contrary, advocates of

[50] Daniel Philpott, "In Defense of Religious Freedom" (paper presented at the annual meeting of the American Political Science Association, August 28, 2014), 2–3.

religious freedom surfaced on the margins of society, often by victims of state-sponsored religious persecution acting in opposition to the governing authorities. On the other hand, there is much evidence that notions of religious freedom predated the modern West. While it is true that the first principled and systematic instantiations of religious freedom emerged in Europe following the Reformation, the idea of religious freedom has historical roots in antiquity.[51] Nearly two thousand years ago, a pair of North African Christian apologists, Tertullian of Carthage and Lucius Lactantius, articulated principled defenses of religious freedom. Writing in the early third century, Tertullian declared, "It is a fundamental human right, a privilege of nature, that every man should worship according to his own convictions" (*Ad Scapulam* 2, 1–2). A century later, Lactantius echoed this view: "For nothing is so much a matter of free will as religion, for if the mind of the worshipper turns away it is carried off and nothing remains" (*Divine Institutes* V, XX).[52] And on an adjacent continent in the third century BC, the Indian emperor Ashoka likewise urged religious tolerance and mutual understanding:

Beloved-of-the-Gods, King Piyadasi, desires that all religions should reside everywhere, for all of them desire self-control and purity of the heart. But people have various desires and various passions, and they may practice all of what they should or only a part of it." One must not exalt one's creed discrediting all others, nor must one degrade these others without legitimate reasons (Fourteen Rock Edicts, 7).[53]

Later, Ashoka cautions that one should avoid "praising one's own religion, or condemning the religion of others without good cause" (Fourteen Rock Edicts, 14) out of concern for the collective well-being of all religions.[54]

---

[51] For an analysis and critique of several recent works by the "new critics" of religious freedom, see Philpott and Shah, "Defense of Religious Freedom," 380–395.

[52] These and other remarkably early arguments for religious freedom in early Christianity are discussed at length in Timothy Samuel Shah and Allen Hertzke, eds., *Christianity and Freedom: Volume 1, Historical Perspectives* (New York & Cambridge: Cambridge University Press, 2016), particularly in the chapters by Robert Wilken, Elizabeth Digeser, and Timothy Shah.

[53] See Ven. S. Dhammika, trans., *The Edicts of King Ashoka* (Sri Lanka: Buddhist Publication Society, 1993), www.cs.colostate.edu/~malaiya/ashoka.html.

[54] This tradition of religious tolerance and pluralism has been incorporated into the modern Indian state, whose constitution guarantees religious freedom for its religiously diverse population.

In view of the threats posed by the global crisis of religious freedom and the new critics, the chapters in this volume are of direct relevance and urgent importance. If religious beliefs and practices arise naturally from the normal development of basic cognitive faculties, as Justin Barrett suggests, then religion is no accidental phenomenon propped up by culture, indoctrination, or mere historical circumstance. If theistic belief strongly coheres with rationality and a justified confidence in the epistemic powers of human beings, as Alvin Plantinga argues, then religion is not diametrically opposed to rationality and scientific modernity but stands in indispensable relation to human reason and experience. If the exercise of religion is intimately tied to the use of core human capacities, as Christian Smith and Nicholas Wolterstorff maintain, then religious freedom represents a vital bulwark of human dignity. If religion can be shown to play a decisive role in human health and happiness, then religion must be regarded as an important contributor to human physical and mental well-being. And if religion is a basic good, as Christopher Tollefsen holds, then respecting the good of religion entails protecting religious freedom.

To be clear, this volume does not purport to represent a definitive resolution of longstanding controversies concerning the nature of religion, human experience, and the foundations of morality and rights. It is precisely because of the dignity, nature, and freedom of human beings that searching inquiry about these questions will and should continue. But we trust that these compelling new studies from a wide range of disciplines will provide good reason to be skeptical of recent efforts to liquidate and deconstruct the categories of "religion" and "religious freedom" into infinitely malleable instruments of power. On the contrary, far from being purely artificial, shifting, and contingent constructs, there is good reason to think that religion and religious freedom may be rooted in some of the most enduring and amazing human capacities – capacities that accord with reason and help to make human beings creatures of extraordinary dignity and worth. Even apart from whether our species of *Homo sapiens* is also in some sense *Homo religiosus*, it may well be, then, that religious freedom at its core is less the right to be religious than the right to be fully human.

I

Are Human Beings Naturally Religious?

Christian Smith

Are human beings somehow naturally religious? Should we take religion to be in some way an innate, instinctive, or inevitable aspect of human consciousness, experience, and life? Or is religion a nonessential, historically contingent aspect of basic human being? Various thinkers in different places in history and life have offered different answers to these questions, without, however, coming to agreement. I here attempt to answer them in a way that I hope incorporates some previous thinking, yet moves beyond earlier answers toward a more realistic and helpful understanding. My answer to these questions is significantly shaped by the philosophy of critical realism, which I think helps us do better social science than the other options for philosophies of social science, especially positivist empiricism and postmodern deconstructionism.

These are not issues of merely academic curiosity. The truth about religion and human being carries big implications for how human personal and social life should be properly ordered. Answers to the questions posed above sometimes imply positions about the truth value of religious and secular claims about reality. Answers and arguments about them are also bound up with massive alternative historical projects that seek to shape social orders today and into the future. These include the neo-Enlightenment project of a rational, secular modernity and various religious projects to build a modernity that socially accommodates if not revolves around religious worldviews. The futures of some world civilizations around the globe are today being contested by movements that are affected by different answers to the questions posed above. The stakes of the answers are therefore high, with significant implications for public policy, institutional practices, and the formation of culture over time. Not surprisingly, many of the players in the discussions, including academics, have personal, ideological, moral, and emotional investments in the issues at hand. I cannot say that I do not. However, as scholars engaged in the shared project of (from a critical realist perspective, at least) seeking to know what is true about what is real, we must let the best available evidence and best thinking about it – rather than what we wish or hope to be true because of personal ideological or theological commitments – determine our conclusions. I proceed on that basis.

FRAMING THE QUESTION

Setting these questions in some historical context is necessary to answer them well, since it is impossible to understand current debates without knowing the history of their emergence during the breakdown of Western Christendom over the last 500 years. My task here is not fundamentally historical, however, and space does not allow my providing that full context. I commend Brad Gregory's book, *The Unintended Reformation: How a Religious Revolution Secularized Society*, as providing a most illuminating background for my discussion.[1] Suffice it to say for present purposes that the mainstream of both the Catholic Church and the Protestant Reformers, especially of the magisterial Reformation, assumed and argued that God has planted in all humans an innate capacity and desire to know, love, and serve God – a capacity which, however, has been more or less marred by the effects of sin. So there is a long theological history to these questions in the West, which over time have been transposed into social science debates. Furthermore, notions of "human nature" cannot be understood in the West apart from their background in Christian theology's discussions of orientation to God, sin, human sociability, moral virtues, etc. Finally, the skeptical Enlightenment's project – to reconstitute social order on rational, secular, scientific grounds rather than on the basis of religion – not only polemicized against religion but forcefully denied that religion was an essential or ineradicable aspect of human nature.[2] These views helped establish some of the deep cultural categories affecting this discussion today in the West.

[1] Brad Gregory, *The Unintended Reformation: How a Religious Revolution Secularized Society* (Cambridge: Harvard University Press, 2012).
[2] James M. Byrne, *Religion and the Enlightenment: From Descartes to Kant* (Louisville: Westminster John Knox Press, 1997).

More recently, the academic study of religion (itself a product of secular modernity reconfiguring academic departments of theology) has been split on the question of religion and human nature. Many older, influential scholars (such as Rudolf Otto, William James, and Mircea Eliade) argued in a quasi-liberal Protestant mode that native to human experience or consciousness is an awareness of, and magnetic attraction to, "the holy," "the numinous," "the sacred," "ultimate concerns," etc., thus locating the naturalness of religion in human subjective experience.[3] More recently, other theorists in religious studies – more postcolonial and postmodern – have argued that "religion" as an entity simply does not exist beyond the relatively recent, contingent constructions of Western modernity, thus calling into question the very idea of "religion" and dissolving the discipline's subject of study.[4] (I find neither of these general approaches to be persuasive, even if they contribute some useful ideas and perspectives.[5])

In the sociology of religion, scholars have also disagreed on the matter. Some, such as Andrew Greeley, Daniel Bell, Rodney Stark, Robert Bellah, and Donald Miller, have suggested variously that humans are inherently "unsecular"; that only religion answers well the most profound of humanity's existential questions and is therefore an inelimible feature of human cultures; that humans wish for benefits that can only be obtained through exchanges with supernatural beings believed to exist in otherworldly contexts; that humans have an innate yearning for ecstasy and transcendence, and so on.[6] On the other hand,

---

[3] William James, *The Varieties of Religious Experience* (New York: Library of America, 2009 [1902]); Rudolf Otto, *The Idea of the Holy* (New York: Oxford University Press, 1958); Mircea Eliade, *The Sacred and the Profane: The Nature of Religion*, trans. Willard R. Trask (New York: Harcourt, 1987 [1957]).

[4] Talal Asad, *Genealogies of Religion* (Baltimore: Johns Hopkins University Press, 1993); Russell McCutcheon, *Manufacturing Religion* (New York: Oxford University Press, 2003); Tomoko Masuzawa, *The Invention of World Religions* (Chicago: University of Chicago Press, 2005); Daniel Dubuisson, *The Western Construction of Religion* (Baltimore: Johns Hopkins University Press, 2007).

[5] With regard to the latter thesis, I agree on these matters with Kevin Schilbrack, "Religions: Are There Any?" *Journal for the American Academy of Religion*, 78 (2010): 1112–1138, as well as with Martin Riesebrodt.

[6] Robert Bellah, "Civil Religion in America," *Daedalus* 96 (1967): 1–21; Andrew Greeley, *Unsecular Man* (New York: Dell Publishing, 1972); Daniel Bell, "The Return of the Sacred?" in *The Winding Passage* (ABT Associates, 1980; repr. New York: Basic Books, 1991), ch. 7; Rodney Stark and William Bainbridge, *The Future of Religion* (Berkeley: University of California Press, 1986); Rodney Stark and Roger Finke, *Acts of Faith* (Berkeley: University of California Press, 2000); Donald Miller and Tetsunao Yamamori, *Global Pentecostalism: The New Face of Christian Social Engagement* (Berkeley: University of California Press,

different theorists – including Bryan Wilson, Steve Bruce, the "old" Peter
Berger, Pippa Norris and Ronald Inglehart, and Phil Zuckerman – imply
or argue that religion is the contingent product of certain historical and
social conditions that can, may, or does dramatically diminish and
perhaps ultimately disappear when social conditions change under the
conditions of modernity.[7] Sociologists of religion thus do not enjoy
a consensus on the question of whether religion is in some way natural
to human being.

THE EVIDENCE

So what ought *we* to think? The empirical data tell us four facts. First, very
many individual people in the world are nonreligious and certain entire
cultures appear to be quite secular, without immediate apparent damage
to human happiness or functionality. Not all people and societies are
religious or apparently have to be in order to remain human, contented,
and functional. That suggests that religion is in some sense not natural to
human being but an accidental or inessential aspect characterizing only
some human beings.

Second, religion generally is not fading away in the modern world as
a whole;[8] even the most determined attempts by powerful states to repress
and extinguish religion (e.g., in Russia, China, Revolutionary France)
have been at least partly unsuccessful.[9] In addition to appearing to be

---

2007); and Robert Bellah, *Religion in Human Evolution* (Cambridge: Harvard University
Press, 2011).

[7] Peter Berger, *The Sacred Canopy* (New York: Anchor Books, 1969); Bryan Wilson,
Contemporary Transformations of Religion (Oxford: Oxford University Press, 1979);
Steve Bruce, *God is Dead* (New York: Blackwell, 2002); Pippa Norris and
Ronald Inglehart, *Sacred and Secular* (Cambridge: Cambridge University Press, 2004);
Phil Zuckerman, *Society Without God: What the Least Religious Nations Can Tell
Us About Contentment* (New York: New York University Press, 2008).

[8] Jose Casanova, *Public Religions in the Modern World* (Chicago: University of Chicago
Press, 1994); Peter Berger, ed., *The Desecularization of the World: Resurgent Religion
and World Politics* (Grand Rapids: Eerdmans, 1999); Monica Duffy Toft, Daniel Philpott
and Timothy Shah, *God's Century: Resurgent Religion and Global Politics* (New York:
W. W. Norton, 2011).

[9] See, for example: Joseph Byrnes, *Catholic and French Forever: Religion and National
Identity in Modern France* (State College: Pennsylvania State University Press, 2005);
Paul Froese, *The Plot to Kill God: Findings from the Soviet Experiment in Secularization*
(Berkeley: University of California Press, 2008); and Fenggang Yang, *Religion in China:
Survival and Revival Under Communist Rule* (New York: Oxford University Press,
2011). East Germany may be one exception, whose hyper-secularity, David Martin
notes, reflects "a bargain struck by its communist victors releasing its demoralized people

primordial in human history[10] and present in one form or another in all human civilizations, religion thus also seems to be incredibly resilient, incapable perhaps of being destroyed and terminated. That suggests that religion is in some sense irrepressibly natural to human being.

Third, even when traditionally religious forms of human life seem to fade in some contexts, new and alternative forms of life often seem to appear in their place that engage the sacred, the spiritual, the transcendent, the liturgical, the implicitly religious, the ecstatic, etc. Many observers have noted, not incorrectly I think, that a vast variety of seemingly nonreligious human activities embody and express at least quasi-religious, if not overtly spiritual, features. New Age ideas and claims to be "spiritual but not religious" are obvious instances. Scholars have also noted the religious dimensions of organizations, movements, and practices as different as "secular" environmentalism, academic economics, modern nation states, and arena sports spectacles.[11] It is also hard to miss the presence of superhuman powers, supernatural realities, and spiritual themes in some of the most popular contemporary films, fiction, and television shows.[12] Furthermore, there is clearly a variety of expressions of arguably religious practices – besides the typical Protestant mode of centralized belief and resulting practices – involved in even traditional religious faiths, including perhaps "vicarious religion," "believing

from Nazi guilt if they accepted the complete secularist package." See David Martin, *The Future of Christianity: Reflections on Violence and Democracy, Religion and Human Rights* (Farnham: Ashgate, 2011), 14.

[10] Colin Renfrew and Iain Morley, *Becoming Human: Innovation in Prehistoric Material and Spiritual Culture* (Cambridge: Cambridge University Press, 2009).

[11] Robert Nelson, *Economics as Religion: From Samuelson to Chicago and Beyond* (State College: Pennsylvania State University Press, 2002); Joseph Price, *From Season to Season: Sports as American Religion* (Macon: Mercer University Press, 2004); Thomas Dunlap, *Faith in Nature: Environmentalism as Religious Quest* (Seattle: University of Washington Press, 2005); Robert Nelson, *The New Holy Wars: Economic Religion versus Environmental Religion in Contemporary America* (State College: Pennsylvania State University Press, 2009); William Cavanaugh, *Migrations of the Holy: God, State, and the Political Meaning of the Church* (Grand Rapids: Eerdmans, 2011). For an argument that even secularization theory itself betrays an "unsecular," quasi-religious, and eschatological view of human nature and history, see Timothy Samuel Shah, "Secular Militancy as an Obstacle to Peacebuilding," in *The Oxford Handbook of Religion, Conflict, and Peacebuilding*, eds. Atalia Omer, R. Scott Appleby, and David Little (New York and Oxford: Oxford University Press, 2015), 380–406.

[12] Margaret Miles, *Seeing and Believing: Religion and Values in the Movies* (Boston: Beacon Press, 1997); Richard Bleiler, *Supernatural Fiction Writers: Contemporary Fantasy and Horror* (New York: Scribner, 2002); Lynn Schofield Clark, *From Angels to Aliens: Teenagers, the Media, and the Supernatural* (New York: Oxford University Press, 2005); Connie Neal, *The Gospel According to Harry Potter* (Louisville: WJK, 2008).

without belonging," and myriad manifestations of "everyday religion."[13] This evidence suggests (though hardly proves) that religion may be in some sense irrepressibly natural to human being.

The fourth fact worth noting is that the fate of religion in the lives of individual persons and shared cultures is variable and highly dependent upon path-contingent personal and historical experiences and developments.[14] Different people and peoples can and do head in quite different directions when it comes to religion. No one narrative or trajectory tells the whole story. There may simply not be a dominant story. At best, scholars can note and interpret broad patterns and associations. But the outcome of religion in human social life is highly dependent upon the particularities of history and context. That suggests that, if religion is in any way natural to human being, which is not certain, then whatever it means to be "natural" has to account for a great deal of variability and contingency.

What should we make of these four empirical facts, which do not seem at first to produce one consistent interpretive conclusion? I believe it is possible to express a theoretical account of religion and humanity that does justice to all of the evidence above. But getting to that account requires sorting out some basic issues first.

PROPERLY DEFINING THE ISSUES

The kind of theoretical account needed to make the best sense of the evidence described above will have to proceed, I am convinced, with

---

[13] Grace Davie, *Religion in Britain Since 1945* (Hoboken: Wiley-Blackwell, 1994); Nancy Ammerman, ed., *Everyday Religion: Observing Modern Religious Lives* (New York: Oxford University Press, 2007); Meredith McGuire, *Lived Religion: Faith and Practice in Everyday Life* (New York: Oxford University Press, 2008); Grace Davie, "Vicarious Religion," *Journal of Contemporary Religion* 25 (2010): 261–266. See also: Slavica Jakelić, *Collectivistic Religion: Religion, Choice, and Identity in Late Modernity* (Farnham: Ashgate, 2010). Furthermore, at least some traditional religions, including Christianity (per St. Augustine, for example), have long argued that many apparently nonreligious activities – including drunken intoxication, wild carousing, promiscuous sex, harsh athletic training, committed political activism, incessant material consumption, drug addiction, and so on – actually represent deeply driven human religious longings and searching, which happen to be misdirected quests for the true religious good. Such claims seem to tend to arise especially from traditions of monotheism and monism, both of which deny the possibility of the *ultimate* metaphysical existence of badness and evil.

[14] David Martin, *A General Theory of Secularization* (New York: Harper, 1978); Martin, *Future of Christianity*.

critical realism and not positivist empiricism operating in the background as the guiding philosophy of social science. Very many of our problems and failures in social science result from research being framed by positivist empiricism. Among many flaws in the latter approach, one is to suppose that social reality normally operates according to certain covering laws that can be expressed in the form of:

if A → (probably) B (all else being equal).

Positivist empiricism thus tells us to look for regular associations between observable empirical events, and defines "explanation" as identifying the strongest, most significant associations between them. It also sets the expectation that once the covering laws have been identified, they will apply to all cases and situations that the laws cover – which is usually assumed, if only by default, to mean (modern) "people" generally. All of that gets researchers thinking in yes/no, either/or, correct/false terms (often modified, however, by the introduction of statistical probabilities and the *ceteris paribus* clause). Applied to the question at hand, the debate as a result normally proceeds on the unquestioned assumption that *either* humans are naturally religious (and so religion will always persist in human societies) *or* humans are not naturally religious (and so modernity may or will profoundly secularize people and society).

Critical realism reconstructs many of our basic assumptions, telling us to ask different questions, and thus opening up new, helpful possibilities of understanding and explanation. Here is not the place to explain the details of critical realism.[15] Suffice it for present purposes to focus our attention on its emphasis on natural capacities, powers, limitations, tendencies, and contingencies. In reality – as critical realism describes it – myriad kinds of real entities exist, each of which possesses particular characteristics by virtue of their ontological makeup. Human beings are

[15] But, see: Roy Bhaskar, *The Possibility of Naturalism* (London: Routledge, 1979); Andrew Collier, *Critical Realism* (London: Verso, 1994); Margaret Archer, *Realist Social Theory: The Morphogenetic Approach* (Cambridge: Cambridge University Press, 1995); Roy Bhaskar, *Critical Realism* (New York: Routledge, 1998); Andrew Sayer, *Realism and Social Science* (New York: Sage, 2000); Mats Ekström et al., *Explaining Society: Critical Realism in the Social Sciences* (New York: Routledge, 2002); Christian Smith, "Future Directions in the Sociology of Religion," *Social Forces*, 86 (2008): 1561–1590; Douglas Porpora, "Recovering Causality: Realist Methods in Sociology," in *Realismo Sociologico*, eds. A. Maccarini, E. Morandi, and R. Prandini (Genoa–Milan: Marietti, 2008); Philip Gorski, "Social 'Mechanisms' and Comparative-Historical Sociology: A Critical Realist Proposal," in *The Frontiers of Sociology*, eds. Björn Wittrock and Peter Hedström (Leiden: Brill, 2009).

one such kind of entity. Crucial among those characteristics are certain structured arrangements of specific features, capacities, powers, limits, and tendencies. Those are in fact what help to constitute entities. Under differing environmental conditions, different combinations of capacities and powers are triggered (or not) into operation, which, depending on their powers, tendencies, and interactions, produce causal effects in the entity and/or its surrounding world. As the various capacities of entities and the different entities themselves interact with other entities in particular ways, "emergent" processes produce in and among them genuinely new features, capacities, powers, and tendencies. Through this process of interaction and emergence, much of reality itself develops in "stratified" and structured form, entailing innumerable, complex processes of multi-causal influence operating at many "levels" or dimensions, in various ways, "upwardly" and "downwardly," giving rise to immensely complex events and outcomes.

Crucial to learn from critical realism for our purposes here are the following points. First, real entities with essential properties exist ontologically in reality, often independent of human mental activity, not in static form but rather through continually dynamic interaction. Second, real entities ontologically comprise the basic difference between potential and actual (or realized). Innate to real entities are certain capacities and powers, existing at a "deep" level of reality, that are triggered only under certain conditions and so activated to actually realize their potential. This means that certain natural features of entities can be entirely real but nonetheless inoperative and unobserved at times. Third, the causal capacities of entities always operate in accordance with certain tendencies, in particular trajectories of force and power. This means that, when the causal energies of entities are released in particular cases, they are *neither* determined, determining, or absolutely predictable, *nor* random, chaotic, or incomprehensible. Fourth, the (social) scientific task is not to discover the covering laws that explain and predict observable associations of conditions and events ("if A → [probably] B [*ceteris paribus*]"). The task rather is for our theorizing minds to use all available empirical evidence and powers of reason to develop conceptual models that as accurately as possible descriptively represent the real causal processes operating at a "deeper," unobservable level of reality, through the agency of real causal mechanisms that produce changes in the material and nonmaterial world (some of which) we observe empirically. Fifth, we must always pay close attention to the particularities of environmental and contextual factors that do and do not activate various causal capacities and powers of different entities in various combinations, which then produce a variety of possible, sometimes observable outcomes. And, in all of this, we have to get ready to deal with real complexity.

Having sketched these few key ideas from critical realism, to which I will return shortly, our next task is to define "religion." This has been a matter of ongoing and vexing dispute among scholars. But I believe that Martin Riesebrodt's recent reformulation of Melford Spiro's older definition proves, for a variety of reasons, the most satisfactory.[16] Riesebrodt defines religion as, "a complex of practices that are based on the premise of the existence of superhuman powers, whether personal or impersonal, that are generally invisible."[17] People are religious, according to Riesebrodt, in order to tap those superhuman powers to help them avert and solve problems they confront – from getting hurt or sick to suffering a bad existence after death. In his approach, Riesebrodt asks us to focus on religious "liturgical" practices rather than abstract belief systems, which avoids a number of problems in other definitions. This substantive (not functional) definition of religion provides traction for identifying when religion is present or absent, stronger or weaker in human life. At the same time, however, it does not focus us on the centrality of religious beliefs, but on religious practices. That deftly sidesteps the misguided thrust of recent radical-constructionist accounts of religion that liquidate the subject. It also complicates the picture described by those, like Zuckerman, who observe that highly secularized societies are often "without God" though "not without religion," as well as the implications of that observation for answering the questions posed here.

Finally, to answer our questions well, we have to clarify what we mean by "naturally" and "by nature." Though at first a seemingly obvious concept, it turns out that "nature" is a quite difficult term to define. I here spare the reader the details of the problems involved and simply assert that critical realism provides the most sensible way to proceed. By "nature," as related to something like "human nature," I as a realist

---

[16] Martin Riesebrodt, *The Promise of Salvation: A Theory of Religion* (Chicago: University of Chicago Press, 2010); see also: Melford Spiro, "Religion: Problems of Definition and Explanation," in *Anthropological Approaches to the Study of Religion*, ed. Michael Banton (London: Tavistock, 1966), 87–126.

[17] "The 'superhumanness' of these powers consists in the fact that influence or control over dimensions of individual or social human life and the natural environment is attributed to them – dimensions that are usually beyond direct human control. Religious practices normally consist in using culturally prescribed means to establish contact with these powers to gain access to them." Riesebrodt, *The Promise of Salvation*, 74–75.

mean the stably characteristic properties, capacities, and tendencies of human beings that obtain by virtue of the ontological character of their personhood. Specific parts of reality are what they are and are not other things. By virtue of being what they particularly are, these parts of reality possess certain given features, causal powers, and dispositions (and not others) that adhere in their being. These properties, capacities, and tendencies are not accidental to particular instances of the entities in question, but rather inhere in the entity itself. Everything in reality has some kind of nature, in this sense, insofar as entities possess and so can express particular characteristics, capacities, and tendencies by virtue of simply being what they are. It is in the nature of real entities to have certain features, causal powers, and dispositions that distinguish them from other entities that they are not. When such features, causal powers, and dispositions are not accidental, random, or unstable characteristics of an entity, but instead typify the entity by virtue of its ontological makeup in ways that are stable and commonly shared by all entities of that type, we can refer to them as their "nature." This approach recognizes that many parts of reality are neither (entirely) humanly constructed nor readily susceptible to intentional change. Different parts of reality happen to have different inherent features, causal powers, and dispositions by virtue of the nature of what they are. Reality itself, therefore, has a certain structure or "grain" in its features, abilities, tendencies, and operations, which one can work either with or against, with varying consequences.

A CRITICAL REALIST ACCOUNT

With the above clarifications in view, I propose the following answer to the question of whether or not humans are by nature religious. I begin by stating my position negatively. First, humans are *not* by nature religious, if by that we mean that all human persons are compelled by some natural and irrepressible need or drive or instinct or desire to be religious. In that sense, some humans are religious and some are not, often quite happily and functionally so, it appears. Thus, to begin, the answer is "no" if the question refers to a universal demand for religion operating at the empirical level of individual persons.

Second, humans are *not* by nature religious, if by that we mean that every human culture has a functional need or intractable impulse to make religion a centrally defining feature of society. Societies, like particular people, vary in how important a role religion plays in their lives. Some are highly religious. Others are quite secular, with religion operating on the margins, in private or in secret, far from the institutional centers of material and legitimate-knowledge production and distribution. At most we might say that total irreligion and complete secularity appear to be impossible among humans at the societal level. But that is a long way from saying that humans are naturally religious.

That said, I do believe that human beings *are* naturally religious when that is understood in a particular way. *All human persons are naturally religious if by that we mean that they possess, by virtue of their given ontological being, a complex set of innate features, capacities, powers, limitations, and tendencies that capacitate them to be religious (i.e., to think, perceive, feel, imagine, desire, and act religiously), and that, under the right conditions, tend to predispose and direct them toward religion.* The natural religiousness of humanity is thus located not in a naturally determined uniformity of empirical religious practice, either by individuals or societies (which is how positivist empiricism would focus our attention). It is instead located in the distinctive, inherent features, capacities, powers, limitations, and tendencies of human persons that are rooted, ultimately, in the human body and the emergent (often nonmaterial) capacities that arise from the body.

Human persons being "religious by nature" in this sense should not be taken lightly. We are speaking here of very powerful causal forces and dispositions rooted in the very nature of reality which are chronically triggered to operate in human life in a variety of human social contexts. That helps to explain religion's primordial, irrepressible, widespread, and seemingly inextinguishable character in the broad sweep of human experience. If true, it also suggests that the skeptical Enlightenment, secular humanist, and New Atheist visions for a totally secular human world are simply not realistic – they are cutting against a very strong "grain" in the nature of reality's structure and so will fail to achieve their purpose.

But that is not the whole story. Humans being "religious by nature" in this sense also does not tell us to expect the eventual "return of religion" everywhere or the incapacity of people to function reasonably well in the absence of religion. Neither does it license observers to decide that non-religious people are really "anonymous" religious believers or somehow pathological or subhuman in their lack of religiousness. Instead, this view tells us that nonreligious humans are persons who, like all persons, possess the natural capacities and possible tendencies toward religion but who, for whatever reasons, have either (1) not had those capacities and tendencies activated by environmental, experiential triggers in the first place or (2) have had them activated but also had them neutralized or deactivated by some other experienced causal forces.

The kinds of natural features, capacities, powers, limitations, and tendencies to which I refer I have already written about at length in my 2010 book, *What Is a Person? Understanding Humanity, Social Life, and the Good from the Person Up.*[18] I will not repeat that book's argument here. Suffice it to say that they start at the "bottom" with capacities for consciousness and unconsciousness, work in processes of upward emergence through a variety of increasingly complex and sophisticated capacities and powers, and culminate with the highest-level capacities of language, symbolization, valuation, creativity and innovation, causal understanding, self-reflexivity, creating and communicating meanings, narration, anticipating the future, identity formation, self-transcendence, truth seeking, abstract reasoning, moral awareness, aesthetic judgments, forming virtues, and interpersonal communion and love. These natural human capacities enable and dispose humans to an immense number and variety of activities and practices. Among them are the distinct abilities and, when activated, tendencies to (1) conceptualize and believe in superhuman powers; (2) engage in activities designed to seek help from superhuman powers (such as prayer, worship, sacrifice, obedience); (3) anticipate alternative futures related to the superhuman powers, dependent in part on different courses of action taken regarding them; (4) subjectively experience communion, union, harmony, or affirmation with or from superhuman powers; (5) engage in human social relationships that reinforce the believed reality of the superhuman powers; (6) learn to interpret the larger world and experience in light of the beliefs involved in interacting with the superhuman powers; and so on. At the same time, those capacities run into major contradictions when they "hit the wall" of natural human limitations, finitude, and constraints. It is the dynamic tension of the meeting and interplay of natural capacities and limitations that helps to give rise to religion.

But what exactly do I mean by natural *tendencies* toward religion that are grounded in the ontology of human personhood? The natural tendencies I mean are caused by an interconnected set of orientations toward life and the world in which humans continually seem to find themselves. In some sense we are here speaking about "the human condition," but not one that is free-floating or psychologically or cognitively autonomous from nature and bodies. The human condition I mean here arises through the process of emergence directly from the innate features of nature's

---

[18] Christian Smith, *What Is a Person? Understanding Humanity, Social Life, and the Good from the Person Up* (Chicago: University of Chicago Press, 2010).

human body as it operates in its material and nonmaterial[19] environment – particularly from the frictional collision of its natural powers and natural limitations. At the same time, this human condition is not absolutely determined and determining – there does exist space for the consequences of the somewhat free play of human desires, emotions, beliefs, and so on.

The first of these natural human tendencies toward religion springs from our universal human *epistemic condition*. That is, in the final analysis all humans are *believers* generally, not knowers with certitude, of what is true about what is real. This point I have argued at length in my previous book, *Moral, Believing Animals: Human Personhood and Culture*[20], and will not repeat here. It is enough to say that everything we humans ever "know" is grounded more fundamentally on presupposed beliefs that are the necessary conditions to ever get inquiry, perception, and knowledge-building off the ground. And those beliefs simply cannot be verified with more fundamental proof or certainty that provides us assurance that they are true and right beliefs. All humans are thus believers before and more basically than we are knowers. That is just as true for atheists as for religious adherents. In the end, none of us can find and build upon certain, indubitable truths that are not dependent upon more basic, presupposed beliefs. The quest for foundationalist certainty, with which we are likely familiar, is a distinctly modern project launched as a response to the instabilities and uncertainties of early-modern Europe, with thinkers such as Hugo Grotius and René Descartes as its pioneers.[21] But that modern, philosophical foundationalist project has failed. There is no universal, rational foundation upon which indubitably certain knowledge can be built. All human knowing is more fundamentally built on believing. That is the human condition. And that means that *religious* commitment, as a human activity, is not fundamentally different, at

---

[19] Meaning things like cultural beliefs, oral communications, shared values (not spirits, angels, etc., necessarily).

[20] Christian Smith, *Moral, Believing Animals: Human Personhood and Culture* (New York: Oxford University Press, 2003).

[21] For a discussion of the nature of Descartes's foundationalism precisely as a response to the divisions and instabilities of early-modern Europe, see Stephen Edelston Toulmin, *Cosmopolis: The Hidden Agenda of Modernity* (Chicago: University of Chicago Press, 2013). For an interpretation of Hugo Grotius as an innovative and radical foundationalist – indeed, preceding Descartes – who sought to identify an indubitable and parsimonious set of rational and moral truths as a means of securing stable consensus amidst Europe's deepening religious and political conflicts in the early seventeenth century, see Timothy Samuel Shah, *Even if There is No God: Hugo Grotius and the Secular Foundations of Modern Political Liberalism* (Oxford: Oxford University Press, forthcoming).

bottom, than *all* human belief commitment, insofar as religion involves belief and trust in, and response to, the existence of believed-in realities that are not objectively verifiable and universally shared by all reasonable people. Religious believing in particular is thus not at odds or variance with the epistemic trajectory of all human believing. And that, under the right conditions, helps tend people toward religion.

A second feature of the human condition that I believe gives rise to a natural tendency toward religion concerns the human *capacity to recognize and desire to solve problems.* Following Riesebrodt's definition of religion above, we see that religion has its deepest roots in the human desire to avert, forestall, and resolve real and perceived problems. Among all the animal species on this earth, human life, being so very complex, is particularly susceptible to encountering a wide variety of problems. Humans are also particularly well capacitated to recognize problems, define them as problems, and desire to overcome them. Finally, humans, being also so very finite in their capacities, are also highly likely to encounter situations in which they have limited or no power to solve their problems. That is, human capacities to know what is happening in life often outstrip human powers to control what is happening. Very regularly, yawning chasms stand between people's problems and their abilities to solve them. Yet humans, for various reasons, have difficulties ignoring their problems. When the prospect of a helpful superhuman power is present in a situation, it is often quite natural for humans to be interested in the possibility of appealing to those powers to help avert or resolve their problems (unless some other stronger causal power neutralizes that interest).[22] Comparatively, the "hamster condition" and even the "chimpanzee condition" are not like the human condition in this respect, which makes them naturally less capacitated for and tending toward religion.

The human *existential condition* also lends itself to the tendency toward religious engagement. Humans recurrently appear to ask and wrestle with answers to what Brad Gregory has called the "Life Questions": "What should I live for and why? What should I believe and why should I believe it? What is morality and where does it come from? What kind of person should I be? What is the meaning of life, and what should I do in order to lead a fulfilling life?"[23] Daniel Bell similarly noted a set of existential life questions that he argued recurrently call

---

[22] See, for example, Lynn Davidman, *Tradition in a Rootless World* (Berkeley: University of California Press, 1991).

[23] Gregory, *The Unintended Reformation*, 74.

humans back to religion in order to answer well, namely, "the core questions that confront all human groups in the consciousness of existence: how one meets death, the meaning of tragedy, the nature of obligation, the character of love – these are recurrent questions which are, I believe, cultural universals, to be found in all societies where men have become conscious of the finiteness of existence."[24] The human existential condition that raises these kinds of questions reflects the fact that humans have both incredible capacities and severe limits, and that contradiction continually raises pressing difficulties. We have the capacity to know we will die but not to know what comes after, for example. We tend to seek truth, goodness, and beauty but find so little of it in this world and oftentimes in ourselves. We are meaning-making and significance-seeking animals, yet find our ability to spin satisfying meanings solely from within the horizons of the immanent world we occupy to be limited. Consequently, religion has been an historically primary way that humans have answered these questions, and I am confident it will continue to be for many people.

But this is also crucial to realize: religion is not the only way for humans to answer these big Life Questions and live seemingly functional, happy lives. The human existential condition does not necessitate that people be religious. Indeed, it does not even mean that all people feel the need to address and answer such questions – many people appear happy to focus on the present, live as well as they can, and not be bothered by The Big Questions. At the same time, however, the capacity to respond to the human existential condition in terms that are not religious does not mean that this existential condition does not exist. It does. Again, we are dealing with causal forces that need to be activated (and not subsequently neutralized) and with tendencies, not with perfect associations or necessities. And such forces and tendencies are highly shaped by the particularities of historical and social conditions and experiences.[25]

Finally, the human *moral condition* inescapably involves the making of "strong evaluations" (in Charles Taylor's words[26]), unavoidably

---

[24] Bell, "The Return of the Sacred?" 333.

[25] See Phillip Gorski, "Historicizing the Secularization Debate," *American Sociological Review* 65 (2000): 138–167; Christian Smith, ed., *The Secular Revolution* (Berkeley: University of California Press, 2003); Ann Taves, *Religious Experience Reconsidered* (Princeton: Princeton University Press, 2009).

[26] Charles Taylor, *Sources of the Self: The Making of the Modern Identity* (Cambridge: Harvard University Press, 1989). For a further argument for the indispensability of strong sources of moral evaluation that are independent of individual preferences, see Taylor's *The Ethics of Authenticity* (Cambridge: Harvard University Press, 2008 [1991]).

operating in relation to moral beliefs that are taken to arise not from our personal preferences and desires but from sources transcending them. It is simply *un*natural in the strongest sense of that word for humans to think that morality is nothing but a charade, that even the asking of moral questions is wrongheaded, that all moral claims are nothing but relative human constructions. Friedrich Nietzsche attempted some version of this, but could not himself finally escape the position of arguing that some things were in fact true, that some positions were actually right – which is why he wrote his powerful works to convince his readers of his views. The transvaluation of all values still ended up committing Nietzsche to certain values, truth claims, and senses of normative good and bad. "Slave morality" was bad, for instance, while the morality of the noble pagan warrior was good. This condition thus puts all (but psychopathic) humans in the position of having to operate with some account for where morality comes from, what makes it real. Some people are clearly able to submerge such questions from consciousness. But the questions recurrently return in cultures and social groups, if not in the lives of distinct persons. Religions are not the only answer to the question of moral sources, but historically they have been foundational and central. Secular modernity is arguably radically incoherent and self-deceived on matters of moral philosophy – I think it clearly is.[27] So, even though few people are moral philosophers who care about intellectual consistency (not that most moral philosophers necessarily prove to be all that consistent either), the questions themselves never disappear. They return again and again in the course of the human experience over time.[28] And this too, under the right conditions, I suggest, leans certain triggered human capacities for religious-like things to be disposed to religious answers and practices.

But how, critics might ask, can we distinguish genuine, natural human tendencies from any other factor that might produce some or another human activity? One way to sort this out is to consider how relatively easy or hard it is for natural human capacities to be expressed in particular ways. The harder people have to work to produce something in human life, the less likely humans have a natural tendency for it. It is a natural tendency, for example, for people to use their capacity for muscle motion in their legs and arms to walk and to feed themselves, but not to crab-walk

---

[27] Among persuasive works arguing this: Robert Kraynak, "Justice Without Foundations," *The New Atlantis* (2011): 103–120; Alasdair MacIntyre, *After Virtue* (Notre Dame: Notre Dame University Press, 1982).

[28] Smith, *Moral, Believing Animals.*

backwards or repeatedly hit themselves in the head with hard objects. When it comes to cultural practices, across human history and societies, it is possible to find a dizzying array of expressions of human potentials. But some of them are rare and difficult to achieve, while others are common and easy. Viewed broadly (i.e., not just thinking of modern Europe), religion tends to fall into the latter category. In most historical situations, it has not been hard for people and cultures to come to believe, embrace, practice, and pass on religions to subsequent generations. It has been much, much harder to extinguish them. In fact, it usually takes some combination of potent religion-undermining experiences, like decades of ideological attacks (as with skeptical Enlightenment polemicists), the traumas of demoralizing wars (as in the early modern so-called[29] "wars of religion"), religiously significant atrocities (such as the Holocaust), sustained internal religious conflicts (as in European Christendom after the Protestant Reformation), or purposive state repression (such as Soviet-enforced atheism), to suppress human religious practices. And even then it does not necessarily work. That tells us something: that humans not only have the potential capacities to be religious, like the capacities for anything else humans might do, including rare and difficult things, but that those capacities are also directed by very strong, natural tendencies that so happen to turn them toward religious expression. In short, humans not only have latent potentials for religion but also very strong natural tendencies toward practicing religion. If so, that contributes to my larger argument that, understood rightly, humans are naturally religious.

My larger argument can thus be summarized as follows (which is a natural way of thinking for critical realists, but problematic for positivist empiricists): simply because some feature of human being is *natural* in or to human ontology or existence, that does *not* mean that it is or needs to be always empirically expressed, acted upon, or found necessary or attractive to all humans or to most humans in any particular culture. Many natural features and capacities in reality, including human reality, are not often activated, in particular cases. Others are activated but subsequently countered or neutralized by the causal power of other factors at work. Thus, we can confidently say that humans are naturally religious or by nature religious – as a matter of real, natural potentiality, capacity, and tendency – while at the same time acknowledging that many humans and even some cultures are not particularly religious at

---

[29] William Cavanaugh, *The Myth of Religious Violence: Secular Ideology and the Roots of Modern Conflict* (New York: Oxford University Press, 2009).

all.[30] The key to understanding that kind of account is to work out of a critical realist, not a positivist empiricist (not to mention postmodern deconstructionist), framework. Such an account entails many implications, theoretical and practical, worth considering. But one it strongly suggests is that we should not expect human societies to become thoroughly secularized on any long-term basis. Secularization as a process will likely be limited, contingent, and susceptible to long-term reversals.

IMPLICATIONS FOR RELIGIOUS FREEDOM

What are the implications of this account for the principles and practices of religious freedom? If my account is correct, then a number of conclusions seem to follow. One is that, when institutions and governments restrict or suppress the religious lives of human persons – people's religious practices, beliefs, and associations – they are thereby violating an ontologically and often existentially innate part of human personhood. To oppose human religion through coercion, instead of reasoned persuasion, is to infringe upon powers, orientations, interests, and tendencies that are inherent to human being and sometimes central to people's human existence. To refuse religious freedom is therefore to deny human persons the ability to actualize their natural religious potentials by acting upon their natural powers and tendencies to engage religion as an expression of their bodily grounded capacities and epistemic, existential, moral, problem-solving human condition.

In this case, we can expect that states will only ever be able to significantly restrict religious freedom in their societies by resorting to highly coercive and violent, and thus illegitimate, and likely reprehensible, means. *If* religion were *not* an innate part of human nature, as I have described it, but rather only inessential or accidental – something like a preference for truancy from school, say, or wishing to ride motorcycles without helmets – then the government suppression or eradication of religion might be possible through the use of prudent, acceptable public policies. An intelligent "choice architecture" intending gently but firmly to "nudge" all people away from any religion or into one religion through a kind of "libertarian paternalism" might be

---

[30] Christian Smith and Brandon Vaidyanathan, "Religion and Multiple Modernities," in *Oxford Handbook of Religious Diversity*, ed. Chad Meister (New York: Oxford University Press, 2010).

effective.[31] But if religion is indeed a part of human nature, as I have argued, then state efforts to restrict religious freedom must work "against the grain" of reality and so inevitably will have to resort to extreme measures to do so. The history of the twentieth century provides us with many lamentable empirical demonstrations of that. Whether a government's policy is societal atheism (as with the Soviet Union, for instance) or a mono-religious monopoly (as with Saudi Arabia), severe state coercion, repression, imprisonment, and executions of dissenters over what must be understood to be matters of conscience have been, are, and will be necessary. That is because humans *by nature* have innate and sometimes irrepressible capacities and tendencies toward religious belief and practice – the sort that, ultimately, governments can control or suppress only with violence.

If this is correct, then institutions and governments that intend not only to not violate but actually to honor and foster the flourishing of human beings as they are in reality need to provide for the proper freedom of religious belief and practice. Both beliefs and practices matter, since religion, when correctly understood (per Reisebrodt), is not merely a system of ideas that people can keep privately in their heads. Religion is at heart about bodily and social practices by which people engage superhuman powers as they understand them. And those practices and the requirements that come from them often require obligatory actions, including some performed in public spaces or with social implications.[32]

Respecting religious freedom in the details is, of course, no easy matter. There are cases, for example, in which granting unfettered religious freedom results in predictable outcomes that even more deeply violate human dignity and flourishing than does the curtailing of religious freedom in those instances, which may justify state intervention – I think, for example, of situations involving *sati* (widow burning), capital punishment for noncapital offenses (e.g., stoning adulterers), the violent persecution of "heretics," the real abuse of children in new religious movements, and so on. Those, however, are extreme cases, which should not serve as

---

[31] Richard Thaler and Cass Sunstein, *Nudge: Improving Decisions About Health, Wealth, and Happiness* (New York: Penguin, 2009).

[32] On this I number myself among the so-called "structural pluralists," about which see: Stephen Monsma and Christopher Soper, *The Challenge of Pluralism: Church and State in Five Democracies* (Lanham: Rowman and Littlefield, 2008); Stephen Monsma, *Pluralism and Freedom: Faith-Based Organizations in a Democratic Society* (Lanham: Rowman and Littlefield, 2012).

baselines to determine standard state policies on religious freedom.[33]
Furthermore, we should never forget that governments are never neutral
actors in any of these matters (which raises questions of the basis of the
legitimacy of religious-liberty-restricting state interventions, which are
beyond my capacity to address here). Finally, all considerations of religious liberty must recognize and speak to the complicated matter of
religious traditions' historically situated needs and capacities (or lack
thereof) for the self-correction of their own unjust practices – based, not
primarily on "external" demands of a liberal state, for example, but on
their own best theological and moral resources. Balancing the strong
imperative of religious freedom with the value of religions being pressured
(ideally from within, but often necessarily from without) to confront their
own internal inconsistencies and contradictions, in order that they can
develop into more genuine, robust versions of themselves – judged by their
own "internal" standards – is difficult but sometimes necessary.

Still, when all is said and done, I think, the default baseline position
must be in favor of extensive religious freedoms for all humans, and the
burden of meeting a high bar of evidence and reason should rest on those
seeking to restrict religious freedom. To do otherwise, if my account
above is correct, inevitably violates something that is, properly understood, natural to humanity in a deep and often very important way.

[33] I am aware that the New Atheists would have us believe that religious faith and practice
per se are inherently abusive and destructive of human dignity and flourishing. I believe
they are wrong about that. In their arguments, their substantive knowledge of religion is
generally terrible, their empirical evidence selective, their confusing of science with
naturalism specious, and their reasoning not entirely coherent, making their case to
directly equate "religion" with evil and destruction ignorant, parochial, and unimpres-
sive. See: Keith Ward, *Is Religion Dangerous?* (Grand Rapids: Eerdmans, 2006);
David Berlinski, *The Devil's Delusion: Atheism and its Scientific Pretensions*
(New York: Crown Forum, 2008); Terry Eagleton, *Reason, Faith, and Revolution:
Reflections on the God Debate* (New Haven: Yale University Press, 2009); David
Bentley Hart, *Atheist Delusions: The Christian Revolution and Its Fashionable Enemies*
(New Haven: Yale University Press, 2010); and Alvin Plantinga, *Where the Conflict
Really Lies: Science, Religion, and Naturalism* (New York: Oxford University Press,
2011).

2

Are Human Beings Naturally Religious?

A Response to Christian Smith

Phil Zuckerman*

In his book, *Natural Atheism*, anthropologist David Eller declares that "all humans are born atheists," and that atheism is the natural default position of all children. Most children, however, subsequently go on to *become* religious because their parents or immediate culture foists religiosity upon them through socialization, whereby "there is a distinct process of instilling in the mind of the child a religious system and thereby transforming that child from a natural question-poser to a socialized question-rejecter."[1] While Eller's position may strike some as extreme, there is in fact extensive evidence from countless studies illustrating the degree to which socialization, particularly family socialization, strongly influences, shapes, and maintains human religiosity.[2] And conversely, studies have shown that when parents *aren't* religious, their children tend to be overwhelmingly secular. For example, Nelson Hart found that – among American families back in the 1980s – if the father was secular but the mother was religious, then about one-sixth of the children of such unions grew up to become secular; if the mother was secular but the father was religious, then about half of such children grew up to be

* I would like to thank Ryan Cragun, Luke Galen, Armin Geertz, Frank Pasquale, Darren Sherkat, John Shook, and Christian Smith for their input, dialogue, and insights that helped me in crafting this paper.
[1] David Eller, *Natural Atheism* (Cranford: American Atheist Press, 2004), 11–12.
[2] For starters, see, for example, Darren Sherkat, "Religious Socialization: Sources of Influence and Influences of Agency," in *Handbook of the Sociology of Religion*, ed. Michele Dillon (New York: Cambridge University Press, 2003); chapter 6 in Benjamin Beit-Hallahmi and Michael Argyle, *The Psychology of Religious Behavior, Belief, and Experience* (New York: Routledge, 1997), 73–96; and chapter 4 in Ronald Johnstone, *Religion in Society: A Sociology of Religion* (Upper Saddle River: Prentice Hall, 1997), 60–88.

secular; if *both* parents were secular, then about 85 percent of such children grew up to be secular themselves.[3] And more recent survey analysis by Steve Bruce and Anthony Glendinning shows that "if someone was not raised in a particular faith, the chances of acquiring one later in life are small." How small? "About 5%."[4]

Thus, some social scientists out there, David Eller among them, argue that atheism specifically, or secularity more broadly, is actually the "natural" state of humanity.

In sharp disagreement, Christian Smith argues that it is religion that is actually natural to the human condition, not atheism or secularity. According to Smith, religion is "irrepressibly natural,"[5] humans have "very strong natural tendencies toward practicing religion,"[6] religiosity is an "ontologically and often existentially innate part of human personhood,"[7] and being religious is, in reality, essentially going *with* "the grain"[8] of what it means to be human.

So who is correct? Eller or Smith? I would argue: *both*. Or rather, *neither*. Humans undoubtedly possess certain natural tendencies to be religious, but they simultaneously *also* possess certain natural tendencies to be secular. Welcome to the messiness of the human condition. Many cultures today are highly religious, such as El Salvador, Zimbabwe, and Bangladesh, while others are highly secular, such as Sweden, the Czech Republic, and Estonia. Some subcultures today are highly secular, such as Americans Jews, while others are highly religious, such as African Americans. Some societies are very religious for centuries, and then religion dramatically fades in a matter of two or three generations.[9] Some societies are relatively secular for a spell, and then religion suddenly erupts with vigor.[10] Some centuries are characterized by relatively high levels of religiosity (such as the sixteenth), while other centuries are characterized

---

[3] Hart M. Nelsen, "The Religious Identification of Children of Interfaith Marriages," *Review of Religious Research* 32 (1990): 122–134.

[4] Steve Bruce and Tony Glendinning, "Religious Beliefs and Differences," in *Devolution: Scottish Answers to Scottish Questions*, ed. Charles Bromley (Edinburgh: Edinburgh University Press, 2003), 86–115. See also Phil Zuckerman, *Faith No More: Why People Reject Religion* (New York: Oxford University Press, 2011).

[5] Christian Smith, "Are Human Beings Naturally Religious?" this volume, pp. 49, 50.

[6] Ibid., 51.   [7] Ibid., 52.   [8] See Ibid., 44, 45, 53.

[9] See, for example, Callum Brown, *The Death of Christian Britain* (New York: Routledge, 2001).

[10] See, for example, the situation in modern Israel: Assaf Inbari, "The End of the Secular Majority," *Haaretz* (Israel), February 3, 2012, www.haaretz.com/israel-news/the-end-of-the-secular-majority-1.410880.

by relatively high levels of secularity (such as the twentieth).[11] Many individuals are strongly religious for decades, and then they suddenly lose their faith, becoming convinced atheists.[12] And many other individuals are secular for many years, and then suddenly find religious faith, becoming extremely pious.[13] And just to add to the complexity, we know that most people are neither totally religious nor totally secular, but maintain and exhibit both orientations simultaneously throughout the course of their lives. Some people find themselves feeling religious or behaving particularly religiously at certain times, and are notably secular at other times. But to suggest, as Professor Smith does, that such people are being more "naturally human" when they are feeling or behaving religiously – and are thus somehow less "naturally human" when they are feeling or behaving in a secular fashion – is simply untenable. Indeed, to privilege either religiosity *or* secularity as somehow more natural, more "with the grain of reality" than the other, is deeply misguided. As cognitive psychologists Armin Geertz and Godmundur Ingi Markusson so astutely argue: "[A]theism … draws on the same natural cognitive capacities that theism draws on" and both "religiosity and atheism represent entrenched cognitive–cultural habits where the conclusions drawn from sensory input and the output of cognitive systems bifurcate in supernatural and naturalistic directions. The habit of atheism *may* need more scaffolding to be acquired, and its religious counterpart may need more effort to kick, but even so, that does not, ipso facto, make the latter more natural than the former."[14]

Thus, my main critique of Professor Smith's paper is that it singles out and privileges religiosity as the "natural" state of being human, which unavoidably mischaracterizes and simultaneously denigrates secularity as somehow "unnatural" – a bit like crab-walking backwards, which is, in fact, the exact analogy Professor Smith uses. To argue, as Professor Smith does, that religious people somehow "walk" properly in accordance with the reality of their human nature, while secular people are "crab-walking backwards" – hampered, strained, clumsily, and awkwardly twisting against their very human natures – no, this will not do. It is not only an

[11] Steve Bruce, *Secularization* (New York: Oxford University Press, 2011).

[12] Zuckerman, *Faith No More.*

[13] Bob Altemeyer and Bruce Hunsberger, *Amazing Conversions: Why Some Turn to Faith and Others Abandon Religion* (Amherst: Prometheus, 1997).

[14] Armin Geertz and Gudmundur Ingi Markusson, "Religion Is Natural, Atheism Is Not: On Why Everybody Is Both Right and Wrong," *Religion* 40 (2010): 152–165.

egregiously biased position, but worse, it is simply unsupportable from a
social scientific perspective.

* * *

I must declare, before continuing, that I do find Professor Smith's paper
quite reasonable in places. The overall tone is admirably sensible, and
even humble, which I appreciate and respect. Professor Smith is truly the
anti-Stark of contemporary sociology of religion. There were many times
when I found myself wanting to sharply disagree with him, yet he couches
his provocative assertions with enough caveats, disclaimers, and sober
acknowledgements of exceptions, that he makes it hard to do so. Just
when I wanted to attack this or that point, he disarmed me with his
thoughtfulness and reasonableness. And indeed, there is so much that I
simply and readily agree with. But, given that I was asked to give a critical
rebuttal, I will do my best to do so.

First off, I find it unwise, generally unhelpful, and potentially quite
dangerous for social scientists to designate certain aspects of human
thought or behavior as "natural" for the simple reason that such designating has been used countless times throughout history to oppress and/
or harm selected groups of people. Certain races have been called
"naturally" inferior to others, with horrific consequences.
Miscegenation laws crippled human flourishing because "mixed race"
marriages were deemed "unnatural." Women have suffered and been
severely hobbled because they have been dubbed "naturally" less capable or intelligent than men. Homosexuals have suffered every kind of
injustice and indignity as a result of being deemed "unnatural." Heck,
just a couple of years ago, Republican (and extremely religious) presidential candidate Rick Santorum declared his opposition to allowing
homosexual couples to adopt parentless children in need of homes
because such families, in his view, are "unnatural." And while I assume
that Mr. Santorum strongly believes in democracy – as well as Professor
Smith, and probably every reader of this essay – it is worth pointing out
that there were times in the not too distant past when democracy itself
was castigated as "unnatural" by men in positions of political power
and scholarly authority.

While I would not go so far as to say that there is *nothing* "essential" or
"natural" about being human, and while I would never deny that all
humans obviously have certain shared universal traits or predispositions
that are the result of our bio-evolutionary, genetic, neurological makeup,
and I while I would furthermore agree that some of those universally

innate traits or predispositions help account for religion's ubiquity,[15] I get nervous – indeed, suspicious – any time a social scientist starts labeling some humans (in this case, the religious) as more in line with the grain of human nature than other humans (in this case, the secular). Such language lends itself easily to political manipulation; I shudder to think of living in a "properly ordered" society (to use Professor Smith's term) in which secular folk are officially deemed "unnatural." Yikes.

A second critique I have is that, as part of his attempt to convince us that religion is natural, Professor Smith argues that it has been present, in one form or another, in all human civilizations. So what? We could say the same thing about rape, incest, humor, sports, xenophobia, teamwork, murder, deceit, illiteracy, dance – but we know that hundreds of millions of humans are not dancers, are utterly uninterested in dance, don't like to dance, and in fact feel incredibly "unnatural" while attempting to dance. We could say the same thing about art. On one hand, art enjoys a certain universality and timelessness. On the other hand, while some people are very artistic, many others are not at all, and a whole slew of people are somewhere in between. We could also say the same thing about violence. It has been present, in one form or another, in all human civilizations. But we know that some people are incredibly violent, while others don't seem to have a violent bone in their body, with many more exhibiting a mixture of both dispositions. Is one more "natural" than the other? Of course not. Violence *and* peacefulness are *both* natural facets of the human condition. Dancers are no more in line with their "natural" humanity than non-dancers. Artists are no more "natural" than non-artists. We find *both* – in abundance – in the human experience. How about polygamy? Or monogamy? Which is "natural"? *Both.* And the same goes with religiosity and secularity: some people are religious, some people aren't. The evidence couldn't be more clear on this front – a fact that Professor Smith admirably acknowledges yet fails to integrate into his theory, because to do so would essentially undo his very enterprise.

A third critique concerns Professor Smith's assertion that religion is "not fading away in the modern world as a whole."[16] There is strong evidence for this assertion. Much of the evidence, however, rests on that most basic cornerstone of demographics: birthrates. Those nations on earth that are highly religious (and also generally quite poor) tend to

---

[15] See, for example, Pascal Boyer, *Religion Explained* (New York: Basic Books, 2002); Stuart Guthrie, *Faces in the Clouds* (New York: Oxford, 1993).

[16] Christian Smith, "Are Human Beings Naturally Religious?" this volume, p. 38.

have the highest birth rates, while the most secular nations on earth (which are often among the most prosperous) tend to have the lowest birth rates. For example, highly religious Niger has a birthrate of 7.6, while highly secular Japan's is only 1.4; highly religious Sierra Leone has a birthrate of 4.6, while highly secular Sweden's is only 1.9.[17] In short, religious people have many more babies than secular people, both globally and within nations.[18] This fact – and no other – accounts for religion's current global maintenance.

But if we set the matter of unequal birthrates aside, we can readily find undeniable evidence of religion's "fading away" throughout much of the modern world. Consider, for example, Canada, where one hundred years ago, only two percent of the population claimed to have no religion. But today, nearly 30 percent of Canadians claim as much,[19] and approximately one in five Canadians does not believe in God.[20] Or consider Australia where, one hundred years ago, less than one percent of the population claimed no religious identity, but today, approximately 20 percent of Australians claim as much.[21] Exploding rates of secularity are even more dramatic in Europe. A century ago in Holland, around ten percent of the population claimed to be religiously unaffiliated; today, it is over 40 percent.[22] And there are now more atheists than theists in Holland – a first in Dutch history.[23] Nonbelievers also outnumber believers in Norway – another historical first for that nation.[24] In contemporary Great Britain, nearly *half* of the people now claim no religious identity at all.[25] And there are now more atheists and agnostics now than theists throughout England, Scotland, and Wales – a

---

[17] "Fertility rate, total (births per woman)," World Bank, accessed July 24, 2016, http://data.worldbank.org/indicator/SP.DYN.TFRT.IN?year_high_desc=true.

[18] Anthony Gottlieb, "Faith Equals Fertility," *Intelligent Life (Economist)*, Winter 2008.

[19] Bruce, *Secularization*, 14.

[20] Bruce Altemeyer, "Non-Belief and Secularity in North America," in *Atheism and Secularity*, ed. Phil Zuckerman (Santa Barbara: Praeger, 2009). See also Reginald Bibby, *Restless Gods* (Toronto: Stoddart, 2002).

[21] Bruce, *Secularization*, 14.   [22] Bruce, *Secularization*, 10.

[23] Taneli Savela, "More Atheists than Believers, but 60 PCT on the Fence," *NL Times* (Netherlands), January 16, 2016, www.nltimes.nl/2015/01/16/atheists-believers-60-pct-fence/.

[24] "For First Time, Majority in Norway don't Believe in God," *The Local* (Norway), March 18, 2016, www.thelocal.no/20160318/majority-of-norwegians-dont-believe-in-god.

[25] Samuel Bagg and David Voas, "The Triumph of Indifference: Irreligion in British Society," in *Atheism and Secularity*, ed. Phil Zuckerman, vol. 2 (Santa Barbara: Praeger, 2010), 97.

first in British history.[26] In Sweden, approximately *half* the population self-identifies as secular.[27] Furthermore, 61 percent of Czechs, 49 percent of Estonians, 45 percent of Slovenians, 34 percent of Bulgarians, and 31 percent of Norwegians do not believe in God.[28] And 40 percent of the French, 27 percent of Belgians, and 27 percent of Germans do not believe in God *or* any sort of universal spiritual life force.[29] Such levels of atheism, agnosticism, and overall irreligion are simply remarkable – not to mention historically unprecedented.

Rates of secularity are also increasing in Latin America.[30] For example, eight percent of adults in Brazil, 11 percent in Argentina, 16 percent in Chile, 18 percent in the Dominican Republic, and 37 percent in Uruguay, now claim to have no religion – the highest rates of secularity ever seen in South America.

Asia is also experiencing widespread secularization. For example, all indicators of religiosity have plummeted in Japan over the past fifty years,[31] and rates of atheism have increased in South Korea.[32] And secularity is truly widespread throughout China, where approximately half of the population is nonreligious.[33]

As for the United States, the percentage of Americans who claim "none" when asked what their religion is has grown from eight percent back in 1990, up to 23 percent today,[34] – some place the percentage of

[26] Nicholas Hellen, "Post-Christian Britain Arrives as Majority Say They Have No Religion," *Sunday Times* (UK), January 17, 2016, www.thesundaytimes.co.uk/sto/new s/uk_news/Society/article1657457.ece

[27] Lars Ahlin, *Pilgrim, Turist, Eller Flykting?* (Stockholm: Brutus Ostlings Bokforlag Symposium, 2005), 94.

[28] Ronald Inglehart et al., eds., *Human Beliefs and Values* (Buenos Aires: Siglo Veintiuno, 2004).

[29] Eurobarometer, "Special Eurobarometer 341: Biotechnology Report," October 2010, 2004, http://ec.europa.eu/public_opinion/archives/ebs/ebs_341_en.pdf.

[30] Pew Research Center, "Religion in Latin America: Widespread Change in a Historically Catholic Region," November 13, 2014, www.pewforum.org/files/2014/11/Religion-in-Latin-America-11-12-PM-full-PDF.pdf.

[31] Ian Reader, "Secularization, R.I.P.? Nonsense! The 'Rush Hour Away from the Gods' and the Decline of Religion in Contemporary Japan," *Journal of Religion in Japan* 1 (2012): 7–36.

[32] WIN-Gallup International, "Global Index of Religiosity and Atheism," 2012, pp. 12–13, www.wingia.com/web/files/news/14/file/14.pdf.

[33] Pew Research Center, "The Future of World Religions: Population Growth Projections, 2010–2050," April 2, 2015, www.pewforum.org/2015/04/02/religious-projections-2010-2050/.

[34] Michael Lipka, "A Closer Look at America's Rapidly Growing Religious 'Nones'," Pew Research Center, May 13, 2015, http://www.pewresearch.org/fact-tank/2015/05/13/a-closer-look-at-americas-rapidly-growing-religious-nones/.

nonreligious Americans even higher, at 28 percent.[35] Among Millennials, rates of irreligion are even higher still – at 35 percent.[36] In absolute numbers, approximately 660,000 Americans join the ranks of those claiming no religion every year.[37] And nearly half of all "nones" are atheist or agnostic in orientation, about a quarter believe in a "higher power," and just over a quarter believe in a "personal God"[38] – so the rise of irreligion also means a simultaneous rise of atheism and agnosticism as well, evidencing the highest rates of secularity even seen in US history.

Given all of the above, it is no wonder that *National Geographic* ran a feature story in 2016 with the headline: "The World's Newest Major Religion: No Religion."[39]

Now, I don't for one minute think that the above information proves that secularization is somehow inevitable or irreversible. But it does prove that it is possible, and that it is occurring. For Professor Smith to deny the reality of religion's fading throughout much of the Western world – and elsewhere – over the course of the last 100 years is downright ostrich-like, and shows that, in his theorizing, he does *not* in fact "use all available empirical evidence," as his own perspective of "critical realism" apparently requires.

My fourth critique concerns the underlying breadth of Professor Smith's argument. His argument is so flagrantly broad, I contend, as to become almost useless. Here is what I mean. Professor Smith writes the following in his explication of what he means when he says that humans are naturally religious:

All human persons are naturally religious if by that we mean that they possess, by virtue of their given ontological being, a complex set of innate features, capacities, powers, limitations, and tendencies which capacitate them to be religious (i.e., to think, perceive, feel, imagine, desire, and act religiously), and which, under the right conditions, tend to predispose and direct them toward religion. The natural

---

[35] Joseph Baker and Buster Smith, *American Secularism: Cultural Contours of Nonreligious Belief Systems* (New York: New York University Press, 2015), 1, 23.

[36] Michael Lipka, "Millennials Increasingly Are Driving Growth of 'Nones'," Pew Research Center, May 12, 2015, http://www.pewresearch.org/fact-tank/2015/05/12/millennials-increasingly-are-driving-growth-of-nones/.

[37] Barry A. Kosmin et al., "American Nones: The Profile of the No Religion Population, A Report Based on the American Religious Identification Survey 2008," Trinity College, 2009, p. 20, http://commons.trincoll.edu/aris/files/2011/08/NONES_08.pdf.

[38] Ibid., 11.

[39] Gabe Bullard, "The World's Newest Major Religion: No Religion," *National Geographic*, April 22, 2016, http://news.nationalgeographic.com/2016/04/160422-athe ism-agnostic-secular-nones-rising-religion/.

religiousness of humanity is thus located not in a naturally determined uniformity of empirical religious practice, either by individuals or societies (which is how positivist empiricism would focus our attention). It is instead located in the distinctive, inherent features, capacities, powers, limitations, and tendencies of human persons that are rooted, ultimately, in the human body and the emergent (often non-material) capacities that arise from the body.

Human persons being "religious by nature" in this sense should not be taken lightly. We are speaking here of very powerful causal forces and dispositions rooted in the very nature of reality which are chronically triggered to operate in human life in a variety of human social contexts. That helps to explain religion's primordial, irrepressible, widespread, and seemingly inextinguishable character in the human experience. If true, it also suggests that the skeptical Enlightenment, secular humanist, and New Atheist visions for a totally secular human world are simply not realistic – they are cutting against a very strong "grain" in the nature of reality's structure and so will fail to achieve their purpose [emphasis in the original].[40]

But we could plug in just about *any* word in place of "religious," and the assertion would still work. Instead of "religious" in the above passage, we could insert "cowardly" (or "heroic"!), "happy" (or "depressed"!), "optimistic" (or "pessimistic"!), "horny" (or "totally uninterested in sex"!), "racist" (or "anti-racist"!), "polygamous" (or "monogamous"!), etc. – and it still works. Just for fun, let's insert "criminality" in place of "religious" and see what happens:

All human persons are naturally [criminal] if by that we mean that they possess, by virtue of their given ontological being, a complex set of innate features, capacities, powers, limitations, and tendencies which capacitate them to be [criminal] (i.e., to think, perceive, feel, imagine, desire, and act [criminally]), and which, under the right conditions, tend to predispose and direct them toward [criminality]. The natural [criminality] of humanity is thus located not in a naturally determined uniformity of empirical [criminal] practice, either by individuals or societies (which is how positivist empiricism would focus our attention). It is instead located in the distinctive, inherent features, capacities, powers, limitations, and tendencies of human persons that are rooted, ultimately, in the human body and the emergent (often non-material) capacities that arise from the body.

Human persons being "[criminal] by nature" in this sense should not be taken lightly. We are speaking here of very powerful causal forces and dispositions rooted in the very nature of reality and are chronically triggered to operate in human life in a variety of human social contexts. That helps to explain [criminality's] primordial, irrepressible, widespread, and seemingly inextinguishable character in the human experience. If true, it also suggests that the [theological], [religious], and [humanistic] visions for a totally [law-abiding] human world are simply not realistic – they are cutting against a very strong "grain" in the nature of reality's structure and so will fail to achieve their purpose.

[40] Christian Smith, "Are Human Beings Naturally Religious?" this volume, p. 45.

Such theorizing is so broad as to be essentially useless as far as the practice of social science is concerned.

Fifth, related to my scrutiny of the above passage, Professor Smith argues that all people possess certain innate features, capacities, and tendencies which, "under the right conditions, tend to predispose and direct them toward religion." The four words "under the right conditions" are pretty important here. In fact, they are supremely important, and lie at the very core of sociology and anthropology. After all, *under the right conditions*, people can be directed toward genocide, organ-donating, communism, graffiti-spraying, extreme consumerism, body-piercing, celibacy, trick-or-treating, vegetarianism, paintball playing, nationalism, TV watching – and on and on and on. "Under the right conditions" is what the social sciences are all about. Thus, to say that "under the right conditions" people tend to be religious isn't saying much of anything at all. In fact, it is admitting that social forces, cultural dynamics, and historical contingencies are extremely crucial in the development of religiosity – *and* secularity – rendering the insistence that one is more "natural" than the other all the more dubious.

* * *

Faith and doubt, credulity and skepticism, theism and atheism, religious fervor and utter religious indifference – these are all parts of the human condition. In some cultures or eras, one is stronger or more pervasive than the other; in other cultures or eras, vice versa. For some individuals, one is more dominant, and in other individuals, it is just the opposite. Attempting to understand why this is the case involves marshaling the best evidence possible – looking at historical developments, neuropsychological predispositions, human evolution, economic and political factors, cultural trends, social forces, family influence, socialization, etc. But designating only one (i.e., religion) as "natural," as Professor Smith does, essentially subverts the very goal of social science, reducing very important and complex questions about religiosity/secularity to nothing more than mere philosophical speculation concerning human ontology, speculation that can readily admit that, sure, not everyone is religious, but heck, not everyone walks properly either.

To argue, as Professor Smith does, that humans are "naturally" religious will most likely have the unfortunate consequence of elevating religious people to a privileged status – as those human beings best in line with their very human natures – while simultaneously denigrating secular people to an inferior status as woefully and pitifully out of sync with the very reality of human nature. Professor Smith's theory would thus reify the notion that religiosity is somehow better or healthier, while secularity is somehow pathological or hazardous (which, even if true – which I would contest – would not in itself mean that one is more "natural" than the other!). Professor Smith's theory unavoidably celebrates religion as an expression of *true* human nature, and castigates secularity as a retardation, obfuscation, or denigration thereof. Religiosity is thus constructed as essentially and ontologically correct, while secularity is constructed as essentially and ontologically wrong. And this is all, frankly, really bad sociology. And it is really bad psychology. But what is much worse, it reveals a shockingly deep lack of imagination concerning the fascinating complexities of the human condition.

* * *

As for the final matter of religious freedom, I will offer the following:

I think the founders of the United States got it right in the First Amendment – democratically elected governments should not be in the business of establishing, funding, running, supervising, or pushing religion, nor should they go about seeking to limit the free exercise of religion by inhibiting, prohibiting, or restricting religiosity, or persecuting people because of their religion. Amen to that.

There is no question that, when we look at the world today, those nations that limit religious freedom tend to be among the most undemocratic of societies – totalitarian, despotic, tyrannical. Indeed, where religious freedom is restricted, we also find limits on women's rights, gay rights, minority rights, political freedoms, civil liberties, freedom of the press, speech, etc. This correlation can't be coincidental. Governments that tell people how or how not to be religious, and enforce such regulations, are undoubtedly bad governments, and usually brutal.

But while I wholeheartedly share Professor Smith's support of religious freedom, my underlying reasons are qualitatively different from his. He seems to think that religion should be protected from government repression because religion is "natural" and thus government restrictions on religious freedom go against inherent, innate qualities of human personhood. I, however, support *religious* freedom simply because I support *human* freedom, and all that entails. Whether religion is "natural" is beside the point. Criminality and violence are also theorizable as "natural," but that doesn't mean governments should therefore "respect criminal and violent freedom." Please. But it is in this very section of Professor Smith's paper that he actually tips his hand and allows us to see most clearly the inevitable and disturbing political implications of his theory. He argues that since religion is dubbed "natural" (but *not* secularity), governments ought to respect religion and leave it alone. But by this logic, since secularity is constructed as "unnatural," then governments surely need not necessarily respect it to the same degree, if at all. While Professor Smith may not personally hold this position, it is inevitably implied, and unavoidably embedded, in his work.

The bottom line is that people have the right to believe in whatever they want (be it Jesus or their friends), worship whatever they want (be it Buddha statues or carrots), assemble however they like (be it at a Mass or a motorcycle parade), pray to whatever they like (be it Allah or Elvis), engage in whatever rituals they like (be it a bar mitzvah or a high school graduation), read whatever they like (be it the *Upanishads* or Stephen King), wear whatever they like (be it a crucifix or shark tooth), so long as these activities do not cause harm to others, and are done within the established legal limits set within our Constitution.

3

On the Naturalness of Religion and Religious Freedom

Justin L. Barrett

Jesse Bering's recent book *The Belief Instinct* and Robert McCauley's *Why Religion Is Natural and Science Is Not* are two of a number of published works promoting what I call the naturalness of religion thesis: because of the nature of human minds, religious expression in beliefs and practices is nearly inevitable in most populations and the majority of individuals within those populations. In this paper I will sketch the sorts of reasons that have been leading scholars to conclude that religion is natural and then offer a few comments regarding the implication of such scientific conclusions for religious freedom. First, I want to dispense with some unhelpful concepts in support of what I believe is a helpful use of the term "naturalness."

The naturalness thesis is often mistaken for the claim that religious beliefs – particularly theistic ones – are "innate" or "hard-wired" into the human brain. Journalists have mistakenly represented me as advocating such a view. Let me be clear: I do not much care for trying to characterize certain cognitive capacities or forms of cultural expression such as religion as *innate* or not. After all, what would it mean for something to be *innate*? It cannot mean determined by our biology because no cognitive capacity or form of cultural expression, strictly, is determined by our biology absent important environmental qualifications. Does *innate* mean present at birth? But what makes birth special – especially now that we regularly schedule and induce birth? And what about predictable but late-arriving capacities such as speech or sexual behaviors?

Similarly, in recent years we have begun to hear cognitive traits referred to as "hard-wired." This problematic metaphor comes from electrical systems. If you have a hard-wired appliance, it is part of the electrical system of (for instance) your house and you cannot simply unplug it. Overhead light fixtures are hard-wired but floor lamps that you plug into the wall are not. Smoke alarms may be hard-wired into the electrical system of the house, but battery-operated smoke alarms are not. Applied to cognitive systems, "hard-wired" is sometimes used to mean invariable or fixed in some way by the circuitry of the brain. For those of us who think that we think through our brain (or, more strongly, that our brain thinks), it is a little odd to say that some cognition is part of our brain circuitry whereas other cognition is not: it is *all* part of our cognitive "electrical system." So the emphasis added by "hard-wired" just means a degree of rigidity, automaticity or invariance. But this is an issue of degree, whereas in reality to be hard-wired (as in electrical systems) is a discrete concept – either hard-wired or not.

I find terms like *innate* and *hard-wired* problematic, but surely they are pointing toward an important consideration regarding human cognition: just how much is a given trait or capacity *variable* from one person to another because of environmental factors, and *variable* across situations in a given individual based on context or volition? To capture these questions, I will use a distinction proposed by philosopher of cognitive science Robert McCauley, but with slight modification. Throughout I will refer to the *naturalness* of a trait or capacity, but naturalness meant in a particular way.

COGNITIVE NATURALNESS

McCauley uses *naturalness* to refer to thought processes or behaviors that are characterized by ease, automaticity, and fluency. Those abilities that require little conscious attention or effort are *natural* in McCauley's sense. Speaking a native language, adding 2+2, and walking are natural for most of us in this respect. McCauley goes on to observe that this kind of naturalness can come about in two basic ways. *Practiced naturalness* arises through lots and lots of practice, training, tuition, and cultural support (including relevant artifacts) as in gaining chess mastery or becoming a concert pianist. In contrast, *maturational naturalness* seems to just appear as a matter of developmental course – as in learning to walk or talk or add small numbers.[1] Of course, many forms of cultural

---

[1] Maturational naturalness may involve heavy repetition or practice. Practice is not a distinguishing feature between these two types of naturalness unless we regard "practice" as indicating deliberate, consciously motivated rehearsal. With this narrower view of

expression that we find "natural" bear some marks of both practiced and maturational naturalness. Literacy, which requires practice, training, tuition, and writing tools, for instance, can get so automatic and fluent that we find it hard to turn off.

Though many (if not all) forms of expression we would call cultural show signs of both practiced and maturational naturalness, not all cognitive systems that underlie these forms of expression have this dual character. Some cognitive capacities are decidedly maturationally natural. I wish to focus on these maturationally natural capacities because they bear the important feature of being present in most all normally developing humans of any cultural group. Indeed, a good rule of thumb McCauley suggests for identifying such maturationally natural cognition is whether its absence in your child would make you worry that an abnormality is present. If your five-year-old child just can't develop chess mastery, even after many lessons and lots of practice, you would probably just shrug, but if your five-year-old were not speaking you would be concerned. Maturationally natural cognitive capacities typically arise early in development (in the first five years of life) as a matter of course.[2] It follows that they are broadly present across cultures in largely similar forms. These capacities are the foundations upon which cultural learning and expertise are built.

Note that this view of maturationally natural cognition does not require that the capacities are present at birth, biologically determined, hard-wired, or innate. Some of these capacities could be largely fixed before birth or impervious to environmental inputs (outside of normal biological needs). Other maturationally natural capacities might be largely a product being tuned up by environmental regularities that occur in any cultural context: rocks are solid everywhere, plants require sunlight, babies have mothers, and so on. We often overlook just how regular many aspects of the world (including the social world) are. Identifying something as maturationally natural doesn't commit one to a hard stance on any of these issues.

"practice" it might be argued that the maturationally natural does not typically require such deliberate efforts to attain.

[2] Some thought and behavior related to reproduction appear later but would still qualify as maturationally natural. I add to McCauley's characteristic features of maturational versus practiced naturalness another type of early development. If a trait or capacity has been part of human prehistory for a long time it is more likely to be maturationally natural. Practiced natural capacities are relative latecomers: mostly in the last 10,000 years. Robert N. McCauley, *Why Religion Is Natural and Science Is Not* (New York: Oxford University Press, 2011).

The regularity and early development of maturationally natural capacities make me think that these capacities map on to what we normally think of as part of human nature or as natural cognition. For this reason, and for linguistic economy, I will use *natural* to mean maturationally natural. In contrast, I will refer to practiced naturalness as *expertise*.

NATURAL GENERAL COGNITION[3]

The most obvious and least controversial features of natural cognition are *general* limitations such as limits on perception, attention, and memory. We know full well from our own experiences that we cannot remember everything we might want to remember, whether it be long-term memory or consciously attended-to *working memory*. We can only attend to so many units of information at one time. In fact, one of the first sallies in the "cognitive revolution" that launched cognitive science was research by George Miller investigating working memory.[4] His experiments led to the claim that working memory is limited to approximately seven-plus-or-minus-two chunks of information – a claim that has undergone some modification but is still in the right ballpark: we can (usually) only keep up to around seven chunks of information in attention at once, and sometimes fewer than that. *Chunks* might sound crude, but it means roughly the largest conceptually meaningful unit a person recognizes. So, the digits [o], [7], [o], [4], [1], [7], [7], [6], may be represented as eight chunks (one for each digit) or recognized as the date July 4, 1776, and be represented as either three chunks, if that is just an arbitrary date with no particular significance, one chunk for [July], one for [4], and one for [1776]; or as just one chunk, [American Independence Day]. Knowledge, then, influences chunk sizes, but big or small, it is still unusual to be able to keep more than seven or so chunks of information in working memory.

This observation about working memory being limited has important consequences for perception, thought, and communication. Applied to perception, a limit on working memory suggests restrictions on how rich

---

[3] In this discussion of natural cognition, I do not specify just how the brain limits the mind. To do so would be premature in most cases and be beside the point. We do not need to specify exactly how my body limits my ability to be a world-class sprinter (does it have something to do with leg length, fast-twitch muscle fibers, or what?) to know that a physical limitation is in play.

[4] George A. Miller, "The Magical Number Seven, Plus or Minus Two: Some Limits on Our Capacity for Processing Information," *Psychological Review* 63, no. 2 (1956): 81–97.

a representation of the world around us we can maintain. Simply too much information comes pouring in at one time for us to attend to it all. We have the *illusion* of a complete representation of the world around us, particularly in familiar environments, because we know what should be there. That is, our knowledge automatically, non-consciously fills in the blanks. We have to attend to only enough details about the environment to trigger the right conceptual information or the right course of actions.

To get around our working memory limitations in thinking we also make heavy use of what might be termed "intuitive" or "tacit" knowledge: ideas we typically don't even know we have but once it is pointed out it just seems right; it is intuitive. To illustrate, we tacitly know that animals have babies like themselves. Dogs, for instance, have baby dogs. Cats have baby cats. This fact is so banal that it is rarely stated, nor does it even need to be stated. If I tell you that a manoby in the local zoo had babies I don't need to tell you that it had baby manobies instead of baby wallabies – that information is there automatically, tacitly, intuitively. In fact, you also tacitly know that the manoby moves to obtain nutrition, has parts inside of it that make it go, is made of organic matter, is a bounded physical object that cannot pass directly through other objects, and a host of other pieces of information – even though you have never heard of a manoby before (because I made it up). This intuitive knowledge is built into the chunk "manoby" and so doesn't take up precious working memory space.

Because this extra conceptual information gets smuggled in "free of charge" to working memory, it serves as an important prop for communication. Real-time face-to-face verbal communication makes working memory demands that could easily outstrip seven-plus-or-minus-two chunks if not for conceptual information that can be assumed. Again, if I tell you that the local zoo has a manoby that gave birth, I don't have to tell you that it grows, requires food, and the rest. The consequence is efficient communication. I only need to communicate enough information to trigger this conceptual background information and trust your mind to fill in the rest.[5] Note, however, that if I am trying to tell you about something for which you don't naturally possess background conceptual

---

[5] In fact, if I set off telling you that the manoby has to eat, grows, is made of organic material, and the like, you will think (rightly) that there is something wrong with me. I have violated the normal expectation governing communication that I will only explicitly tell you information that might be novel, important, and meaningful to you – an expectation Dan Sperber and Deidre Wilson have argued to be a natural part of human cognition pertaining to communication. See: Dan Sperber and Deirdre Wilson, *Relevance: Communication and Cognition,* 2nd ed. (Oxford: Blackwell Publishing, 1995).

information that can flesh out the skeleton of verbal communication, I have the increased burden of detailing all of this information and you have the burden of keeping enough of it in working memory at a time that it can be sufficiently comprehended to be encoded into long-term memory for later use. It follows that ideas that are largely composed of the conceptual building materials we already have are more easily and readily communicated. Ideas that deviate from our intuitive knowledge require more effort, attention, and repetition (or other devices) for successful communication.

Working memory and attendant attentional limitations cause us to depend on intuitive knowledge for rapid reasoning, communicating, and learning. As ideas that make good use of existing intuitive knowledge will be easiest to acquire, use, and communicate, then knowing something about what kind of intuitive knowledge people are likely to have is critically important in knowing what they can readily acquire, use, and communicate. And, it may come as no surprise that the intuitive knowledge that virtually all people will share has its origins in (maturationally) natural cognition.[6]

NATURAL CONTENT-SPECIFIC COGNITION

In contrast to *general* cognition, we also have limitations and tendencies when it comes to specific domains of cognitive content, what might be called *content-specific cognition*. Not all information about all topics is treated the same. In my experience, this claim is more surprising and more controversial, so allow me to provide two examples to make the point.

Humans (and monkeys) have a natural disposition to become afraid of snakes. It is very easy for a person to become afraid of snakes compared to flowers or butterflies. People have been shown to rapidly detect snakelike objects, and to be readily conditioned to fear snakes – even when they are not consciously aware of having seen the snake. Infants readily associate snakes with fearful stimuli: when presented with a photo of a snake and another animal (e.g., a hippo) along with a voice speaking in a frightened

---

[6] Not all intuitive knowledge is necessarily (maturationally) natural. As suggested in the discussion of practiced versus maturational naturalness, expertise can bring with it deeply ingrained, automatic associations and ideas that become "intuitive." This expertise-based intuitive knowledge, however, will be irregularly acquired by humans and highly variable, whereas the intuitive knowledge that springs from natural cognition will be available to nearly everyone and from an earlier age. For this reason, generally *intuitive* refers to natural cognition as opposed to expertise in the study of cognitive development.

tone, they preferentially look at the snake, but not when the voice uses a happy tone. If you suspect that this rapid fear-association with snakes is due to cultural peculiarities, consider this: monkeys raised without exposure to snakes (in captivity) can acquire a long-lasting fear of snakes merely by watching another monkey react in fear to a snake. Not so with watching a monkey react in fear to a bunny. Monkeys and humans alike have a *preparedness* to become afraid of snakes. Why might this be? As snakes might prove dangerous and are rarely a dominant source of food or other survival aid, a good survival strategy is simply to avoid snakes. Having a natural bias to become afraid of snakes would be adaptive for monkeys, humans, and other animals.[7]

Newborn babies differentially detect faces and imitate their expressions. From immediately following birth (within hours) human babies already attend more to human faces in their environment than to most other sorts of things out there. The baby in the delivery-room bassinet would rather look at mother's face than a pile of rags, the colorful wallpaper, or the nearby sphygmomanometer. Even more surprising is that within a few hours after birth babies can imitate some facial expressions such as sticking out the tongue.[8] Think what is involved in this feat: among the blurry mass of novel stimuli a baby detects something in her environment (the face) and maps the thing's appearance and movement onto her own facial musculature to create a comparable expression. And the baby doesn't even know she has a face yet! Again, as impressive as this is for a newborn with very poor visual acuity, the finding makes sense. Spotting and recognizing other humans is terribly important for human social success. Having some natural biases that give an advantage in processing faces (as compared with, say, trees, potatoes, or the faces of cows or chickens) would be helpful. This content-specific facility with human faces persists into adulthood: most adults are remarkably facile

---

[7] For more information on the relevant experiments see: Arne Öhman and Susan Mineka, "Fears, Phobias, and Preparedness: Toward an Evolved Module of Fear and Fear Learning," *Psychological Review* 108, no. 3 (2001): 483–522; Arne Öhman and Susan Mineka, "The Malicious Serpent: Snakes as a Prototypical Stimulus for an Evolved Module of Fear," *Current Directions in Psychological Science* 12, no. 1 (2003): 5–9; and Judy S. DeLoache and Vanessa LoBue, "The Narrow Fellow in the Grass: Human Infants Associate Snakes and Fear," *Developmental Science* 12, no. 1 (2009): 201–207.

[8] Andrew N. Meltzoff and N. Keith Moore, "Newborn Infants Imitate Adult Facial Gestures," *Child Development* 54 (1983): 702–709. Exactly which gestures and at which (early) age children can imitate them is debated but does not change the point that such imitation is a very early emerging and essentially universal capacity.

with identifying and remembering thousands of faces when compared with comparably complex and varied visual stimuli.

These two areas of content-specific natural cognitive bias – fearing snakes and detecting faces – are just the tip of the iceberg, but I hope they are sufficient to illustrate a key point: the mind as a whole is not helpfully compared to a blank slate only limited by capacity. Rather, our minds preferentially attend to and differentially process some types of information over others, handling different domains of information in different ways.

Based upon these considerations about human cognition – particularly that we have processing limitations that force us to rely upon tacit knowledge for perception, communication, and learning – we would not expect religious ideas concerning supernatural agents to be massively widespread and enduring (as they are) unless they had close relations with knowledge structures that humans naturally possess.

REFLECTIVE BELIEFS AND INTUITIONS

Reflective beliefs – our consciously entertained and affirmed ideas and propositions – oftentimes are obtained through the automatic deliverances of intuitions. As Nobel Laureate Daniel Kahneman's work has shown, if an idea readily comes to mind – has that familiar, intuitive ring – it seems right to us and we are inclined to accept it. This is what he calls *accessibility bias*.[9] Ideas that are part of content-specific natural cognition will be the large pool of ideas that people have in common across cultures. Thus, natural cognition anchors and informs the range of likely reflective beliefs people will hold. In other words, natural cognition provides default positions for reflective beliefs. It is hard work to reason, and so we are inclined to just accept intuitions for reflective beliefs. For instance, when confronted with a question that they have never consciously considered – such as, "Do you believe snakes are dangerous?" – people may have no explicit, reflective belief one way or the other but must come to a decision. Unless relevant information, such as from previous education in zoology, comes to mind, the most likely reflective belief will be that option consistent with relevant natural cognition. If thinking about snakes triggers an association with fear and danger, as is often the case, then the non-reflective intuition, "Snakes are scary," seems right and

---

[9] Daniel Kahneman, "A Perspective on Judgment and Choice: Mapping Bounded Rationality," *American Psychologist* 58, no. 9 (2003): 697–720.

serves as the starting point or default for the reflective belief, "Snakes are scary and dangerous." Consider the question of whether other people have conscious thoughts. Maybe it has never occurred to me to think explicitly about whether other people have conscious thoughts and I have not been exposed to related philosophical ruminations. So, how do I form a reflective belief on the subject? I tap my intuitions and discover the intuitive idea, "People have conscious minds." Finding no reason to reject or override such an intuition, I accept it (at least initially) as my reflective belief. In the absence of salient, relevant, consciously accessible reasons not to do so, reflective beliefs are simply read-offs of natural intuitions.[10] For more complex propositions, or those not immediately delivered by our natural cognition, credence increases with the cumulative support of various ideas automatically delivered by natural cognition. An idea that manages to resonate with many different natural intuitions will just seem right. As we shall see, my argument is that beliefs in gods often have just this type of cumulative cognitive support.

What, then, are the features of natural cognition that support belief in gods or other religious ideas and, hence, make religion *natural*?

WHAT MAKES RELIGION NATURAL?

Cognitive scientists of religion have identified a number of features of human minds that combine to make religion natural, particularly the way we identify intentional agents, the way we reason about minds and about bodies, and our tendency to search for purpose in the natural world. Importantly, all are cognitive faculties that are foundational for the way humans make sense of their world and life in it. These faculties are not add-ons to human nature or systems that we can simply turn off.

Humans have a strong natural propensity to focus particular attention on the difference between the actors and the props in the world, or between agents and objects. Agents are beings with minds – or "minded" beings – that act based on mental states such as beliefs, desires, and precepts. Objects only react to what goes on around them and so cannot

---

[10] See: Chapter 1 of Justin L. Barrett, *Why Would Anyone Believe in God?* (Lanham: AltaMira Press, 2004); Chapter 9 of Pascal Boyer, *Religion Explained: The Evolutionary Origins of Religious Thought* (New York: Basic Books, 2001); Dan Sperber, "Intuitive and Reflective Beliefs," *Mind and Language* 12 (1997): 67–83.

initiate action. From infancy babies are sensitive to this difference between agents and objects.[11]

Arguably, as social beings, both selective attention to agents and trying to understand and predict their actions are critically important for human thriving. For this reason, our cognitive system for detecting agents and our system for thinking about their actions might be especially eager and active. This hypertrophied social mind has been noted by many cognitive scientists of religion as playing a critical role in religious expression.[12]

I have termed the system for detecting agents and their activity the Hypersensitive Agency Detection Device (HADD). Evidence that humans have such a system and that it can be easily triggered is strong.[13] Stewart Guthrie has argued that the human perceptual and conceptual tendency to see humanlike agents and agency everywhere – even in situations we later recant – is an example of better-safe-than-sorry tuning,[14] also known as *error management*.[15] Guthrie has argued that this tendency to find humanlike agency even where it does not actually exist is a primary generator of belief in gods. We have *HADD-experiences*, experiences in which we detect agency for which the type of agency is unclear, and then sometimes regard them as evidence of a god or gods. Our natural cognitive systems find "minded" agency even where there may not be any, and are likewise attracted to intentional explanations for natural events and states of affairs. Gods, by these lights, may be false positives.[16]

---

[11] György Gergely and Gergely Csibra, "Teleological Reasoning in Infancy: The Naive Theory of Rational Action," *Trends in Cognitive Sciences* 7, no. 7 (2003): 287–292; Philippe Rochat, Tricia Striano, and Rachel Morgan, "Who is Doing What to Whom? Young Infants' Developing Sense of Social Causality in Animated Displays," *Perception* 33 (2004): 355–369.

[12] Stewart E. Guthrie, *Faces in the Clouds: A New Theory of Religion* (New York: Oxford University Press, 1993); Robert N. McCauley and E. Thomas Lawson, *Bringing Ritual to Mind: Psychological Foundations of Cultural Forms* (Cambridge: Cambridge University Press, 2002); Boyer, *Religion Explained*; Jesse M. Bering, *The Belief Instinct: The Psychology of Souls, Destiny, and the Meaning of Life* (New York: W. W. Norton & Company, 2011); Barrett, *Why Would Anyone Believe in God?*; Barrett, *Born Believers: The Science of Childhood Religion* (New York: Atria Books, 2012).

[13] Brian J. Scholl and Patrice D. Tremoulet, "Perceptual Causality and Animacy," *Trends in Cognitive Sciences* 4 (2000): 299–309.

[14] Guthrie, *Faces in the Clouds*.

[15] Ryan T. McKay and Daniel C. Dennett, "The Evolution of Misbelief," *Behavioral and Brain Sciences* 32 (2009): 493–561.

[16] Guthrie's argument raises an interesting epistemological problem. How do we know that these are "false positives"? The agency detection cognitive system (or HADD) would have to be checked against a different, reliable system for identifying when agency has been

Even if one is uncomfortable with Guthrie's decidedly dismissive approach concerning the possible existence of one or many gods, his general point is helpful. Our natural cognition readily applies purposive and mentalistic construals to a broad range of objects, states, and events even given only ambiguous evidence that mental agency is in fact at play. If one has been exposed to a god concept – and if in principle the god's activities are detectable in the world – one's agency detection system has a good likelihood of detecting evidence of the god's activity at least occasionally. Similarly, given that HADD is more forgiving of false positives than failures of detection, one will occasionally encounter events or conditions that *seem* to cry out for an explanation in terms of the activity of an intentional agent, and a regular human or animal will clearly be insufficient. Such events might occasionally lead to the postulation of a god (or support the existence of a known god).

Once an agent is "detected," the Theory of Mind system (ToM) generates a host of intuitions regarding the motivations for the alleged actions of the agent. ToM or *folk psychology*, as it is sometimes called, includes intuitions about what others are thinking, what they perceive, what they want, their emotional states and beliefs, and the relationships among these various mental states. For instance, we typically think that people act to satisfy desires through means that are informed by beliefs, which are guided by percepts. ToM eagerly wants to know why agents did what they did and what they will do next. Though thinking about the minds of other people might be the most prominent activity for ToM, ToM does not require the agent in question to be physically present or visible, even in young children, as research on imaginary friends shows.[17]

accurately detected. Do we have such a system, or do we just have the one agency detection system? Maybe it is at the point we decide we do *not* detect intentional agency that a mistake is sometimes made. Though evidence for some HADD-like system is strong, whether and how it contributes to belief in gods requires more empirical attention.

Guthrie uses different language in presenting his argument. He favors the term *anthropomorphism* to capture the tendency to attribute events and states to intentional agents. I avoid this term for three reasons. First, it carries the connotation that all intentional agency is humanlike, whereas this is an open question. In many cases it is not human agency that is being postulated but something different. Second, anthropomorphism is often associated with importantly different approaches such as Freudian or Piagetian, and can carry the assumption that the agency in question is thought to have a humanlike bodily form. My third concern is that the term anthropomorphism dodges an important theological question: To what extent is human agency a reflection of divine agency – theomorphism – rather than the other way around?

[17] Marjorie Taylor, *Imaginary Companions and the Children Who Create Them* (New York: Oxford University Press, 1999); J. Bradley Wigger, Katrina Paxson, and

If an event or state of affairs is processed as being the product of an intentional agent by HADD, ToM picks up the task of determining why the agent in question did it. A common class of states for which such reasoning seems natural is the arrangement of the natural world. Through numerous experiments, Deborah Kelemen and colleagues have produced considerable evidence that children exercise what she calls *promiscuous teleology*: a tendency to find design and purpose in the natural world beyond what parents license. For instance, children are inclined to say rocks are "pointy" not because of some physical processes but because being pointy keeps rocks from being sat upon and crushed.[18] Using teleological reasoning to account for the origins or causes of things extends to living things such as plants and animals and non-living natural things such as rocks and rivers, but is less applicable to natural events such as thunderstorms.[19] Interestingly, Kelemen has recently produced evidence that adults that have not been formally educated show a preference for teleological explanations that is similar to that of even scientifically educated adults under conditions of hurried response.[20] These results suggest that promiscuous teleology is not outgrown but only tamped down in some cultural contexts. Perhaps not surprisingly, this teleological reasoning often finds a comfortable fit with the idea that the purpose was brought about by an intentional agent or creator. This conceptual space seems to invite a god or gods to fill it. Replicating Piaget's investigations into children's ideas about who should be credited with the natural world's apparent design and purpose,[21] contemporary researchers have found that preschoolers show no confusion: humans make pencils and chairs, but God makes animals and stars.[22]

Lacey Ryan, "What Do Invisible Friends Know? Imaginary Companions, God, and Theory of Mind," *International Journal for the Psychology of Religion* 23 (2013): 2–14.

[18] Deborah Kelemen, "Why Are Rocks Pointy? Children's Preference for Teleological Explanations of the Natural World," *Developmental Psychology* 35 (1999): 1440–1452.

[19] Deborah Kelemen, "Are Children 'Intuitive Theists'? Reasoning about Purpose and Design in Nature," *Psychological Science* 15 (2004): 295–301.

[20] Deborah Kelemen and Evelyn Rosset, "The Human Function Compunction: Teleological Explanation in Adults," *Cognition* 111 (2009): 138–143; Deborah Kelemen, Joshua Rottman, and Rebecca Seston, "Professional Physical Scientists Display Tenacious Teleological Tendencies: Purpose-based Reasoning as a Cognitive Default," *Journal of Experimental Psychology: General* 142 (2013): 1074–1083.

[21] Jean Piaget, *The Child's Conception of the World*, trans. Andrew Tomlinson (Patterson: Littlefield, Adams, 1960).

[22] Susan A. Gelman and Kathleen E. Kremer, "Understanding Natural Cause: Children's Explanations of How Objects and their Properties Originate," *Child Development* 62 (1991): 396–414.

Taking Guthrie and Kelemen's work together, we see that humans have natural, intuitive impetus for postulating gods. Events and things in the world appear purposeful, designed, or otherwise the product of minded, intentional activity. It has been speculated that events of unusual fortune or misfortune likewise provide motivation to consider the existence and activities of gods.[23] When some improbable event happens that seems meaningful, we might readily assume that someone, perhaps a divine someone, is responsible.[24]

Such thinking could be reinforced by moral intuitions as well. Psychologists have discovered some evidence that we easily think about the world as operating on some kind of reciprocity principle, what is called *Just World Reasoning*.[25] If someone does something morally wrong, something bad is more likely to befall him. But why? One way of theologically elaborating this intuition is to postulate a punishing and rewarding force such as karma, as we see in many Asian religions. Alternatively, a fairly intuitive account would be that someone knows about the wrongdoing and punishes it. As gods might know even what is done in secret, and can use natural forces and things to reward or punish, gods may serve an explanatory purpose in these cases of unusual fortune or misfortune. Even gods that have little concern about human interactions may be vengeful when humans trespass against them.

The natural tendency to see agency around us, to see purpose in the world, to demand explanation for uncommon fortune or misfortune, and

---

[23] Bering, *The Belief Instinct.*

[24] More evidence for such a claim is needed but the idea has been entertained by several cognitive scientists of religion, see: Boyer, *Religion Explained;* Barrett, *Why Would Anyone Believe in God?;* D. Jason Slone, *Theological Incorrectness: Why Religious People Believe What They Shouldn't* (New York: Oxford University Press, 2004); Jesse M. Bering and Dominic D. P. Johnson, "'O Lord ... You Perceive my Thoughts from Afar': Recursiveness and the Evolution of Supernatural Agency," *Journal of Cognition & Culture* 5 (2005): 118–142. Note that, from a psychological perspective at least, when an improbable event happens, such as winning the lottery, pointing out that given enough time or enough people playing the lottery someone is bound to win does not necessarily remove the desire for an explanation of why. Sure, someone had to win, but why me? Sure, people get struck by lightning, but why me and why now?

[25] Adrian Furnham, "Belief in a Just World: Research Progress over the Past Decade," *Personality and Individual Differences* 34, no. 5 (2003): 795–817; Melvin J. Lerner, *The Belief in a Just World: A Fundamental Delusion* (New York: Plenum Press, 1980).

to connect fortune or misfortune to reward and punishment may conspire to make gods readily understandable and provide impetus for entertaining their existence and activities. One further set of considerations deserves mention as well.

HOW DEAD PEOPLE BECOME GODS

Many, if not most, of the world's gods (broadly construed) bear some relation to deceased humans. The theory of euhemerism holds that gods, ancestor-spirits, and ghosts were, at one time, humans.[26] In small-scale and traditional societies, warding off ghosts and malevolent spirits, propitiating the ancestors, or garnering the support of (deceased) saints, often takes on far greater importance in regular practice than concerns about creators or cosmic deities. What might account for this cross-cultural recurrence?

Psychologist Paul Bloom has argued that humans are naturally "intuitive dualists." That is, they regard minds and bodies as separable entities because of representational conflicts between two different conceptual systems that generate inferences regarding the properties of humans.[27] One system, variously termed naïve or folk physics or mechanics, deals with solid, bounded physical objects and is present in the first few months of life.[28] This system registers human bodies as objects with certain physical properties such as having to be contacted to be moved, moving continuously through space, and the like. The second system, dealing with minded agents (Theory of Mind), is not concerned with bodies in the same way but with minds. Bloom argues that these two systems, with their different developmental schedules, different evolutionary histories, and different input–output conditions, are only ever tenuously united in

---

[26] Euhemerus was a Greek philosopher born in the fourth century BCE who is known primarily for his radical view that the gods were originally historical figures who won acclaim and worship after their deaths. Only fragments of Euhemerus's works survive, so we know of his views chiefly through references to him in other writers, such as the Christian rhetorician Lactantius, who refers approvingly to Euhemerus in his influential treatise, *The Divine Institutes*, ca. 303–311 CE.

[27] The term "intuitive dualism" may be misleading in a certain sense. Bloom's account leaves open whether thinking that "I have a separable mind and body that are different substances" is an intuitive idea as opposed to it being a reflective idea that is strongly informed by the dynamics of intuitive reasoning about minds and bodies and is thus an idea we find very intuitive once it is suggested. Or perhaps we tend to reason as if we are dualists without necessarily recognizing that we are.

[28] Elizabeth S. Spelke and Katherine D. Kinzler, "Core Knowledge," *Developmental Science* 10, no. 1 (2007): 89–96.

reasoning about humans. For this reason they easily accommodate thinking about disembodied minds and something of us persisting after death (such as souls or spirits).

If we accept that our natural cognitive equipment makes us intuitive dualists as Paul Bloom has suggested, then the idea that an immaterial something – mind, body, spirit, or some combination thereof – is left behind after death is not radically counterintuitive. Even if such dualism is not an intuitive default but is merely an easily accommodated idea, the point remains that mind- and soul-related ideas are not difficult to decouple from bodily reasoning, and the fact that someone's body has stopped working need not be conceptually incompatible with reasoning about the person's thoughts, feelings, desires, and other properties. Further, as Pascal Boyer has noted, when we consider someone we know intimately, it is clear that we know a lot about his or her tastes, desires, preferences, personalities, and the like; and upon death these mind-based properties remain untouched. Our Theory of Mind (ToM), informed by such information, continues generating inferences and predictions even after someone has died.[29] Add to these considerations the occasional, emotionally gripping experiences related to the deceased, such as dreams, hallucinations, or strange sounds, which trip our enthusiastic agency detection system (HADD), and you have a recipe for supposing that the recently deceased is still active without his or her body. Indeed, the distinct sense that someone who has passed away is still somehow present is not uncommon even among people who explicitly reject belief in ghosts and spirits of the dead.[30] As the dead no longer have visible physical bodies, they may satisfy the search for an intentional agent in the many cases in which our agency detection system detects agency, but it is clear a visible human or animal could not have been responsible (HADD experiences). It follows that little cultural encouragement is needed to develop the idea that some form of the dead is still around and active among the living in some cases.[31]

---

[29] Boyer, *Religion Explained.*

[30] Jesse M. Bering, "The Folk Psychology of Souls," *Behavioral and Brain Sciences* 29 (2006): 462–498; Junwei Huang, Lehua Cheng, and Jing Zhu, "Intuitive Conceptions of Dead Persons' Mentality: A Cross-Cultural Replication and More," *International Journal for the Psychology of Religion* 23 (2013): 29–41.

[31] In one case in which a close friend died, I can remember hearing sounds – actual sounds, not hallucinations – that I automatically assumed were from him approaching, and had to consciously remind myself that he was dead and the sounds must have a different cause. Similarly, I had chilling dreams of him returning and trying to participate in regular life. It is easy to see how such experiences could set one to wondering whether the deceased really are still active and trying to interact, especially if people have convergent experiences that they share with each other.

Further, Jesse Bering suggests that the impossibility of imagining no longer having certain classes of mental states makes it natural to assume that minds do continue at least some operations after death. Added to this "simulation constraint" is the natural human tendency to seek existential meaning in events and subtle events after the death of a loved one (such as surprising sights or sounds or dreams), which may be taken as evidence of the persistence of the other after death.[32] In one set of experiments Bering and collaborators showed that American children have stronger commitments to an afterlife earlier in childhood, suggesting that enculturation would have to lead people out of, rather than into, such beliefs.[33] Bering further argues that such a strong predisposition to have afterlife beliefs was encouraged in the course of evolution by selective pressure, because holding such a belief can promote reputation-enhancing behavior. If you believe ghosts or ancestor spirits might be around and watching, you are more inclined to behave in ways good for your social reputation, thereby making you a more attractive exchange partner. Other scholars hold that while ordinary cognition may be configured in such a way as to make afterlife reasoning easy and attractive, it still is not fully "intuitive," and they have presented evidence that its prevalence may increase instead of decrease with maturation.[34]

Placing together these various cognitive dispositions, belief in gods and perhaps the afterlife is relatively natural. Propositions about there being one or more gods that are responsible for some of the purpose we detect in the natural world fits easily with ordinary natural cognition. Either our brains or our environments need to change in important ways for people to cease having a natural disposition toward some kinds of religious ideas. The naturalness of religion story does not end there, however. It could be that once these cognitive factors converge on ideas about gods and produce what we might call religious behaviors, these behaviors prove adaptive and are hence reinforced through natural selection.[35]

---

[32] Bering, *The Belief Instinct*. Bering, "The Folk Psychology of Souls," 462–498.

[33] Jesse M. Bering and David F. Bjorklund, "The Natural Emergence of Reasoning about the Afterlife as a Developmental Regularity," *Developmental Psychology* 40 (2004): 217–233.

[34] Rita Astuti and Paul L. Harris, "Understanding Mortality and the Life of the Ancestors in Rural Madagascar," *Cognitive Science* 32 (2008): 713–740.

[35] Ara Norenzayan, *Big Gods: How Religion Transformed Cooperation and Conflict* (Princeton: Princeton University Press, 2013).

The most common evolutionary strategy in the study of religion is to focus on the potential adaptive value of religious practices, particularly collective rituals. If a community performs a ritual that engenders trust, goodwill, and cooperation, such a community could be larger (thus benefitting individuals with greater labor specialization, greater protection against enemies and predators, access to harder to get resources such as large game) and more likely to share resources and engage in long-term exchange agreements that help prevent bouts of personal misfortune. Individuals in such a community would enjoy greater fitness than comparable individuals living in smaller, less cooperative communities. Hence, the genotype that gives rise to the ritual phenotype will be selectively encouraged.

Why would religious rituals encourage group cohesion? "Signaling" explanations are the most prominent candidates. Religious rituals and other collective practices might serve as indexes of commitment that would be hard for a skeptic to feign. These indexes might be emotional reactions to the ritual such as ecstasy or weeping indicative of being a true believer.[36] Empirical studies, particularly those by Richard Sosis and collaborators, have provided some supportive evidence for a connection between ritual participation and in-group cooperation, trust, and/or altruism.[37]

IMPLICATIONS FOR RELIGIOUS BELIEFS AND FREEDOM

The exact details of how religion might be natural are far from settled, but current thinking by most researchers in the cognitive and evolutionary

---

[36] Joseph Bulbulia, "Charismatic Signaling," *Journal of Religion and Culture* 3, no. 4 (2009): 518–551.

[37] Richard Sosis and Eric Bressler, "Cooperation and Commune Longevity: A Test of the Costly Signaling Theory of Religion," *Cross-Cultural Research* 37 (2003): 211–239; Richard Sosis, "The Adaptive Value of Religious Ritual: Rituals Promote Group Cohesion by Requiring Members to Engage in Behavior that is Too Costly to Fake," *American Scientist* 92 (2004): 166–172; Candice Alcorta and Richard Sosis, "Ritual, Emotion, and Sacred Symbols: The Evolution of Religion as an Adaptive Complex," *Human Nature* 16 (2005): 323–359; Bradley J. Ruffle and Richard Sosis, "Cooperation and the In-Group-Out-Group Bias: A Field Test on Israeli Kibbutz Members and City Residents," *Journal of Economic Behavior and Organization* 60 (2006): 147–163; Bradley J. Ruffle and Richard Sosis, "Religious Behaviors, Badges, and Bans: Signaling Theory and the Evolution of Religion," in *Where God and Man Meet: How the Brain and Evolutionary Sciences Are Revolutionizing Our Understanding of Religion and Spirituality*, ed. Patrick McNamara (Westport: Praeger, 2006); B. Ruffle and R. Sosis, "Does it Pay to Pray? Costly Ritual and Cooperation," *The B. E. Journal of Economic Analysis and Policy* 7 (2007): 1–35 (Article 18).

sciences of religion converge on the idea that by virtue of being a byproduct of ordinary human cognition, or by virtue of being an adaptation promoting group living, or by a combination of the two, religion is a relatively natural form of cultural expression. Does this naturalness bear upon whether religious expression should be afforded special freedoms (for instance, in contrast with other forms of cultural expression such as sport, art, and music)?

If this scientific research into the causes of religion entail that religious expression, thus explained, is therefore false or irrationally held, we might not be comfortable with affording it special liberties. Do such explanations "explain away" religion? Some scientists think so. Jesse Bering, a cognitive scientist of religion, writes:

So it would appear that having a theory of mind was so useful for our ancestors in explaining and predicting other people's behaviors that it has completely flooded our evolved social brains ... What if I were to tell you that God's mental states, too, were all in your mind? That God ... was in fact a psychological illusion, a sort of evolved blemish etched onto the core cognitive substrate of your brain? It may feel as if there is something grander out there ... watching, knowing, caring. Perhaps even judging. But, in fact, that's just your overactive theory of mind. In reality, there is only the air you breathe.[38]

Many New Atheists, drawing upon the cognitive science of religion to attack religious belief, seem to be committing a version of the genetic fallacy that William James warned against at the start of his *Varieties of Religious Experience*,[39] noting that from methodological naturalism, all mental states have a bio-psychological cause. Yet identifying this cause says nothing one way or the other about whether the mental states in question are good or useful:

According to the general postulate of psychology just referred to, there is not a single one of our states of mind, high or low, healthy or morbid, that has not some organic process as its condition. Scientific theories are organically conditioned just as much as religious emotions are; and if we only knew the facts intimately enough, we should doubtless see 'the liver' determining the dicta of the sturdy atheist as decisively as it does those of the Methodist under conviction anxious about his soul. When it alters in one way the blood that percolates it, we get the Methodist, when in another way, we get the atheist form of mind.[40]

---

[38] Bering, *The Belief Instinct*, 37.
[39] William James, *The Varieties of Religious Experience* (London: Longmans, Green, and Co., 1902).
[40] Ibid., 14.

For cognitive or evolutionary explanations of religion to bear upon the question of what one ought to believe about religion, they would have to do more than explain that the brain, or evolution, or cognition was involved in the formation of religious beliefs. That isn't new information.

Pointing out that these scientific findings imply that people would have religious beliefs whether or not they were true won't do the job either. First, it is far from obvious that this claim is an implication of the science at all. It could be that religious beliefs are a byproduct of evolved cognition only because of a divine mind behind the natural order, and if there were no such god, our minds and beliefs would be very different. Second, a huge number of natural beliefs would be undercut by the same logic. We appear to have natural, evolved dispositions to regard others as having minds, causation to be unidirectional and real, color to be a real quality of objects, and so on. Arguably, we would (and sometimes do) believe such things whether or not they were true. If so, should we jettison such beliefs as well? If we were to do so, would we have enough pre-scientific commitments still available to get the scientific enterprise (that allegedly undercuts such commitments) off the ground?

Arguments from the naturalness of religion against religion need to show that the psychological antecedents are untrustworthy or otherwise suspect in their belief-forming activities, and it isn't clear that one can do this without already taking some stand on the quality of their products. Consider a household scale. I might suspect that it gives bad readings for any number of reasons, but I cannot determine that it is in fact error-prone without independently determining the weight of an object and then showing that the scale does not give its true weight. Just dropping a bag of potatoes on the scale and saying, "See, the scale says 10 kilos. That's not right. This scale is no good," would only be convincing if we knew already that the sack of potatoes does not in fact weigh 10 kilos. If our cognitive systems "weigh" our experiences and conclude that there is at least one god out there, we cannot take this conclusion as evidence that the cognitive systems are mistaken unless we have independent reason to think there are no gods. Indeed, normally we would regard such a "weighing" as evidence that there is indeed at least one god.

It seems to me, then, that at best the anti-religionist is left with building a case from worldview coherence – i.e., that these particular findings from the cognitive and evolutionary sciences are more at home with a materialist worldview than with a religious one.

Building such a successful argument might be possible but it faces some formidable challenges. Most difficult might be the problem that the naturalness of religion seems to be underwritten by the same cognitive systems that give us a host of mundane commitments (such as the existence of other conscious minds, orderly intelligibility of the natural world, and predictable causation) that are required for most materialist worldviews as well as religious ones. If religious thought were born of a wholly unique cognitive mechanism or adaptation that could be cut away without broader epistemic costs, the anti-religious project would surely have an easier chance at success.[41]

While we wait for the anti-theistic argument to be developed, how should we, then, regard the naturalness of religion thesis? How should we treat our apparently natural propensity to have religious beliefs and beliefs about supernatural agents in particular? I suggest we do what we do with all other intuitive beliefs: regard them as "innocent until proven guilty." Insofar as beliefs in the existence of gods are fairly direct, natural outcomes of ordinary human cognition, they may be regarded as justified until reasons arise to reject them.[42]

For instance, our natural tendency to see design and purpose in the natural world, and regard that design and purpose as the product of intentional agency, seems to be cognitively natural and, hence, innocent until proven guilty. Likewise, in many situations our agency detection system tells us that someone has acted, and we are justified in this belief until we acquire good reasons to reject it.

Freedom of Religious Expression

Let us suppose that scientific accounts of the naturalness of religion are on the right track and do not entail the proposition that religious beliefs are false or irrational. What implications, then, does the naturalness of religion have for religious freedom? I confess no special expertise in this area and defer to informed scholars of religious liberty. I offer only brief comments for the sake of stimulating reflection. For the purposes of my discussion I will take religious freedom to refer to the political freedom to exercise some kind of religious beliefs and practices, privately and

---

[41] Justin L. Barrett and Ian M. Church, "Should CSR Give Atheists Epistemic Assurance? On Beer-Goggles, BFFs, and Skepticism Regarding Religious Beliefs," *The Monist* 96 (2013): 311–324.

[42] And reasons often do arise. Suppose someone believes his god is fully visible under normal conditions and lives on the top of Mt. Olympus. Repeatedly, he climbs Mt. Olympus and fails to see the god. Either the belief that the god lives on Mt. Olympus or that the god is fully visible or that the specified god exists becomes suspect.

publicly, but I will leave aside issues concerning religious pluralism. The converse of religious freedom as I understand it is disallowing *any* religious expression (at least in the public sphere).

Suppose that adaptationist (or exaptationist) accounts of religion such as signaling theory are correct and that belief in gods and the afterlife serves to make people more cooperative and prosocial (at least toward their own community's members). Suppose, too, that religious expression was a device that helped humans build larger-scale societies, as has been suggested by various evolutionary theorists.[43] What, then, would be the consequence of forcefully removing religion's cohesive presence from society? We might imagine that some new devices could be engineered to serve the same function. But if religion is indeed part of an evolved gene-culture complex, then we should have no optimism that artificially invented substitutes for religion would successfully serve the same role, particularly without creating friction with the natural dispositions that religious cultural expression rides upon. Arguably, we have seen such attempts to replace religion with other socio-political devices, but for them to be successful, they have ended up taking on many of the trappings of religion. I have in mind here leader cults of the Leninists, Maoists, and Kimists (of North Korea). Even with some successes, it appears that all of these movements have been unable to suppress religious expression entirely and, to boot, have brought horrific oppression and human rights abuses in the name of the social transformation they sought.[44]

Even if religion does not play any natural social function that cannot be supplanted, what about the natural cognitive dispositions toward religious expression? In most people and in most cultural environments, we might predict that people will continue to entertain religious beliefs, engage in religious practices and identifications of various sorts, and link these religious expressions to core personal values that bear upon one's

[43] Jesse M. Bering, Katrina McLeod, and Todd K. Shackelford, "Reasoning about Dead Agents Reveals Possible Adaptive Trends," *Human Nature* 16 (2005): 360–381; Dominic D. P. Johnson, "God's Punishment and Public Goods: A Test of the Supernatural Punishment Hypothesis in 186 World Cultures," *Human Nature* 16 (2005): 410–446; Dominic D. P. Johnson, "God Would be a Costly Accident: Supernatural Beliefs as Adaptive," *Behavioral and Brain Sciences* 32, no. 6 (2009): 523–524; Bering, *The Belief Instinct*; Norenzayan, *Big Gods*.

[44] On the determined Soviet effort to stamp out religion and the respects in which this aggressive atheist campaign assumed the trappings of a religious crusade, see Paul Froese, *The Plot to Kill God: Findings from the Soviet Experiment in Secularization* (Berkeley: University of California Press, 2008).

public actions. What governmental discouragement of religious expression is likely to do in such situations is to move people away from developed, established forms of religious expression to more idiosyncratic or marginal forms of religious expression, or toward the adoption of proto-religious ideas and practices. Sociologist Rodney Stark reports evidence of such a shift already beginning to take place in secularized Western Europe. As traditional Christianity has declined in prominence, astrology, spiritualism, and paganism have expanded.[45] The difficulty, however, is that the newer, idiosyncratic, and more "spiritual" religious forms associated with the New Age Movement, for example, do not appear to be very effective in promoting community, cooperation, and cohesion, which, as noted above, both signaling theory and evolutionary theory have highlighted as one of religion's most important traditional functions across human history.[46]

I recognize that these musings regarding the naturalness of religion and freedom of religious expression do not directly address the normative question of whether the naturalness of religion supports (or challenges) the position that religious expression *ought* to be afforded basic rights and freedoms. Rather, I am speculating with regard to what the consequences of religious suppression might be. If, as a general matter, religious suppression is difficult or impossible to achieve without undesirable unintended outcomes, then this alone may constitute a pragmatic argument for refraining from religious suppression and respecting at least a modicum of religious freedom.

---

[45] Rodney Stark, "Europe's Receptivity to New Religious Movements: Round Two," *Journal for the Scientific Study of Religion* 32 (1993): 389–397; and Rodney Stark and Laurence R. Iannaccone, "A Supply-Side Reinterpretation of the "Secularization" of Europe," *Journal for the Scientific Study of Religion* 33 (1994): 230–252.

[46] The idiosyncratic and under-institutionalized features of New Age spirituality receive compelling treatment in Steve Bruce, "Secularization and the Impotence of Individualized Religion," *The Hedgehog Review* 8 (2006): 35–45; and in chapter 4 of Steve Bruce, *God Is Dead: Secularization in the West* (Oxford: Basil Blackwell, 2011), 75–103.

4

Sacred Versus Secular Values

Cognitive and Evolutionary Sciences of Religion and Their Implications for Religious Freedom

Richard Sosis and Jordan Kiper

INTRODUCTION

In his chapter for this volume, Justin Barrett develops the view put forward by Robert McCauley that "religious expression in beliefs and practices is nearly inevitable in most people."[1] This view is based on recent advances in the cognitive and evolutionary sciences of religion (CESR, henceforth), and is otherwise known as the *naturalness of religion thesis*: the claim that because religion is part of the phylogenetic and ontogenetic history of human beings, it is natural to humanity. The purpose of this chapter is to examine this claim and explore some of its implications for religious freedom, the principle that people are free to choose their own religious beliefs, and governments should not enforce a uniform state religion or seek to eliminate all religious expression. The primary question we wish to address is: if religion is indeed natural to humanity, should it be afforded special political protections safeguarding its expression? At first blush, it may appear that the answer to this question depends on how the alleged naturalness of religion is understood. We argue, however, that regardless of where religion lies on the naturalness spectrum, CESR offers few convincing normative reasons *per se* for protecting religious expression in terms of naturalism, and, on the contrary, it may provide compelling reasons to be cautious about blanket protections of religious expression. Our central thesis is that religious freedom may be a fundamental political right that deserves legal protection, but the

---

[1] R. N. McCauley, *Why Religion Is Natural and Science Is Not* (New York: Oxford University Press, 2011).

justification and the level of such protections cannot be derived from the naturalness of religion alone. What CESR can offer is a materialist account of religious beliefs, practices, and systems. This may prove useful for explaining religion in secular terms, resolving conflicts between religious adherents and secularists, and highlighting the potentially negative unintended consequences of manipulating or interfering with religious systems from the outside.

Barrett has initiated a discussion on naturalism from the perspective of cognitive science;[2] we hope to complement his outstanding contribution by focusing on recent advances in the evolutionary sciences. Together, these approaches have ushered in a renaissance in religious scholarship, including the emergence of new academic societies, conferences, and journals. Indeed, over the past decade the cognitive and evolutionary sciences have merged into what appears to be an interdependent and mutually beneficial long-term collaboration.[3] Still, these areas of study began as independent approaches, and despite a flourishing relationship, they continue to maintain distinct research methodologies and foci.[4] As the following discussion illustrates, the two approaches often yield divergent conclusions over the evolution of religion, even when considering the very same issue.

To summarize the outline of this chapter, we first offer a brief overview of the evolutionary study of religion and its relationship to the cognitive science of religion. We then describe one evolutionary theory of religion, namely, signaling theory, which is acutely pertinent to the discussion that follows. Next, we examine the implications of evolutionary signaling

---

[2] J. L. Barrett, *Cognitive Science, Religion, and Theology* (West Conshohocken, PA: Templeton Press, 2011), and J. L. Barrett, *Born Believers: The Science of Children's Religious Belief* (New York: Simon and Schuster, 2012). See also Barrett's contribution to this volume: Chapter 3, "On the Naturalness of Religion and Religious Freedom," pp. 67–88.

[3] R. Sosis, "The Road Not Taken: Possible Paths for the Cognitive Science of Religion," in *Religion Explained? The Cognitive Science of Religion After Twenty-Five Years*, eds. L. Martin and D. Wiebe (London: Bloomsbury Press, forthcoming).

[4] J. Bulbulia, et al., eds., *The Evolution of Religion: Studies, Theories, and Critiques* (Santa Margarita: Collins Foundation Press, 2008); R. Sosis and J. Bulbulia, "The Behavioral Ecology of Religion: The Benefits and Costs of One Evolutionary Approach" *Religion* 41 (2011): 341–362; J. Watts, et al., "Broad Supernatural Punishment but not Moralizing High Gods Precede the Evolution of Political Complexity in Austronesia," *Proceedings of the Royal Society of London B: Biological Sciences* 282.1804 (2015): 20142556; B. G. Purzycki, et al., "Moralistic Gods, Supernatural Punishment and the Expansion of Human Sociality," *Nature* 530 (2016): 327–330; D. Johnson, *God Is Watching You: How the Fear of God Makes Us Human* (New York: Oxford University Press, 2015).

theory for the naturalness of religion thesis. We then conclude with a short discussion about the implications of this work for religious freedom. Because of the numerous fields of study that our topic touches upon, we note here that our discussion is conveyed amidst considerable intellectual ferment, diversity, and debate in the science and philosophy of religion. Undoubtedly, then, many issues such as religious epistemology, the moral right to religion, and the nature of religious freedom are beyond the limits of our analysis. Nonetheless, we hope our contribution is able to traverse disciplinary divides and speak to scientists, philosophers, and policy-makers alike.

EVOLUTIONARY SCIENCE OF RELIGION: AN OVERVIEW

Eminent theorists from David Hume to Max Weber have long recognized that religion evolves; that is, it changes and develops over time. For instance, in his *Natural History of Religion*, Hume commented that there is a kind of flux and reflux to religion such that, in due time, it changes with individuals and societies.[5] Likewise, Weber noted that a community's religious system tends to become embedded in its political structure, thus changing with its military and economic prosperity.[6] But despite recognizing the ebb and flow of religion, these theorists, like most scholars of their day, remained in the dark about the exact mechanism responsible for change; it was not until the advances of Charles Darwin that light was shed on the matter.

The evolutionary study of religion rightly originates with Darwin, who offered a mechanism that could explain change in nature, including changes in human behavior over time. That mechanism is natural selection, which Darwin described as follows: "[I]f variations useful to any organic being do occur, assuredly individuals thus characterized will have the best chance of being preserved in the struggle for life; and from the strong principle of inheritance they will tend to produce offspring similarly characterized."[7] Building on this observation, Darwin considered human evolution in *The Descent of Man, and Selection in Relation to Sex* (1871), where he argued that, similar to other adaptations, human beliefs

---

[5] David Hume, "The Natural History of Religion," in *Dialogues and Natural History of Religion*, ed. J. A. C. Gaskin (New York: Oxford University Press, 1993 [1757]), 158–159.

[6] Max Weber, *The Sociology of Religion* (Boston: Beacon Press, 1991[1922]), 17.

[7] Charles Darwin, "On the Origin of Species," in *Darwin: The Indelible Stamp*, ed. J. D. Watson (Philadelphia: Running Press Book Publishers, 2005 [1859]), 413.

and behaviors evolved by differential survival and reproduction. Remarkably though, when considering religion Darwin failed to apply his own selectionist logic and thought the problem of the origin of religion was relatively easy and obvious. He wrote: "As soon as the important faculties of the imagination, wonder, and curiosity, together with some power of reasoning, had become partially developed, man would naturally crave to understand what was passing around him, and would have vaguely speculated on his own existence."[8] According to Darwin, then, once humans evolved the ability to reflect on their own existence they needed answers to existential questions, and religion was born to provide those answers.

Darwin was a careful scientist and his detailed descriptions of the structure and form of numerous species remain an inspiration to scientists today. Yet, in spite of his keen observational skills, he seems to have completely missed the structure and form of religion. For simply contemplating existential questions does not lead one to build elaborate monuments, undergo circumcision, renounce sexual activity for a lifetime, or turn dinner into charcoal on an alter for beings that have never been seen. Darwin deserves credit for launching the evolutionary science of religion, but, admittedly, it was not a strong beginning. Indeed, only in the past decade have evolutionary scholars begun to understand why selection has favored the many remarkable beliefs and behaviors that constitute religious expression.

While Darwin may have thought the causal factors favoring religion's evolution were obvious, the evolutionary study of religion faces a number of significant challenges. Here we mention two that are particularly relevant to the discussion that follows. The first challenge is that patterns of religious behavior, like other areas of social life, have undergone considerable change over our evolutionary history, making generalizations about them somewhat tenuous. British anthropologist E. E. Evans-Pritchard was explicit on this point when he argued that dramatic historical changes in religious behavior render it impossible to generalize across categories of religions such as tribal, chiefdom, and contemporary world religions.[9] To overcome this challenge, the evolutionary science of religion offers the

[8] Charles Darwin, "The Descent of Man, and Selection in Relation to Sex," in *Darwin: The Indelible Stamp*, ed. J. D. Watson (Philadelphia: Running Press Book Publishers, 2005 [1871]), 678.

[9] E. E. Evans-Pritchard, *Theories of Primitive Religion* (Oxford: Oxford University Press, 1965).

following three observations. First, religion is describable by means of methodological naturalism, which simply means that the supernatural and normative need not be invoked to explain any set of religious phenomena. Second, the ethnographic record indicates that religious behavior is quite costly, but nonetheless rampant across cultures, including modern societies.[10] Third, given that religion is costly, natural selection must have favored its survival only if it provided potential benefits to its practitioners, such as enhancing cooperation, assuaging existential concerns, or improving health and healing.[11] Hence, evolutionary scientists of religion do generalize across time and space because they presume that religious behaviors are natural phenomena that are responsive to the range of selective pressures humans have experienced throughout their varied evolutionary history, and the costs and benefits of these behaviors can be analyzed from an adaptationist perspective.

The second challenge for evolutionary scientists is how to define religion. Put simply: what is religion? And, more specifically, when considering the evolution of religion, on what exactly is selection operating, and what precisely is evolving? With regard to what religion is, scholars have offered countless definitions. However, those definitions range from individual experiences to collective beliefs, from ritual practices to social institutions. Alternatively, they are specific to particular research topics, which can be as diverse as Neanderthal burials and contemporary religious fundamentalism. It is not clear, then, whether religion is a coherent set of phenomena or an artifact of various disciplines and discourses, imposed on disparate human activities. Acknowledging these difficulties, evolutionary scholars propose that religion, if anything, is an inherently fuzzy category with unclear boundaries.

Accordingly, rather than defining religion per se, many evolutionary scholars have concluded that it can best be studied by considering its

---

[10] J. Bulbulia, "The Evolution of Religion," in *The Oxford Handbook of Evolutionary Psychology*, eds. R. I. M. Dunbar and Louise Barrett (New York: Oxford University Press, 2007), 622.

[11] R. Sosis and C. S. Alcorta, "Signaling, Solidarity and the Sacred: The Evolution of Religious Behavior" *Evolutionary Anthropology* 12 (2003): 264–274; R. Sosis, "Religious Behaviors, Badges, and Bans: Signaling Theory and the Evolution of Religion," and J. Bulbulia, "Nature's Medicine: Religiosity as an Adaptation for Health and Cooperation," in *Where God and Science Meet: How Brain and Evolutionary Studies Alter Our Understanding of Religion, Vol. 1*, ed. P. McNamara (Westport: Praeger, 2006), 61–86 and 87–122; and J. Bulbulia and Sosis, "Signaling Theory and the Evolution of Religions" *Religion* 41 (2011): 363–388.

constituent parts.[12] For despite its diversity, religion consists of recurrent core features that receive varied emphasis across cultures. For instance, although Christian cultures place great emphasis on the afterlife, Judaic cultures put less emphasis on the afterlife and more on human responsibility in this life.[13] Furthermore, while some cultures focus on mystical experiences, others focus on creeds and doctrine.[14] The task for evolutionary scholars is therefore to shift attention away from providing a conclusive definition of religion, and to focus instead on demarcating its recurrent features. In doing so, one finds that such features include – among others – ritual, myth, taboo, emotionally charged symbol, music, altered consciousness, commitment to supernatural agents, and belief about the afterlife. Developing a list of religion's core features is of course fraught with its own difficulties; scholars will undoubtedly continue to debate fiercely about what should be included and excluded from the list. We wish to point out, however, that even if a list of features were universally accepted, religion would remain a fuzzy category, as there are always human activities on the fringes that will defy strict definitional boundaries.

With that said, breaking the social category of religion down into its more easily definable core elements has several advantages. First, it avoids endless disputes concerning whether Marxism, science, patriotism, sports and so on are religions. After all, it is clear that religion shares several core elements with these cultural institutions, especially in terms of promoting group commitments, involving ritual, assuaging anxieties, and inculcating myths. Second, it allows researchers to take a comparative approach to religion, and thereby identify and explain why some groups emphasize different aspects of

---

[12] S. Atran and A. Norenzayan, "Religion's Evolutionary Landscape: Counterintuition, Commitment, Compassion, Communion," *Behavioral and Brain Sciences*, 27 (2004): 713–770; C. S. Alcorta and R. Sosis, "Ritual, Emotion, and Sacred Symbols: The Evolution of Religion as an Adaptive Complex," *Human Nature* 16 (2005): 323–359; J. Bulbulia, "Are There any Religions? An Evolutionary Exploration," *Method and Theory in the Study of Religion*, 17 (2005): 71–100; H. Whitehouse, "Cognitive Evolution and Religion: Cognition and Religious Evolution," in *The Evolution of Religion: Studies, Theories, and Critiques*, 31–42; R. Sosis, "The Adaptationist-Byproduct Debate on the Evolution of Religion: Five Misunderstandings of the Adaptationist Program," *Journal of Cognition and Culture* 9 (2009): 315–332; R. Sosis "Religions as Complex Adaptive Systems" in *Mental Religion: The Brain, Cognition, and Culture*, ed. N. Clements (Farmington Hills: Macmillan, forthcoming), 219–236.

[13] L. Baeck, *Judaism and Christianity* (Philadelphia: Jewish Publication Society, 1958).

[14] H. Whitehouse, *Modes of Religiosity: A Cognitive Theory of Religious Transmission* (Walnut Creek: AltaMira Press, 2004).

religion above others. Third, and most importantly, by breaking religion down into its basic elements it becomes obvious that these elements did not evolve together. Ritual, for example, has antecedents in many other species[15] and presumably has a much deeper evolutionary history in our lineage than many other core elements, such as myth. Therefore, "When did religion evolve?" is a poor question because it assumes that at some point in our evolutionary history religion simply "appeared." But this is not the case. Religion did not just appear, but rather consisted of uniting cognitive processes and behaviors that for the most part already existed. And although these elements evolved separately, at some point in our evolutionary history they began to coalesce and appear together with regularity. With regard to timing, then, the appropriate question is: "When did the features of religion coalesce?" At the moment we do not have a clear answer to this question, and we know surprisingly little about the dynamic interrelationship between the many core features of religion. Of course, understanding why these features coalesce as they do should provide us with insights about *when* they began to do so.

Finally, breaking religion down into its constituent parts also clarifies what selection has operated on – i.e., a coalescence of cognitive, emotional, and behavioral elements. It also directs us to the questions one needs to ask in order to analyze the adaptive value of religion. Put simply, even if religion is merely a Western construct, as some have argued,[16] it *is* nonetheless a collection of cognitive processes and behaviors that form an appropriate unit of adaptationist analysis. For it is the functioning of these processes in coordination with each other that makes religion an adaptive system. Specifically, religion is an adaptive system similar to – but no less complex than – the respiratory, circulatory, or immune systems. These too are Western constructs that probably lack counterpart in the lexicon of traditional populations, yet they are no less interpretable through an evolutionary lens. With this in mind, it is clear why evolutionary scholars avoid the murky waters of defining religion, and focus instead on pinpointing its recurrent set of core elements. In short, evolutionary scholars do isolate and study specific core elements of religion in order to

---

[15] E. G. D'Aquili et al., *The Spectrum of Ritual* (New York: Columbia University Press, 1979); Alcorta and Sosis, "Ritual, Emotion, and Sacred Symbols," 323–359; C.S. Alcorta and R. Sosis, "Rituals of Humans and Animals," in *Encyclopedia of Human-Animal Relationships*, vol. 2, ed. Marc Bekoff (Westport: Greenwood, 2007).

[16] M. Klass, *Ordered Universes: Approaches to the Anthropology of Religion* (Boulder: Westview Press, 1995).

understand their fitness effects and how they function. But it is the religious system itself, which is the coalescence of these elements, that must be the focus of an adaptationist analysis.[17]

EVOLUTIONARY SIGNALING AND RELIGION

From an adaptationist standpoint, the most striking feature of any religious system is its costs. This is particularly noticeable in terms of the ritual practices that throughout the world are often torturous and terrifying.[18] For instance, consider just a few of the initiation ceremonies historically performed by Native Americans: Apache boys were forced to bathe in icy water, Luiseño initiates were required to lie motionless while being bitten by angry hordes of ants, and Tukuna girls had their hair plucked out. Of course, not all communities demand such sacrificial behavior of their members. Indeed, the most common religious activities in Western world religions, namely, prayer and scriptural study, are comparatively benign compared to the above rituals. It deserves mentioning, however, that even in religious communities that place few demands on their adherents, religious activities still require time and energy – time and energy that will thus become unavailable for other activities.

But this begs an important question: why is there so much variance across religious communities with regard to the costs imposed on adherents? Furthermore, what are the determinants of this variance? In trying to understand why selection would favor costly religious behaviors, evolutionary scholars have used two main insights drawn from cultural anthropology, which we address briefly here.

First, anthropologists have often approached religion as a form of communication, typically viewing ritual as the primary expression of religious belief.[19] However, it was not until anthropologist Roy Rappaport's pioneering work that ritual was clearly shown to be

[17] B. G. Purzycki, O. S. Haque, and R. Sosis, "Extending Evolutionary Accounts of Religion Beyond the Mind: Religions as Adaptive Systems," in *Evolution, Religion, and Cognitive Science: Critical and Constructive Essays* (Oxford: Oxford University Press, 2014), 74–91; B. G. Purzycki and R. Sosis, "The Extended Religious Phenotype and the Adaptive Coupling of Ritual and Belief," *Israel Journal of Ecology & Evolution* 59.2 (2013): 99–108; and J. Kiper and R. Sosis, "Moral Intuitions and the Religious System: An Adaptationist Account," *Philosophy, Theology and the Sciences* 1.2 (2014): 172–199.

[18] A. Glucklich, *Sacred Pain: Hurting the Body for the Sake of the Soul* (New York: Oxford University Press, 2001).

[19] E. E. Evans-Pritchard, *Nuer Religion* (Oxford: Clarendon Press, 1956); E. Leach, *Culture and Communication: The Logic by Which Symbols Are Connected* (New York:

a unique form of communication.[20] Based on his ethnographic accounts of the Maring of New Guinea, Rappaport demonstrated that rituals serve as a non-linguistic mode of expression, insofar as the ritual act itself conveys and instills social conventions among members of a community. This is because participating in ritual is equivalent to accepting what it represents, which, for Rappaport, is commitment to the community and its social way of life. As such, rituals serve as the very foundation of society, and even the origin of the social contract.[21]

Secondly, while researchers have long maintained that religion promotes group solidarity, it is Durkheim's key insight into the nature of social life that remains a central tenet for the anthropology of religion.[22] That is, because we are born into groups, we develop an underlying sense of the basic social structures that promote group solidarity. For instance, we learn through enculturation to abide by the general morals and legal traditions of our group, and we do so not only to avoid punishment but also to benefit from harmonious social operations. Recognizing this, Durkheim argued that from a social-scientific perspective, the primary characteristic of religion is not supernatural belief but rather collective behaviors that serve the needs of the group. After all, seemingly religious behaviors such as worship services or rituals are actually social behaviors that reinforce group solidarity through collective effervescence. This was made clear by Durkheim's analysis of totemism among the Australian Aborigines. There he showed that the totem is at once the symbol of god and society – just as, for instance, the cross represents Christ and the Church for Christian communities. Thus, when individuals collectively served the totem, they inadvertently served the group, thereby strengthening its underlying social structures.

Cambridge University Press, 1976); N. Luhmann, *The Religion of Society*, ed. A. Kieserling (Frankfurt: Suhrkamp, 2000).

[20] R. Rappaport, *Pigs for the Ancestors* (New Haven: Yale University Press, 1968); R. Rappaport, "The Obvious Aspects of Ritual," in *Ecology, Meaning and Religion*, ed. R. Rappaport (Berkeley: North Atlantic Books, 1979), 173–222; and R. Rappaport, *Ritual and Religion in the Making of Humanity* (Cambridge: Cambridge University Press, 1999).

[21] Rappaport, *Ritual and Religion in the Making of Humanity*, 132.

[22] E. Durkheim, *The Elementary Forms of Religious Life*, trans. Karen E. Fields (New York: The Free Press, 1995 [1912]); V. Turner, *The Ritual Process: Structure and Anti-Structure* (Chicago: Aldine, 1969); H. Whitehouse, "Immortality, Creation and Regulation: Updating Durkheim's Theory of the Sacred," in *Mental Culture: Classical Social Theory and the Cognitive Science of Religion*, eds. Dimitris Xygalatas and William W. McCorkle Jr. (New York: Routledge, 2014), 66–79.

For evolutionary scholars, the above accounts highlight the fact that religion promotes communication and group solidarity. But these accounts alone are not entirely satisfactory for those who wish to understand religious behavior in terms of its evolution. To understand how natural selection could have favored ostensibly costly religious behaviors, evolutionary scientists have turned to evolutionary signaling theory, which aims to explain the adaptive value of signals used in animal communication.[23] Of central interest to signaling theorists are the conditions under which selection will favor reliable signals, on one hand, and deceptive signals, on the other.[24] Based on costly signaling models, communication between individuals with conflicting interests can be reliable when there is a link between the quality of a signaler and the signal being produced, which typically depends on the cost of the signal. Under conditions where the signal is costly to produce, selection can favor those whose qualities enable audiences to distinguish reliably between honest and dishonest signalers. As a result, natural selection provides the means to discriminate by exacting demands that are more costly for low-quality signalers than they are for high-quality ones.[25] For instance, numerous reliable signaling systems have evolved – such as the stotting of Thomson's gazelles, the plumage of peacocks, the frequency calls of frogs, and so forth – that involve organisms that possess the energetic resources to display signals that are too hard to fake for those with low energetic resources.[26] Put concisely, signals expressing phenotypic condition can be honest if the costs to lower-quality individuals of imitating the signals of higher-quality individuals outweigh the benefits that can be achieved.

Applying these insights from evolutionary biology and cultural anthropology, evolutionary anthropologists Lee Cronk and William Irons began to investigate religion as an evolved and dynamic signaling system. Irons

---

[23] L. Cronk, "Evolutionary Theories of Morality and the Manipulative Use of Signals," *Zygon* 29 (1994): 81–101; W. Irons, "Religion as a Hard-to-Fake Sign of Commitment," in *Evolution and the Capacity for Commitment*, ed. R. Nesse (New York: Russell Sage Foundation, 2001), 292–309.

[24] W. Searcy and S. Nowicki, *The Evolution of Animal Communication: Reliability and Deception in Signaling Systems* (Princeton: Princeton University Press, 2005).

[25] A. Grafen, "Biological Signals as Handicaps," *Journal of Theoretical Biology* 144 (1990): 517–546; Amotz Zahavi and Avishag Zahavi, *The Handicap Principle: A Missing Piece of Darwin's Puzzle* (New York: Oxford University Press, 1997).

[26] T. J. Polnaszek and D. W. Stephens, "Why Not Lie? Costs Enforce Honesty in an Experimental Signalling Game," *Proceedings of the Royal Society of London B: Biological Sciences* 281.1774 (2014): 20132457; Eileen A. Hebets, et al., "A Systems Approach to Animal Communication," *Proceedings of the Royal Society of London B: Biological Sciences* 283.1826 (2016): 20152889.

argued that the costliness of religious behaviors enables them to serve as honest signals of commitment to the group.[27] This is because only those who are committed to the group's beliefs and goals will be willing to incur the time, energy, and opportunity costs of such actions. The solidarity created within religious communities enables them to offer community members significant benefits, including social networks, insurance, materials, and even marital partners. These benefits, however, can be exploited by free-riders who are not committed to the community yet nonetheless reap the group's benefits. To avoid the free-rider problem, communities must therefore impose a cost on potential group members. Accordingly, religious performance serves to demonstrate an individual's commitment and loyalty to the group, thereby allowing them to benefit from the social and material resources it offers.[28]

ON THE NATURALNESS OF RELIGION

The salient point that emerges so far is that evolutionary scholars seek to describe religion in natural terms. But the word *natural* among evolutionary scholars remains ill-defined, unless we cling to the preconception that whatever science investigates is simply natural. Thus the meaning of the term is an open question. Of course, there is a prevailing definition in philosophy that centers on the concept of ontological naturalism. This is the view that the real world is nothing more than the physical world – that is, the objective world around us is causally limited to physical antecedents and physical consequences.[29] While most evolutionary scientists

---

[27] Irons, "Religion as a Hard-to-Fake Sign of Commitment," 292–309.

[28] For more detailed accounts of the application of costly signaling theory to religion see: R. Sosis, "Why Aren't we all Hutterites? Costly Signaling Theory and Religion," *Human Nature* 14 (2003): 91–127; J. Bulbulia, "Religious Costs as Adaptations that Signal Altruistic Intention," *Evolution and Cognition* 10 (2004): 19–42; R. Sosis, "Does Religion Promote Trust? The Role of Signaling, Reputation, and Punishment," *Interdisciplinary Journal of Research on Religion* 1 (2005): 1–30; Sosis, "Religious Behaviors, Badges, and Bans," 61–86; J. P. Schloss, "He Who Laughs Best: Involuntary Religious Affect as a Solution to Recursive Cooperative Defection," in *The Evolution of Religion: Studies, Theories, and Critiques*, 197–209; Bulbulia and Sosis, "Signaling Theory and the Evolution of Religions," 363–388; E. A. Power, "Building Bigness: Religious Practice and Social Support in Rural India" (doctoral dissertation, Stanford University, 2015).

[29] D. M. Armstrong, "The Causal Theory of Mind," in *Philosophy of Mind: Classical and Contemporary Readings*, ed. D. J. Chalmers (New York: Oxford University Press, 2002), 80–87 (originally published in D.M. Armstrong, *The Nature of Mind and Other Essays* [Brisbane, Australia: Queensland University Press, 1981], 16–31); D. Lewis,

embrace such a perspective, they operate on a slightly different conception of *natural*, which is best described as methodological naturalism: the view that metaphysical commitments of any kind outside of logical analysis and empirical data have no place in science, for science adopts no particular metaphysical account of the phenomena it investigates.[30] If that is right, then a definition of "natural" for many evolutionary scholars is simply the commitment to the scientific method. For the study of religion, however, it is necessary to turn basic definitions like these, in which *natural* is an essentially methodological assertion, into a defensible understanding of religious behavior as natural phenomena. In this section, we wish to examine the novel approach McCauley and Barrett pursue in order to demonstrate the naturalness of religion. After discussing their view, we will briefly provide our own take on the matter.

Drawing on McCauley, Barrett defines "naturalness" in his contribution to this volume as "thought processes or behaviors that are characterized by ease, automaticity, and fluency."[31] To illustrate, we must first explain McCauley's position, which distinguishes between two basic types of naturalness: maturational and practiced naturalness. Maturational naturalness arises as a natural consequence of normal development, such as learning to walk or talk. Practiced naturalness, on the other hand, arises not through the normal course of physical and psychological development, but rather through repeated practice and training, such as learning to play a musical instrument. Barrett further clarifies that maturational and practiced naturalness should be considered along a continuum. At one end of the continuum are maturationally natural behaviors, such as walking, which require little environmental input. At the other extreme are practiced behaviors, which Barrett refers to as expertise, which require extensive training, such as science.

"Psychophysical and Theoretical Identifications," in *Philosophy of Mind: Classical and Contemporary Readings*, 88–94 (originally published in the *Australasian Journal of Philosophy* 50 [1972]: 249–258); D. Papineau, *Philosophical Naturalism* (Oxford: Blackwell, 1993); D. Papineau, "Mind the Gap," *Nous Supplement: Philosophical Perspectives* 12 (1998): 373–389; and J. Kim, *Mind in a Physical World: An Essay on the Mind-Body Problem and Mental Causation* (Cambridge: MIT Press, 1998).

30 P. Draper, "God, Science, and Naturalism," in *The Oxford Handbook of Philosophy of Religion*, ed. William J. Wainwright (New York: Oxford University Press, 2005), 272–303.

31 Barrett, "On the Naturalness of Religion and Religious Freedom," this volume, p. 68. See McCauley, *Why Religion Is Natural and Science Is Not*.

Barrett argues that religion lies toward the maturational end of the naturalness continuum. To defend his view, Barrett relies on an emerging set of studies suggesting that core elements of religious expression – such as supernatural agent beliefs, teleological reasoning, and afterlife beliefs – are the natural outcome of normal cognitive development.[32] Accordingly, Barrett comments in this volume that "[t]he regularity and early development of maturationally natural capacities make me think that these capacities map on to what we normally think of as part of human nature or as natural cognition."[33] While we also find this outlook and the accumulated body of research undergirding it compelling, we suggest that religion actually lies more toward the practiced end of the naturalness continuum. In what remains of this section we defend this view.

To begin, we agree with Barrett that the cognitive structures that produce religious concepts – hypersensitive agency detection device, theory of mind, mind–body dualism, and so forth – are indeed at the foundation of religious thoughts and behaviors.[34] These are essential ingredients of what we call the *religious system*, that is, the recurrent set of core religious elements on which selection operates.[35] But the underlying cognitive structures of religion comprise only the seeds that provide the potential for the system.[36] After all, theory of mind, mind–body dualism, and other cognitive features are necessary but not sufficient to produce religion. To be sustained across the life course and across generations, religious beliefs require reinforcement, and religious behaviors require practice. Therefore, without further qualification, we doubt that religious behaviors are

---

[32] Pascal Boyer, *Religion Explained: The Evolutionary Origins of Religious Thought* (New York: Basic Books, 2001); S. Atran, *In Gods We Trust: The Evolutionary Landscape of Religion* (New York: Oxford University Press, 2002); Justin L. Barrett, *Why Would Anyone Believe in God?* (Walnut Creek: AltaMira Press, 2004); A. Norenzayan, *Big Gods: How Religion Transformed Cooperation and Conflict* (Princeton: Princeton University Press, 2013); H. De Cruz and J. De Smedt, *A Natural History of Natural Theology: The Cognitive Science of Theology and Philosophy of Religion* (Cambridge: MIT Press, 2015).

[33] Justin L. Barrett, "On the Naturalness of Religion and Religious Freedom," this volume, p. 70.

[34] Barrett, *Born Believers*.

[35] Sosis, "Religions as Complex Adaptive Systems," 219–236.

[36] R. Sosis and J. Kiper, "Religion is More Than Belief: What Evolutionary Theories of Religion Tell Us About Religious Commitment," in *Challenges to Religion and Morality: Disagreements and Evolution*, eds. Michael Bergmann and Patrick Kain (New York: Oxford University Press, 2014): 256–276.

"nearly inevitable" as Barrett contends in this volume. Religious expression requires cultural inputs and cultivation, not just cognitive potential. Whether one believes in Zeus, Vishnu, or Allah will depend on the cultural environment in which one is raised. But mere exposure to teachings and rituals focused on these figures is not enough to generate a commitment to them as supernatural. What is needed to generate this kind of religious commitment? Adherents throughout the world believe in their gods and not other people's, regardless of exposure, because adherents perform rituals for their particular deities.[37] In other words, while humans possess the cognitive machinery to believe in gods, a commitment to particular gods requires cultivation. In this regard, belief is not automatic but rather achieved through ritual behaviors, such as supplications to a particular god, ritual presentations of myth, ascetic practices, and healing ceremonies, all of which instill an experience of what religious persons would call the "sacred." This notion is aptly expressed by Karen Armstrong: "Religious discourse was not intended to be understood literally ... People were not expected to 'believe' it in the abstract; like any mythos, it depended upon the rituals associated with the cult of a particular holy place to make what is signified a reality in the lives of participants."[38] That is to say, religious practices are technologies that are critical for performers to understand and experience their community's shared religious outlook.[39]

In terms of cultivating religious experience, religious ritual is universally used to identify the sacred, and in so doing separate it from the profane. As Durkheim argued, the sacred emerges through ritual and reflects issues concerning the social order, such as group interests and welfare amid the threats and uncertainties of the universe, which take on a seemingly cosmic significance in light of religious discourse.[40] On the other hand, the profane centers on the issues of the individual, such as the daily routines of work and consumption. Additionally, as noted by Rappaport, ritual does not merely identify that which is sacred – it *creates* the sacred.[41] For instance, *prasada*, or food that serves as a religious

---

[37] Alcorta and Sosis, "Ritual, Emotion, and Sacred Symbols," 323–359.
[38] Karen Armstrong, *The Case for God* (New York: Random House, 2009), 15.
[39] C. Severi, "Learning to Believe: A Preliminary Approach," in *Learning Religion: Anthropological Approaches*, eds. D. Berliner and R. Sarro (London: Berghahn Books, 2007), 21–30; Tanya Luhrmann, *When God Talks Back: Understanding the American Evangelical Relationship with God* (New York: Vintage, 2012).
[40] Durkheim, *The Elementary Forms of Religious Life*.
[41] Rappaport, *Ritual and Religion in the Making of Humanity*.

offering in both Hinduism and Sikhism, is not simply food that has been discovered to be blessed by deities, or substance that has been rationally demonstrated to have special qualities; it is rather food that has been *transformed* through ritual. This is because the sanctifying ritual of *prasada* collectively alters the participants' cognitive schema of food itself, rendering them with a template for differentiating sacred, blessed food from profane consumables. Most importantly, from a behavioral perspective the emotional significance of sacred and profane food is quite distinct: not only is it inappropriate to treat *prasada* as one treats profane food; it is emotionally repugnant to do so. The central point can thus be summarized: while religious adherents differentiate sacred and profane things, their cognitive discrimination would be empty without having an emotional reaction to the sacred, for it is the emotional significance of the sacred that underlies "faith," and it is ritual participation that invests the sacred with emotional meaning.[42]

Though we return to signaling theory in the next section, it is also worth pointing out here that costly signaling is central to cultivating religious experience. This is due to the fact that ritual technologies, which separate the sacred from the profane and invest emotional substance into otherwise arbitrary symbols, are often purposefully difficult to perform. Specifically, they are physically demanding, time-consuming, and often dangerous. While the cognitive foundations of these behaviors may be maturationally natural, it would be inaccurate to describe such behaviors as "natural" in McCauley's sense of the term; that is to say, as "easy, automatic, or fluent."[43] Armstrong, for example, describes how the "yogin had to do the opposite of what came naturally. He sat so still that he seemed more like a plant or statue than a human being; he controlled his respiration, one of the most automatic and essential of our physical functions, until he acquired the ability to exist for long periods of time without breathing at all."[44] And ritual performers recognize the difficulty in carrying out their ritual routines. As one Chasidic Jew informed Sosis during his fieldwork in Israel, "Do you think keeping these *mitzvoth* is easy? It's hard work doing God's commandments!"[45] With regard to the naturalism spectrum, such behaviors do not come with ease, automaticity

---

[42] Alcorta and Sosis, "Ritual, Emotion, and Sacred Symbols," 323–359.
[43] McCauley, *Why Religion Is Natural and Science Is Not.*
[44] Armstrong, *The Case for God,* 21.
[45] R. Sosis, "Why are Synagogue Services so Long? An Evolutionary Examination of Jewish Ritual Signals," in *Judaism and Biological Perspective: Biblical Lore and Judaic Practices,* ed. R. Goldberg (Boulder: Paradigm Publishers, 2009), 200.

or fluency, and thus they are best characterized by the practiced rather than maturational side of the continuum.

Nonetheless, while we wish to emphasize the importance of cultivation in the development of religious beliefs and commitments, we are not claiming that religious expression is at the far *practiced* end of the naturalness continuum, which is inhabited by activities such as science and chess mastery. These are activities that seem to be at odds with our natural cognition, given the immense effort they require. Consider, for example, the challenge of acquiring statistical expertise. Statistical reasoning appears to conflict with fundamental cognitive algorithms to such an extent that even researchers, including those who regularly employ statistical models in their own work, frequently consult statisticians for advice. Of course, such difficulties are consistent with what we know about our evolved minds. As shown by Gigerenzer and Hoffrage, humans have difficulty with Bayesian reasoning when data are presented as probabilities; but when presented as frequencies, Bayesian problems are much easier to solve.[46] Accordingly, our minds are designed to handle and manipulate frequency information, because frequency formats correspond to the sequential way information has been naturally acquired throughout our evolutionary history. Extensive training is thus necessary to attain statistical expertise, for our cognitive algorithms are not naturally consistent with Bayesian reasoning. We fully recognize that statistical reasoning is different from religious cognition. Where the former requires overriding or circumventing normal cognition, the latter requires moderate cultivation to nurture underlying cognitive propensities. This is witnessed by the fact that religious systems everywhere involve the same modes of human cognition, such as the penchant for beliefs in the afterlife, magical or supernatural causation, and supernatural agents.[47] At any rate, although religion may not be at the far *practiced* end of the naturalness continuum, we wish to stress that it still requires repeated articulation and performance to manifest itself in human communities.

This leads us to a final point on naturalism. Following McCauley, Barrett claims that maturational naturalness is characterized by a lack of variation within populations, whereas practiced naturalness is marked by high variance in expertise. To illustrate, while most human beings learn to

---

[46] G. Gigerenzer and U. Hoffrage, "How to Improve Bayesian Reasoning Without Instruction: Frequency Formats," *Psychological Review* 102 (1995): 684–704.

[47] Ilkka Pyysiäinen, *Magic, Miracles, and Religion: A Scientist's Perspective* (Walnut Creek: AltaMira Press, 2004).

walk in the same manner, they rarely learn the same trades or talents in identical ways. Therefore, we agree with Barrett that the cognitive foundations of religious beliefs are universal and lack significant variation within and across populations. However, we contend that populations exhibit high levels of variance in religious expression, as countless ethnographies have shown, which is precisely what we would expect if practiced naturalness characterized religion. Even in highly religious communities variation is evident, although it tends to be underappreciated by outsiders, who see people dressed similarly and performing the same rituals. Insiders, however, seem to be well aware of such variation.[48] And there is good reason for group members to pay close attention to internal variation: an individual's deviation from community norms indicates deficient group commitment. Evolutionary signaling theory suggests that this variance in belief and practice is likely to have fitness consequences – a topic we would like to address briefly before concluding this discussion on naturalness.

SIGNALING THEORY AND PRACTICED NATURALNESS

In a brief commentary on group selection, anthropologist Lee Cronk raised an intriguing evolutionary puzzle: "Considering the phenomenal reproductive rates of Hutterites, the real mystery for evolutionary biology is why the rest of us are not trying to join their colonies."[49] Indeed, given the extraordinary reproductive success of Hutterites,[50] and provided that natural selection designed us to maximize our fitness, why are most of us unwilling to pay the costs of joining the Hutterites to achieve these reproductive gains? In considering this question, let us consider first the costs and benefits of the Hutterite lifestyle. Hutterites engage in a variety of ritual practices, such as fasting, daily church worship, and thrice-daily communal meals that are preceded and followed by prayer. They also face a wide assortment of restrictions on their behavior, such as prohibitions on owning or using musical instruments, radios, jewelry, tobacco, and other material items. Additionally, dancing and gambling are also forbidden, and colonies impose constraints on contact and communication

---

[48] Luhrmann, *When God Talks Back*, 132–226; Sosis, unpublished data.
[49] L. Cronk, "Group Selection's New Clothes," *Behavior and Brain Sciences* 17 (1994): 615.
[50] S. M. Evans and P. Peller, "A Brief History of Hutterite Demography," *Great Plains Quarterly* 35.1 (2015): 79–101.

with non-Hutterites.[51] Collectively these requirements of the Hutterite lifestyle are rather costly, but presumably these costs have few, if any, negative impacts on their fertility.[52] Furthermore, while Hutterite rituals are often costly, nonbelievers *can* perform them, which raises additional inquiries. If membership in a group that requires ritual practices genuinely results in net fitness gains, why do others not simply perform the rituals required for membership, even if they do not believe the doctrine that gives meaning to the rituals? If the net gains from joining a group outweigh any ritual costs that are required to join the group, how do the costs of the ritual practices serve as deterrents of free-riders who do not believe in the teachings of a religion? Conversely, if rituals must be costly enough to prevent free-riders from entering a population, why is it beneficial for anyone to pay the costs of group membership?

The answer to these questions is straightforward: Hutterites are Hutterites and we are not because of fundamental differences in how they and we were raised. We are not Hutterites because we do not believe in the teachings of the Hutterites, and the only way to perceive the *net* in-group benefits of the Hutterites is to truly believe in their way of life. This of course begs the question of why we do not believe in Hutterite theology. It seems that the only way to achieve such devoutness is to actually live like a Hutterite *and* initially possess either beliefs similar to their own or highly ambiguous ones. Otherwise, simply attempting to observe Hutterite religious obligations will be perceived as too costly, and hence will be avoided or discontinued if attempted. In other words, there are genuine gains to be achieved by joining the Hutterites. But without "belief" our assessment of these potential gains suggests significant costs. Hutterites, on the other hand, are able to maintain their faith and consequently experience a range of short-term benefits through the performance of the many rituals that fill their lives. Ritual performance during childhood minimizes the opportunity costs perceived by group members later in life, increasing their ability to tolerate costly constraints on their lives. As a Hutterite man from Montana commented, "It seems you have to be born with the Hutterite way, to be brought up from childhood on, to abide by these rules... If you are brought up like this, you're not used to all these things you see in

---

[51] J. Hostetler, *Hutterite Society* (Baltimore: Johns Hopkins University Press, 1997); R. Janzen, *The Prairie People: Forgotten Anabaptists* (Hanover: University Press of New England, 1999); and L. Wilson, *Hutterites of Montana* (New Haven: Yale University Press, 2000).

[52] R. Sosis and E. Bressler, "Cooperation and Commune Longevity: A Test of the Costly Signaling Theory of Religion," *Cross-Cultural Research* 37 (2003): 211–239.

town."[53] As the Hutterite example indicates, ritual performance fosters and maintains religious beliefs, and beliefs in turn enable rituals to be effective signals of commitment by lowering the perceived costs of ritual performance, thus preventing free-riders from reaping the benefits of religious-group membership. Accordingly, religious belief is undoubtedly important for group membership, but belief itself is a proximate mechanism that facilitates the production of adaptive ritual behaviors.

To summarize, Barrett places religion toward the maturational side of the naturalness continuum, whereas we have argued that religion lies toward the practiced end of the continuum. This difference in perspective is primarily a function of our respective disciplinary trainings and affiliations. As a cognitive scientist, Barrett is interested in uncovering the universal cognitive architecture that produces religious beliefs. Thus, Barrett perceives religion lying toward the maturational end of the naturalness continuum because he is focused on the cognitive mechanisms producing religious beliefs and behavior, and it is indeed the case that our cognition naturally produces religious expression. As evolutionary anthropologists we are struck by the extraordinary plasticity of human behavior in contrast to other organisms. Consequently, we perceive religion lying toward the practiced end of the naturalness continuum because our attention is focused on the diversity of religious expression and how religious behaviors are critical for forming and sustaining belief and commitment.

IMPLICATIONS FOR RELIGIOUS FREEDOM

In the previous section it was argued that religion entails both cognitive tendencies and ritual behaviors, which together make the cultivation of religious belief a form of practiced naturalism. Our present concern is whether this naturalness bears on religious freedom. In particular, the question we wish to consider is: if religion is a natural part of what it means to be human, as it seems to be, does it deserve special protections? Should its free expression be afforded special rights and safeguards? To answer these questions, we suggest that several factors related to religious freedom must be kept in mind, including the place of religion in liberal democracies, the implications of the naturalness thesis for religious freedom, and the distinct boundary between scientific description and normative prescription. Based on these factors, the suggestion we put

---

[53] Wilson, *Hutterites of Montana*, 22.

forward is that CESR cannot directly speak to religious freedom, but it may be able to illuminate the nature of sacred and secular values, thereby helping others appreciate the pervasiveness of religious practices and the holistic nature of religious systems.

When discussing religious freedom, it is important to recognize that we are generally speaking from the perspective of liberal democracy. This is not to say that religious freedom does not exist outside of liberal-democratic political systems, but rather that, on the world stage, it is a value that emerged in a robust and institutionalized form with liberal democracies. And, in general, it continues to be defended most vigorously by liberal democracies. As such, religious freedom holds a special place in the West because it goes hand-in-glove with the fundamental legal rights associated with an expansive notion of political freedom. This expansive sense of political freedom includes the freedom to seek, receive, and share information and ideas, as well as the right to vote, hold office, petition the government, and participate in religion as one sees fit.[54] Religious freedom is included with these other political rights because the history of Western governments suggests that imposing a single religion on a society has always resulted in political turmoil.[55] As articulated in this volume by Wolterstorff,[56] the practical aim of not singling out a religious order for society is related to the idea that political rights serve to protect citizens from abuses. For instance, the free exercise of religion prevents the power-ful – even the government itself – from abusing the freedom held by individuals to adopt religion as he or she sees fit. However, the idea of freely adopting and exercising a religion, in turn, is traditionally rooted in the philosophical notion of natural rights, that is, that some rights are held by individuals not by virtue of any positively instituted laws but rather the dignity of the person, usually bestowed by a divine creator. Hence, when James Madison and Thomas Jefferson articulated the legal conception of religious freedom they did so with both the ideas of natural law in mind but also with the practical aims of protecting the commonwealth. For prohibiting a state-enforced or established religion serves a governmental interest: namely, political order. In his analysis of failed governmental

---

[54] M. Perry, *The Idea of Human Rights: Four Inquiries* (New York: Oxford University Press, 1998); M. Perry, *The Political Morality of Liberal Democracies* (Cambridge: Cambridge University Press, 2010).

[55] Douglas Laycock, "Religious Liberty as Liberty," *Journal of Contemporary Legal Issues* 7 (1996): 313–356.

[56] Nicholas Wolterstorff, "Why There Is a Natural Right to Religious Freedom," this volume, pp. 195–229

attempts to establish a single religion, legal scholar Michael Perry expresses the notion in this way: "government is not to be trusted as an arbiter of religious (or anti-religious) truth ... As Locke put it, 'the business of laws is not to provide for the truth of opinion, but for the safety and security of the commonwealth, and every particular man's goods and persons.'"[57] Religious freedom is therefore protected in liberal democracies because, in part, it is practical to do so, as history attests.

Moreover, although religious freedom may be a category restricted to legal rights, liberal democracies and many religious faiths seem to express the same philosophical value at their core: that human beings possess inherent dignity.[58] In other words, liberal democracies and most religious faiths recognize that human beings have an inherent value, which has a normative force that compels individuals and governments to treat human beings with respect. Furthermore, both religions and democracies design rules and guidelines to protect human beings accordingly. Even though both kinds of systems often find ways to overlook that value, they nevertheless share a common ground by affirming and valuing human dignity, a ground that is also shared by international human rights documents.[59]

With these caveats in mind, we consider the notion that discoveries in CESR may have an impact on our understanding and protection of religious freedom. For example, one could develop an argument for protecting religion in light of its naturalness. Specifically, if religion lies on the maturational side of the naturalness continuum, then one could argue that religious expression deserves protection. After all, international law safeguards many human rights because they are in fact basic rights, meaning that they are natural to human life and thus inherent to all other freedoms.[60] Here, the terms "human rights" and "natural rights" are not entirely synonymous. While natural rights are often grounded on the metaphysical claim that they are God-given, human rights are human

---

[57] Perry, *The Political Morality of Liberal Democracies*, 76–77.   [58] Ibid.

[59] See, for example, the Universal Declaration of Human Rights of 1948, which affirms in its Preamble that "recognition of the inherent dignity and of the equal and inalienable rights of all members of the human family is the foundation of freedom, justice and peace in the world," and goes on to declare that "the peoples of the United Nations have in the Charter reaffirmed their faith in fundamental human rights, in the dignity and worth of the human person and in the equal rights of men and women and have determined to promote social progress and better standards of life in larger freedom." Available at www.un.org/en/universal-declaration-human-rights/, accessed on February 20, 2017.

[60] Henry Shue, *Basic Rights: Subsistence, Affluence, and U.S. Foreign Policy* (Princeton: Princeton University Press, 1980).

constructs that are grounded on other basic rights – that is, those basic human needs without which all other rights cannot be enjoyed. Examples include positive rights such as the access to water and negative rights such as the freedom from rape or torture. Without these basic rights, all other rights, such as economic or social rights, cannot be enjoyed.[61] Many basic rights appear to be human behaviors that are maturationally natural. For instance, it is maturationally natural for human beings to defend themselves from life-threatening harm and bodily injury, to avoid slavery or servitude, to object to torture and cruelty, to abhor arbitrary confiscation of property, and to eschew several other violations. With each, it seems that being maturationally natural is an element of basic human rights, which indeed receive protection under international law. If so, then religious belief and expression would seem equally deserving of similar protections.

Is the above argument sound? That is to say, can religion be protected along the same lines as other basic rights? We suspect not for at least two reasons. First, even if religion did lie on the maturational side of the naturalness continuum, as Barrett and McCauley contend, it would not be at the far end of the continuum with other natural needs that are associated with human rights. The right to freedom from torture, the right to water, and so forth, are basic rights insofar as other rights cannot exist without them. In other words, it is literally self-defeating to hold that human beings possess rights of any kind without ensuring that their basic rights are protected.[62] We observe that religious freedom is indeed a right – a human right – but it is not a basic right; for other rights can be enjoyed without it. Second, we contend that the political freedom of religion could be on slippery ground if it were justified by virtue of the naturalness of religion. This is because scientists will most likely continue to find new insights and evidence that will further inform our sense of where precisely religion lies on the naturalness continuum. But the freedom of religious belief and expression should not wax and wane with the discoveries of science. It is an essential legal right and an important political freedom, not a scientific proposition subject to continual revision and discovery.

Moreover, if religion lies on the practiced end of the continuum, as we have argued, it is difficult to see how its naturalness could justify special protections. There are countless human activities that build upon natural cognitive mechanisms in much the way religion does, but these require

---

[61] Ibid, p. 21.   [62] Ibid.

practice to gain expertise, thus rendering them forms of practiced naturalness. Just to name a few, these activities include gambling, dancing, playing an instrument, mastering a craft, and excelling at sports. However, unlike basic rights, these activities are rarely protected by societies, because they are not basic human needs. What makes religion different from these activities is that it has a long history of being abused, oppressed, and manipulated by governments. Perry puts the point succinctly: "This, then, is the fundamental warrant for liberal democracy's commitment to the right to religious freedom: Political majorities are not to be trusted (i.e., beyond a certain point) as arbiters of religious truth; moreover, the coercive imposition of religious uniformity is (beyond a certain point) more likely to corrode than to nurture the strength of a democracy. The warrant, which is rooted in historical experience, is fundamental in the sense that it is ecumenical: Both citizens who are religious believers and those who are not can affirm the warrant. And that the warrant is ecumenical is ideal: Liberal democracies are religiously pluralistic."[63] Accordingly, liberal democracies seek to protect religious expression, a form of practiced expertise, because the varieties of human experience produce countless forms of religious belief, which, arguably, cannot be verified or falsified. It is thus arbitrary for any majority to impose the supposed truth of its religious beliefs on others. We do not see how the science of practiced naturalness could speak louder than history or philosophy when it comes to this issue.

A final point: the descriptive endeavors of science can rarely speak to the prescriptive enterprise of ethics or law. For that reason, it is important to emphasize that there is a yawning explanatory gap between what *is* according to science and what *ought to be* according to ethics and law. To be exact, the protection of religious freedom – what ought to be – cannot be derived from the adaptationist analysis of religion – what is. Even if religion provides adaptive benefits in the form of positive health outcomes[64] and facilitates collective action,[65] it still does not tell us how

---

[63] Perry, *The Political Morality of Liberal Democracies*, 79.

[64] H. Koenig, M. McCullough, and D. Larson, eds., *Handbook of Religion and Health* (New York: Oxford University Press, 2001); Connor Wood, "Ritual Well-Being: Toward a Social Signaling Model of Religion and Mental Health," *Religion, Brain & Behavior* (2016), published electronically July 21, 2016, doi: 10.1080/2153599X.2016.1156556.

[65] M. Soler, "Costly Signaling, Ritual and Cooperation: Evidence from Candomblé, an Afro-Brazilian Religion," *Evolution and Human Behavior* 33.4 (2012): 346–356.; R. Sosis, H. Kress, and J. Boster "Scars for War: Evaluating Alternative Signaling Explanations for Cross-Cultural Variance in Ritual Costs," *Evolution and Human Behavior* 28 (2007): 234–247; R. Sosis and B. Ruffle, "Religious Ritual and

religion ought to be handled in liberal democracies. Moreover, determining that a trait is adaptive does not imply that the trait is "good" or offers individual or societal benefits worth protecting. Under conditions of extreme resource stress, for example, infanticide is likely to be adaptive,[66] but few would claim that it deserves protection. In the same way, the adaptive value of religion ultimately says little about whether we ought to protect religious freedom.

SACRED VERSUS SECULAR VALUES

But does the naturalness thesis yield any significant and useful insights regarding problems of religious freedom? In this volume, Barrett explores the implications of the naturalness thesis for two issues: complete freedom of religious expression and disallowing any religious expression. Rather than focus on these extreme conditions, here we examine the gray areas where sacred and secular values conflict. There are several related but separable issues that could be raised, but we focus on just one: can CESR help to resolve conflicts between sacred and secular claims and values? To make progress on that question, let us first consider several examples where basic religious activities appear to conflict with secular values.

In April 2011, the *New York Times* reported that Hindu communities in Queens, New York were using the bay in Gateway National Recreation Area for religious ceremonies, including births, deaths, and festivals.[67] The water of the bay is believed by local Hindus to possess healing powers that can cure sickness, pain, and suffering. But unlike the Ganges, where Hindus traditionally perform religious rites, the enclosed bay does not sweep away refuse. Consequently, park rangers found the remains of Hindu rites on the banks of the bay, such as clothing, statues, coconuts, and clay bowls. Furthermore, during cremation ceremonies human ashes were tossed into the bay. Park rangers and conservationists were of course concerned about the environmental impact of performing these religious rites in a fragile ecosystem.

Cooperation: Testing for a Relationship on Israeli Religious and Secular Kibbutzim," *Current Anthropology* 44 (2003): 713–722; and Y. Hartberg, M. Cox, and S. Villamayor-Tomas, "Supernatural Monitoring and Sanctioning in Community-Based Resource Management," *Religion, Brain & Behavior* (2016): 95–111.

[66] S. B. Hrdy, *Mother Nature: Natural Selection and the Female of the Species* (London: Chatto & Windus, 1999).

[67] Sam Dolnick, "Hindus Find a Ganges in Queens, to Park Rangers' Dismay," *New York Times*, April 21, 2011, accessed May 29, 2015, www.nytimes.com/2011/04/22/nyregion/hindus-find-a-ganges-in-queens-to-park-rangers-dismay.html.

The Jewish holiday of Hanukah offers a second example. In 2007 an Israeli environmentalist organization launched a "Green Hanukah" campaign in which they encouraged Jews to light seven rather than eight candles during the "festival of lights."[68] In an extensive internet campaign, environmentalists argued that every candle produces 15 grams of carbon dioxide and thus the millions of Jews celebrating Hanukah over eight days were "irresponsibly" contributing to climate change. Similar concerns have been raised by American environmentalists over the energy costs of fueling Christmas lights.

However, not all conflicts between religious and secular values involve environmental issues. Jehovah's Witnesses have been at the center of numerous court battles concerning conflicts between their beliefs and secular values. Witnesses, for example, have refused to salute the American flag, which they believe would constitute idolatry, and in a 1943 decision (*West Virginia State Board of Education v. Barnette*), Witnesses were granted the right to refuse to salute the flag and recite the Pledge of Allegiance.[69] A more recurrent conflict centers on battles over their right to refuse blood transfusions, which their faith prohibits because it is equated with drinking blood. Their right to refuse blood transfusions, even if it means certain death, has been upheld in numerous court cases. In response to a 2011 lawsuit, a court ordered the state of Kansas to provide, at considerable expense, a bloodless liver transplant for a patient, based on her beliefs as a Jehovah's Witness.[70]

The courts, of course, have not only handled sacred and secular conflicts among Jehovah's Witnesses. For example, in 2009, eleven Old Order Amish families filed a religious discrimination lawsuit against the town of Morristown, New York.[71] The families were denied building permits by the town because they refused to abide by established building codes that conflicted with their religious restrictions on the use of electronic appliances. The town, for example, demanded full compliance with fire codes,

---

[68] "'Green' Hanukkah Sparks Criticism," *United Press International*, December 5, 2007, accessed May 29, 2015, www.upi.com/Top_News/2007/12/05/Green-Hanukkah-sparks-criticism/52981196902639/.

[69] *West Virginia State Board of Education v. Barnette*, 319 U.S. 624 (1943).

[70] J. Gordon Melton, "Religious Freedom and Bloodless Liver Transplants," *Wall Street Journal*, May 13, 2011, accessed May 29, 2015, www.wsj.com/articles/SB10001424052748703730804576317110673663444.

[71] Associated Press, "Amish Sue New York Town for Discrimination Over Building Code Enforcement," *Fox News.com*, January 6, 2009, accessed May 29, 2015, www.foxnews.com/story/2009/01/06/amish-sue-new-york-town-for-discrimination-over-building-code-enforcement.html.

but the Amish families contended that their faith did not allow electronic smoke detectors in their homes.

Legal conflicts between religious and secular values are manifest in other social arenas as well, including sexuality,[72] wearing religious items,[73] commercialization,[74] and ritual practice.[75] Before considering what CESR can do in these situations, it is worth considering what it cannot do. In line with what we have argued throughout this paper, CESR cannot offer any fine-grained adjudication of such conflicts because it employs methodological naturalism not as a way to discern matters of value or policy but as a way to acquire knowledge. Methodological naturalism in this regard is simply an epistemic outlook, which presumes that all phenomena can be impartially studied using the systematic methods of observation, testing, and replication.[76] Because methodological naturalism attempts to eliminate from science the influence of human biases – such as religious and moral beliefs – it is widely considered the most objective way to approach the natural world. Hence, employment of this approach is the surest way for CESR to maintain its legitimacy as a viable science among the greater scientific community. To offer judgments on conflicts of value, then, especially in the name of naturalism, would not only breach the is–ought barrier, but also pose a risk to the objectivity and credibility of CESR.

In spite of our numerous caveats and objections, we think that CESR does have something valuable to contribute: the resolution of conflicts between sacred and secular values. How so? One causal factor that pervades most conflicts between the religious and secular, as in most disputes, is a lack of understanding and appreciation for the beliefs and behaviors of the opposing side. Suggesting that observant Jews, for example, should light one candle fewer during Hanukkah indicates a complete lack of understanding and appreciation for the deep conviction that

---

[72] "Peter and Hazelmary Bull, British Hotel Owners Who Rejected Gay Couple, Sell Property," Queer Voices, *Huffington Post*, September 19, 2013, accessed March 3, 2017, www.huffingtonpost.com/2013/09/19/peter-hazelmary-bull-sell-hotel-_n_395543 3.html.

[73] "British Airways Christian Employee Nadia Eweida Wins Case," *BBC News*, January 15, 2013, accessed March 3, 2017, www.bbc.com/news/uk-21025332.

[74] S. Nissenbaum, *The Battle for Christmas* (New York: Vintage, 1996).

[75] *Merced v. Kasson*, 577 F.3d 578 (5th Cir. 2009); Jane Sutton, "Santeria Animal Sacrifice Underpins Guantanamo Legal Challenge," *Reuters*, April 18, 2012, www.reuters.com/article/us-usa-guantanamo-chickens-idUSBRE83H1H320120418.

[76] Paul Kurtz, *Philosophical Essays in Pragmatic Naturalism* (Buffalo: Prometheus Books, 1990).

underlies religious beliefs and practices. If CESR can offer anything in such a dispute, it is the explanation of religious beliefs and behaviors in materialist terms. Of course, CESR theories and data are unlikely to be satisfying for many religious adherents, because they fail to capture the full depth of meanings in their convictions. But such interpretations of religion are likely to provide satisfying materialist explanations for secularists. Above all, CESR should not aim to justify such beliefs and practices, but it can open up a fruitful dialogue to facilitate conflict resolution by clarifying why humans possess such strong religious convictions and how those convictions undergird a wide variety of religious beliefs and sometimes demanding religious rituals.

ON RELIGIOUS SYSTEMS

Coming full circle, we conclude our discussion of religious freedom with a brief examination of the adaptive nature of religion and its implication for society writ large. One of the most important aspects of CESR research is understanding religion as an adaptive system.[77] Religious systems are dynamic and complex. We have little understanding of how the feedback mechanisms of religions operate, but religious systems are clearly organic – that is, they are signaling and self-sustaining processes.[78] Altering one part of the system, then, will likely have significant effects on other parts. At the same time, those effects are difficult to predict even for those most familiar with the system, such as religious leaders. To illustrate, sociologists Rodney Stark and Roger Finke have argued that when the Second Vatican Council in 1962 repealed many of the Catholic Church's prohibitions and reduced the level of strictness in the church, it had unforeseeable consequences.[79] Presumably, the Vatican Council was an attempt to

---

[77] Alcorta and Sosis, "Ritual, Emotion, and Sacred Symbols," 323–359; B. G. Purzycki and R. Sosis, "The Religious System as Adaptive: Cognitive Flexibility, Public Displays, and Acceptance," in *The Biological Evolution of Religious Mind and Behavior*, eds. E. Voland and W. Schiefenhövel (Berlin: Springer, 2009), 243–256; Sosis, "The Adaptationist-Byproduct Debate on the Evolution of Religion," 315–332; R. Sosis, E. J. Philips, and C. S. Alcorta, "Sacrifice and Sacred Values: Evolutionary Perspectives on Religious Terrorism," in *Oxford Handbook of Evolutionary Perspectives on Violence, Homicide, and War*, eds. Todd K. Shackelford and Viviana A. Weekes-Shackelford (New York: Oxford University Press, 2012), 233–253.

[78] Rappaport, *Pigs for the Ancestors*; Rappaport, *Ritual and Religion in the Making of Humanity*; Sosis, "Religions as Complex Adaptive Systems," 219–236.

[79] R. Stark and R. Finke, *Acts of Faith: Explaining the Human Side of Religion* (Berkeley: University of California Press, 2000).

regain the commitments of wavering Catholics, but it inadvertently initiated a decline in church attendance among American Catholics, and reduced the overall enrollments in seminaries. Indeed, in the late 1950s almost 75 percent of American Catholics were attending Mass weekly, but since the Vatican's actions there has been a steady decline to the current rate, which is below 35 percent.[80] Such consequences are not exclusive to the Catholic Church. A similar reduction in commitment followed the purging of ritual obligations in Reform Judaism as well.[81] Though many other instances could be referenced, what these two examples illustrate is that religions grow organically – from the bottom up. Therefore, tampering with them either through external intervention or internal transformation can result in unexpected changes, even stunted growth or collapse.

Viewing religion in this light has implications for sacred versus secular conflict. External secular pressures that aim to change religions sometimes result in dangerous consequences. For example, religious radicalization, as exemplified by the emergence of the Muslim Brotherhood in Egypt, Turkey, and elsewhere, appears to be a response to aggressive secular campaigns.[82] If so, minimizing religious extremism in the future may require secularists to accept and tolerate religious traditions and their public expression, and design policies accordingly. This will not be easy, for even externally imposed changes that are intended to benefit religious communities can have long-term negative consequences.

For example, on March 3, 1948, during a period of civil war prior to the Israeli War of Independence, Ben Gurion established a military exemption for yeshiva students. His motives have been debated ever since, but he presumably felt he was saving a cultural remnant of European Jewry that was otherwise headed toward extinction with the birth of the secular Israeli state.[83] As the yeshiva population has grown exponentially because of the extraordinary birth rates of Israeli Ultra-Orthodox Jews, not serving in the military has emerged as a costly signal of one's commitment to

---

[80] W. V. D'Antonio et al., *American Catholics Today: New Realities of their Faith and their Church* (Plymouth: Rowman and Littlefield, 2007); C. K. Hadaway and P. L. Marler, "How Many Americans Attend Worship Each Week? An Alternative Approach to Measurement," *Journal for the Scientific Study of Religion* 44 (2005): 307–322.

[81] L. R. Iannaccone, "Why Strict Churches Are Strong," *American Journal of Sociology* 99 (1994): 1180–1211; B. Lazerwitz and M. Harrison, "American Jewish Denominations: A Social and Religious Profile," *American Sociological Review* 44 (1979): 656–666.

[82] Karen Armstrong, *The Battle for God* (New York: Random House, 2000); M. Ruthven, *Fundamentalism: The Search for Meaning* (Oxford: Oxford University Press, 2004).

[83] N. J. Efron, *Real Jews: Secular vs. Ultra-Orthodox and the Struggle for Jewish Identity in Israel* (New York: Basic Books, 2003).

the community. For Jewish Israelis, not serving in the military is a stigma with consequences in the labor market. But this stigma serves as a gatekeeper within the religious community: one way of demonstrating one's religious commitment is staying in yeshiva not only until the possibility of being drafted has passed due to age but even several years after one is no longer eligible.[84] As a result, yeshiva students and their families are exceedingly poor because they are permitted only minimal employment under the terms of their military exemption. Due to a lack of understanding of how the military exemption has been transformed into a religious commitment signal, the government has attempted to alleviate the financial plight of these yeshiva students by increasing their subsidies. But this has only exacerbated the problem.[85] By increasing payments to yeshiva students, the government has increased the amount of time yeshiva students must remain in the yeshiva to serve as an effective signal of commitment. In short, the government subsidies have effectively decreased the costs of the signal.

These examples suggest there are strong reasons to be cautious about tampering with religions, as if they were simple constructs for viewing the world rather than highly complex, unified, and organic systems. In fact, CESR confirms that religion is much more complicated than is generally appreciated. It is safe to say that, like other systems in nature, religion is dynamic, emergent, and unpredictable. By recognizing that religion is a complex adaptive system, it is our hope that scholars and policymakers will come to appreciate that if there are compelling reasons to control or reform religion, we currently have little understanding of how to do so. Naïve policies seeking change are likely to yield unintended consequences.

CONCLUSION

In this paper, we argued that the cognitive and evolutionary sciences of religion do not provide theoretical or empirical support for the proposition that religion's naturalness warrants the special rights and protections of religious freedom. Our contention was not that religious expression should go without protection, however, but rather that the findings of CESR do not provide support for the political right in question.

---

[84] E. Berman, "Sect, Subsidy and Sacrifice: An Economist's View of Ultra-Orthodox Jews," *Quarterly Journal of Economics* 115 (2000): 905–953.

[85] E. Berman, *Radical, Religious and Violent: The New Economics of Terrorism* (Cambridge: MIT Press, 2009).

Nevertheless, we suspect that research on religious markets may offer relevant and supportive data for religious protection. We conclude our discussion by briefly pursuing this line of thought.

There is considerable debate among sociologists and economists regarding the effects of competition on the strength and health of religions.[86] It has been argued that when religions enjoy an open competitive playing field they are responsive to the demands of religious consumers, improving the quality of what they offer, and thus increasing religious activity and commitment. On the other hand, where religious monopolies eliminate or minimize competition, religions fail to adapt to current needs. In short, they become stagnant and obsolete. The relatively high levels of religiosity in the United States, and low levels of religiosity in Western Europe, are often cited as support for this interpretation of the religious marketplace.[87] But state-sponsored religious monopolies that enjoy privilege not only foster religious lethargy, but also create environments that are ripe for religious extremism. As Iannaccone notes, "Genuinely violent sects tend to arise in countries where the civil government has suppressed religious freedom, favoring one form of religious expression over all others. Within these environments, an unfavored sect is strongly motivated to despise the established religion, and covet the privileges that come with state support."[88] In contrast, where religions can compete freely for members, violent religious extremism is rare. Indeed, Iannaccone and Berman observe that "the most striking feature of American sects may well be their near total lack of militancy."[89]

If this understanding of religious markets is correct, it would seem to provide a strong argument in support of special protections for the freedom of religious expression. We would add, from a selectionist perspective, that the benefits that a religion can offer will be critical to its health and adaptability.[90] The primary benefits that most religions confer on members, and the protections they offer from potential free-riders, derive

---

[86] Pippa Norris and Ronald Inglehart, "Are High Levels of Existential Security Conducive to Secularization? A Response to Our Critics," in *The Changing World Religion Map: Sacred Places, Identities, Practices, and Politics*, ed. Stanley D. Brunn (Dordrecht: Springer Netherlands, 2015): 3389–3408.

[87] L. R. Iannaccone, R. Stark and R. Finke, "Deregulating Religion: The Economics of Church and State," *Economic Inquiry* 35 (1997): 350–364.

[88] L. R. Iannaccone, "Religious Extremism: Origins and Consequences," *Contemporary Jewry* 20 (1999): 23.

[89] L. R. Iannaccone and E. Berman, "Religious Extremism: The Good, the Bad, and the Deadly," *Public Choice* 128 (2006): 122.

[90] Sosis and Bulbulia, "The Behavioral Ecology of Religion," 341–362.

from social networks that provide mutual insurance. If governments can step in to provide such a safety net for their citizens and obviate their need for the material support offered by some religious networks, they can minimize the threat of violent religious extremism even in cases where there is a state-sponsored religious monopoly.

In reference to the theory of natural selection, in the final passage of *On the Origin of Species*, Darwin concluded, "There is grandeur in this view of life..."[91] We entirely agree. We believe that cognitive and evolutionary perspectives do not trivialize religion, explain it away, or attempt to dismantle it. Rather, CESR can lead to a new appreciation of religion. While we doubt that a defensible normative argument that religious freedoms deserve special protections can be built on the sole basis of CESR research, we do believe that CESR research can help facilitate the understanding and appreciation of religion's nature as a complex and adaptive system, can illuminate the potentially dangerous unintended consequences of tampering with religious systems, and can help to resolve conflicts between sacred and secular claims and values.

ACKNOWLEDGEMENTS

We thank the John Templeton Foundation and the James Barnett Endowment for Humanistic Anthropology for generous funding of this research.

---

[91] Charles Darwin, *On the Origin of Species by Means of Natural Selection* (Cambridge: Cambridge University Press, 2009 [1859]), 429.

5

Theism, Naturalism, and Rationality

Alvin Plantinga

My objective in this chapter is to respond to two questions. First, to what extent is belief in God properly basic to human rationality? That is, to what extent is theism rationally innocent until proven guilty – a fully rational default position for human beings? Second, to what extent is belief in God foundational to rationality? That is, to what extent is theism an essential prior condition for regarding our rationality and reasoning powers as trustworthy and reliable?

So the first question is: to what extent is theism rationally innocent until proven guilty? Perhaps another way to ask this question is: can theistic belief be rational even if it is not held on the evidential basis of other beliefs? To answer this question, obviously enough, we have to be clear about the terms "rational" and "rationally." How are we to take these terms here? We're thinking of them as applied to beliefs: some beliefs are rational and some aren't. The term "belief," here, is ambiguous. On the one hand, the term sometimes refers to the act of taking a certain epistemic attitude toward a proposition, and on the other, it sometimes refers to the proposition itself. Consider your belief that all men are mortal. On the one hand, there is the proposition that all men are mortal; on the other, there is your believing that proposition. The term "rational," I take it, refers in the first instance to the believing of a proposition, not to the proposition itself. And it's pretty clear that rationality is supposed to be a good thing, or at least not a bad thing. To say of a belief (a believing) that it is irrational, on the other hand, is to condemn it in some way. It's rational to believe that 7 + 5 = 12; it's irrational to believe that it's turtles all the way down, or that horses are really witches in a clever disguise, or that the next president of the USA will be a five-year-old girl. What makes the difference?

We can begin with a bit of etymology. The term "rational" comes from the Latin word "ratio." *Ratio* has many meanings, but perhaps the one of greatest present interest is *reason*. Man (not to mention woman) is a rational animal. That is, human beings are creatures with reason, creatures with the ability to believe and know. They are also creatures with the ability to draw inferences and thus to *reason* (where here this term is a verb). Reason (*ratio*) is a power or faculty; on earth, at any rate, it seems to be largely confined to human beings.

So a rational animal is one that has reason. But what about beliefs? When are beliefs rational? Not just any belief held by one of us rational animals is by that token a rational belief. People like Dawkins and Dennett, who condemn Christian belief as irrational, are not claiming that those who hold such beliefs are not in fact human beings, or not in fact rational animals. Rational animals can hold irrational beliefs.

Reason is a power or a faculty, and sometimes people speak of the *deliverances* of reason. A belief that is among the deliverances of reason will be rational, while one whose *denial* is among the deliverances of reason, i.e., contrary to reason, is irrational. But here we confront an ambiguity in the word "reason," or at least a plurality of usage. On the one hand, we can think of reason narrowly, as contrasted with experience. What we know by reason is what we know prior to experience (or, better, independent of experience); what we know by reason is what we know *a priori*. Reason taken this narrow way is the faculty by which we know truths of logic and mathematics as well as an assortment of other truths – for example, "Nothing can be red and green all over," and "There aren't any things that do not exist." It's usual to think that what we know *a priori* is *necessarily* true, true in all possible worlds (although it has also been suggested that some contingent propositions are known *a priori*). Some of these propositions we know are *self-evident*; upon a bit of reflection we can just see them to be true. Simple propositions of logic and mathematics – for example, "2 + 1 = 3," "nothing is both a horse and a non-horse," are self-evident. Some argument forms – for example, *modus ponens* – are also self-evidently valid; we can just see on reflection that they lead only to true conclusions, given true premises. Examples would be *modus ponens, modus tollens*, hypothetical syllogism, and the like.

The deliverances of reason, presumably, will be self-evident truths, together with what follows from them by self-evidently valid forms of argument. A complicating factor here is that self-evidence comes in degrees. "2 + 1 = 3" is more obvious than "6 + 2 = 8," but each is self-evident. "7 + 5 = 12" is more obvious than "19 + 13 = 32," but each is self-evident (at least for some people). Hence, the first member of each of these pairs has more by way of self-evidence than the second. Or perhaps we should say not that self-evidence comes in degrees but that self-evidence is the highest degree of something else – intuitive support, we could call it. Then we can say that, for example, "There are no things that don't exist" has some degree of intuitive support, but it has less intuitive support than "There are no things that both exist and don't exist."

Shall we say that the deliverances of reason include all those propositions for which there is some degree of intuitive support? Here we encounter a problem. Consider the Russell paradox specified to properties. Some properties exemplify themselves – for example, the property of being a property. Other properties do not exemplify themselves – for example, the property of being a horse. Those properties that do not exemplify themselves have the property of *non-self-exemplification*. Sadly enough, however, *non-self-exemplification* both does and does not exemplify itself. "There are no properties that both do and do not exemplify themselves" has maximal intuitive support; "there is such a property as non-self-exemplification" has somewhat less intuitive support, which is why rejecting that proposition is a better resolution to the Russell paradox than acquiescing in the proposition that there is such a property as *non-self-exemplification*, which both does and doesn't exemplify itself. Each of the premises of the Russell paradox seems to have some degree of intuitive support, and each of the argument forms by which the unhappy conclusion is reached seems self-evidently valid. But the conclusion is certainly not among the deliverances of reason. What are we to make of this? I don't have the space to go into this problem here, and shall leave it as homework.

We've been taking *rational* beliefs to be those that are among the deliverances of reason, and irrational beliefs to be those whose denials are among the deliverances of reason; and we've been taking "reason" in the narrow sense as a name for that faculty or power by virtue of which we know *a priori* truths. But this isn't how we are to think of rationality and irrationality in the present context. Those who denigrate religious belief as irrational are not ordinarily claiming that the denial of such beliefs is self-evident, or a consequence of self-evident propositions by way of self-evident argumentative forms. Many beliefs are irrational, in a sensible sense, even though their denials are not among the deliverances of reason, taken narrowly. For example, the belief that "If a princess kisses a frog, it will turn into a prince" is irrational for most of us; its denial is not among the deliverances of reason.

What we need is a broader notion of rationality, with an accompanying notion of irrationality. Return to the fact that man is a rational animal. A rational animal is any animal that has *ratio*; but *ratio* is not just reason in the narrow sense. It also includes the rest of the faculties or powers by way of which we have knowledge: memory, perception, and introspection, for example, but also Reid's sympathy, by which we know what others are thinking and feeling, and induction, by which we can learn from experience. Reason would include all the powers or faculties that are involved in the scientific enterprise. Perhaps there is also a moral sense, by virtue of which we can tell right from wrong. And, as we'll see later, perhaps there is also such a thing as Calvin's "*sensus divinitatis*," by virtue of which we can know something about God.[1]

We can speak of the deliverances of reason in this case just as in the case of reason taken in the narrow sense. Note that the deliverances of reason taken broadly can vary from person to person and from time to time for the same person. In fact, a given proposition can be among the deliverances of reason for one person, and its denial among the deliverances of reason for another. It's perfectly rational for a small child to believe in Santa Claus; it is not rational for me to do so, and it is rational for me to believe that there is no such person as Santa Claus. It's rational for you to believe that I live at such and such an address, because that's where I told you I live. I lied, however; and it's rational for me to believe that I do not live at that address. It is rational for me, given my evidence, to believe that Harry is left-handed; still, my evidence may be misleading, and it may be rational for Harry to believe that he is not left-handed. As a consequence, a proposition might be among the deliverances of reason for one person, and its denial may be among the deliverances of reason for someone else.

So how shall we think of the deliverances of reason, the latter taken broadly? As we've already seen, the deliverances of reason vary from person to person; they are relative to a person's experience and other beliefs. I believe that Harry is left-handed; I enter the room, see Harry

---

[1] "That there exists in the human minds and indeed by natural instinct, some sense of Deity, we hold to be beyond dispute, since God himself, to prevent any man from pretending ignorance, has endued all men with some idea of his Godhead, the memory of which he constantly renews and occasionally enlarges, that all to a man being aware that there is a God, and that he is their Maker, may be condemned by their own conscience when they neither worship him nor consecrate their lives to his service." John Calvin, *Institutes of the Christian Religion*, bk. 1, chap. 3, sec. 1, trans. Henry Beveridge (Peabody: Hendrickson Publishers, 2008), 9.

there, and form the belief that there is at least one left-handed person in the room. That belief is presumably among the deliverances of reason, and it is among them in part because of my previous belief that Harry is left-handed. So we should think of the deliverances of reason as relative to a particular profile of experience and belief. We could put it like this: the deliverances of reason, with respect to a particular profile of experience and belief, are the beliefs that would be formed by a properly functioning person enjoying that profile – a person whose rational faculties are at that time subject to no malfunction.

But that's not enough. I might suffer from no cognitive malfunction, but still arrive at a belief that is not among the deliverances of reason. Perhaps I am a victim of the wish-fulfillment Freud speaks of. We are also all aware of the way in which beliefs can be skewed by pride or excessive self-esteem or vainglory. By virtue of such skewed affections, I may form an absurdly mistaken view of the importance of my work, thinking it doesn't get nearly the attention it deserves, even though in fact it is widely overrated. In a *Wall Street Journal* review of Jerry Coyne's *Why Evolution Is True*, Philip Kitcher laments the public's rejection of evolution: "For thoughtful and accomplished scientists, however, the public's inclination is a sign of a dismal attitude toward science, a blind stubbornness in response to evidence–in short the triumph of prejudice over reason."[2] A person can be blinded by hate, but also by loyalty to a friend, or mother love. Beliefs formed under these conditions won't be among the deliverances of reason. We must therefore add another condition: the deliverances of reason, with respect to a given profile of belief and experience, will be the beliefs that could be formed by a person occupying that profile whose cognitive faculties are (1) functioning properly, and (2) are also not overlaid or impeded by wish-fulfillment or pride or any other of these affections that sometimes skew the operation of our cognitive or rational faculties. In other words, there are two sides to cognitive proper function here: on the one hand, there must be no problem with the faculty itself; on the other, no factor like undue self-love (or self-hate) that interferes with the operation of the faculty in question.

So the deliverances of reason, for me, are relative to what I believe. But what if a relevant belief is itself contrary to the deliverances of reason? I believe that Harry is left-handed and thus form the belief that there is a left-hander in the room, but what if I acquired the belief that Harry is

² Philip Kitcher, "Following the Evidence," *The Wall Street Journal*, January 29, 2009, available at www.wsj.com/articles/SB123318971717526863.

left-handed in a wholly disreputable way? I've been reliably informed that he's right-handed. Nevertheless, I suffer from a cognitive quirk that causes me to believe, of anyone I admire (I admire Harry), that he or she is left-handed. Then what? Is the belief that there is a left-hander in the room still a deliverance of reason for me? It's pretty clear, I think, that this belief, thus arrived at, is not among the deliverances of reason for me. A further condition must be added. Say that an *ancestor* of a belief B is any belief on the evidential basis of which B was formed together with any belief on the evidential basis of which an ancestor of B was formed. Then a belief is a deliverance of reason only if none of its ancestors was contrary to a deliverance of reason.

What about the fact that some people are smarter than others? Dawkins and Dennett call themselves and other atheists "brights," suggesting that those of us who believe in God are a little dim – we are running a quart low, perhaps, or the elevator doesn't go all the way up to the top floor. How does stupidity figure in? Clearly you can have considerable variations within proper function, even in the same circumstances. Some college students are much better at math than others. That doesn't mean that the merely average student's faculties aren't functioning properly when he fails to see, for example, that if a set is always composed of preexisting elements, then there can't be a universal set.

Clearly, therefore, affections can skew the operation of reason. It is also obvious, however, that affections can enable someone to see more and know more than she otherwise would. I love my child; this is likely to make me more attentive to her needs, and interests, and joys, and disappointments, so that I will have a more accurate opinion of them than I otherwise would. I'm more interested in mountain climbing than in stamp collecting. It is therefore likely that I will know a good deal more about the one than about the other. And just as hate can skew one's vision on some occasions, on others it can make one more perceptive – better able to see your enemy's weak points, for example.

One final question. Does *ratio*'s proper function *require* affection of some kind or other? Clearly affection can skew cognitive function; clearly it can also enhance it. But is it *required* for proper function? Is there some affection such that its absence makes proper function impossible or unlikely? That's a hard question, and perhaps it's a psychological rather than a philosophical question. I'll venture an opinion anyway. There is the phenomenon of *interest*. I am interested in some topics and not in others. I am interested in mountain climbing, but not in the question of how many blades of grass there are in my backyard. Note that interest can be negative as well as positive; I'm interested in philosophy of religion in that, roughly, I think it is important and I enjoy working in it. But I could also be "a person of interest" in a police investigation; that doesn't mean that the police approve of me or want to promote me or my welfare. I learn that one of my coronary arteries is blocked; this certainly attracts my attention and interest, but not because I think that this is a good thing and needs to be promoted. And, of course, interest comes in degrees; I am interested in mountain climbing, but more interested in epistemology and philosophy of religion.

Interest thus illustrated, furthermore, seems to be an affection, a sort of affective stance with respect to a topic or situation or state of affairs. I therefore suggest, both tentatively and timorously, that cognitive proper function requires at least some interest in the topics at hand. If you have no interest at all in what I am telling you (I'm droning on and on about my nephew's mildly sprained ankle), you'll be subject to a lot of auditory stimulation but will learn very little about my nephew's condition. If I hear about the first World Series game but am not interested, I probably won't remember what I heard. I'll pay little or no attention. So I'd say there is an affection that's a necessary condition of cognitive proper function: taking some interest in, or paying attention to, the subject at hand.

But might it not be perfectly proper not to pay attention? If I'm not interested, why think I'm not functioning properly? Maybe there's no good reason to pay attention. Right now I'm paying no attention to the question of how many papers there are on my desk (except to note that my wife thinks there are too many). Am I as a result convicted of lack of cognitive proper function? Presumably not. So how to put this? Well, suppose I'm just not interested in *anything* – I suffer from complete cognitive apathy or indifference. Complete apathy or indifference is an affective disorder. I take it that the absence of this condition is a necessary condition of proper cognitive function.

Given these preliminaries, we can turn to the question at hand: is religious belief – belief in God, say, to make the question more concrete – rational? First, is the belief that there is such a person as God contrary to reason in the narrow sense? There are some arguments designed to prove that the notion of an omnipotent, omniscient wholly good person is inconsistent or incoherent. For example, there is the claim that the notion of omnipotence is incoherent, the so-called paradox of the stone. There is also the vaguely Wittgensteinian argument that it's not possible that there be a person without a body. These arguments, however, are neither impressive nor widely accepted, and I'll assume that belief in God isn't contrary to the deliverances of reason in the narrow sense. There are further questions here, but let's press on.

Is belief in God contrary to the deliverances of reason, with "reason" taken in the broad sense? Recall that the deliverances of reason, taken this way, differ widely from person to person. It is contrary to reason for me to believe that H_2O never takes a solid form; not so for a Brazilian tribesman. So whose deliverances of reason are we talking about here? Let's just arbitrarily suppose we are talking about educated contemporaries – people who have gone to college, maybe graduated from college, maybe even have PhDs. Many people suppose that belief in God is irrational for such people, and that if they do believe in God, it will be by virtue of some kind of lack of cognitive proper function. According to Freud, the believer *wants* theism to be true, and this desire blinds her to the fact that there is no such person. She can't face reality as it is – nature, says Freud, rises up against us, cold, pitiless, implacable, blind to our needs and desires. She delivers hurt, fear, and pain; in the end, she demands our death. Paralyzed and appalled, we invent (unconsciously, of course) a Father in Heaven who exceeds our earthly fathers as much in power and knowledge as in goodness and benevolence; the alternative would be to sink into depression, stupor, paralysis, and finally death. On this account, belief in God is irrational; the proper function of cognitive faculties, in the believer, is impeded or overlaid by this powerful unconscious desire.

Many believers in God think the shoe is on the other foot – that atheism or unbelief is sometimes a result of cognitive faculties being impeded. According to Paul's *Epistle to the Romans*, chapter 1,

What may be known about God is plain to them, because God has made it plain to them. For since the creation of the world God's invisible qualities – his eternal power and divine nature – have been clearly seen, being understood from what has been made...[3]

Here the suggestion is that in some way God's presence is clear to us. This passage is a source of John Calvin's doctrine of the *"sensus divinitatis."* So why is it that some don't believe? They "suppress the truth in unrighteousness." Theism severely limits human autonomy. According to theism, we human beings are also at best very junior partners in the republic of mind and agency. We are not autonomous, not a law unto ourselves. Furthermore, we are completely dependent upon God for our

---

[3] Romans 1:20 (New International Version).

being and for our next breath. Still further, some find in theism a sort of intolerable invasion of privacy: God knows my every thought, and indeed knows what I will think before I think it. (There is even a hint of this attitude in Psalm 139.) These thoughts so rankle some people that as a result they go against theistic promptings and reject belief in God altogether.

Atheists or agnostics, therefore, are likely to think belief in God is irrational. It results from cognitive impedance by fear, or inability to face this cruel world, or something else. And this seems a sensible attitude for an atheist to take. From that perspective, theists are dead wrong about the most important question facing us human beings. So how to account for the fact that many otherwise apparently intelligent people fall into this colossal error? Freudian wish-fulfillment or some other kind of impedance seems the most plausible explanation. Similarly, theists sensibly attribute atheism to cognitive malfunction of one kind or another, perhaps some kind of blindness – "I was blind but now I see." Or they may attribute atheism to an inordinate desire for autonomy,[4] or perhaps an unwillingness to play nth fiddle for very high n.

Who's right? Each thinks the other irrational. Is there a way to decide between them? Note first that the question of the rationality or lack thereof of a belief is often independent of the truth of the belief. It's irrational for me, given my circumstances, to have a firm belief that the number of stars is even; and this is so whether or not the number of stars *is* even. Given my circumstances, it's irrational for me to believe that you are really an alien from outer space, and this is true even if, remarkably, you are an alien from outer space. But the question of the rationality of belief in God is not like these two. Here, I believe, the right answer is that, in the typical case, belief in God is rational if and only if it is true.

We can see this as follows. Suppose theism is true. There really is an omnipotent, omniscient, and perfectly loving God who has created us and our world, and has created us in his own image. Suppose, furthermore, that the human cognitive economy is such that the vast majority of human beings believe in God or something like God. Our cognitive faculties are such that there is this powerful tendency toward belief in God or something like God. Given these things, it's very likely that God has endowed us with faculties or cognitive processes that enable us to be aware of him and his presence. As I mentioned above, Calvin speaks of a *sensus*

---

[4] If Richard Rorty is to be believed (and perhaps he isn't), Martin Heidegger felt deeply guilty for existing in a universe he had not himself created.

divinitatis, a natural faculty or cognitive process that enables us to know of God's presence and something of his character; Aquinas speaks of something similar: "To know that God exists in a general and confused way is implanted in us by nature, inasmuch as God is man's beatitude."[5] This cognitive process, no doubt, has been damaged and skewed by sin. Augustine speaks here of the "smoke of our wrong-doing," which blinds us to God and obscures his presence from us. Still, the most likely scenario, given theism together with the vastly widespread belief in God or something like God, is that he has created us in such a way that we have cognitive or epistemic access to his existence and his presence to us. It is natural, still further, to think that if God has given us such cognitive access to him, then probably the way in which we human beings come to believe in God is roughly, at any rate, how he intends us to know of him and his presence. But that means that the way in which we come to believe in God is (ordinarily, at any rate) the way in which he intends our faculties to work; hence when they work in that way they are functioning properly; hence the beliefs they produce are in fact rational.

Of course this doesn't mean that *all* belief in God is rational. It is compatible with this scenario that belief in God is ordinarily rational, but in some special cases is not. Perhaps the *sensus divinitatis* fails to work in someone, but he so deeply dislikes his fervently atheist parents that he comes to accept a belief they hold in contempt, and does so just because they hold it in contempt. On balance, however, if theism is true, then theistic belief is ordinarily rational.

On the other hand, if theism is false – if there is no such person as God – then, probably, theistic belief is irrational. If theism is false, then probably belief in God is produced by cognitive faculties that are malfunctioning, or impeded by one thing or another. Again, there may be exceptions. Perhaps someone believes in God on the basis of an argument that is actually misleading, but on the face of it plausible. Perhaps someone rationally believes that it is at any rate possible that there be a greatest possible being, and sees, furthermore, that if that is possible then it follows that indeed there is a greatest possible being – which being would be the God of theism. For the most part, however, it is likely that if theism is false, then most theistic belief is irrational.

There is one complication here. According to classical theism (Aquinas, for example) God is a *necessary* being. That is, there is no possible world

[5] Thomas Aquinas, *Summa Theologica* (1485; New Advent, 1920), part 1, question 2, article 1, www.newadvent.org/summa/1002.htm.

in which God does not exist. But then the proposition "If theism is false, then very likely most theistic belief is irrational" is a subjunctive or counterfactual conditional with a necessarily false antecedent. Now according to the most influential accounts of subjunctives or counterfactuals, a counterfactual with a necessarily false antecedent is necessarily true, no matter what the consequent. So while "If theism is false, then very likely most theistic belief is irrational" is certainly true, the same can be said for "If theism is false, then very likely most theistic belief is rational."

I don't have the space, here, to deal properly with this complication. We should note, however, that it's far from obvious that any counterfactual with a necessarily false antecedent is true. It's true that if I were to prove Gödel's Theorem false, logicians everywhere would be astonished; it's not true that if I were to prove Gödel's theorem false, logicians everywhere would yawn in boredom. Suppose God is necessarily omniscient; it doesn't follow that if God were not omniscient, then he would know that he doesn't exist. Much more needs to be said, but I don't have the space to say it here. In response to the first part of my assignment, therefore, I conclude that, probably, belief in God is rational if and only if theism is true.

II

I turn now to the second question: to what extent is belief in God foundational to rationality? That is, to what extent is theism an essential prior condition for regarding our rationality and reasoning powers as trustworthy and reliable?

First, let's take "our rationality and reasoning powers" to be our cognitive faculties as we were thinking of them above. Then we can see that there is more than one question here. For example, we might be asking: could someone rationally believe that our cognitive faculties are reliable[6] only if she also believed in God? I won't take the question this way, since it's pretty obvious that the answer to this question is "no." Cognitive proper function, I think, requires believing or perhaps implicitly assuming that our faculties are reliable, in the absence of defeaters for that belief. But clearly an atheist need not, just as such, have a defeater for this assumption. I do believe there is a defeater lurking in the neighborhood, but it doesn't arise just as such for an atheist.

---

[6] I take it our cognitive faculties are *reliable* if and only if they produce an appropriate preponderance of true beliefs in this and nearby possible worlds.

What I do think is that a reflective naturalist gets a defeater for the proposition that our cognitive faculties are reliable (call it "R"). I take naturalism to be stronger than atheism: you can be an atheist without rising to the full heights (or descending to the murky depths) of naturalism, but you can't be a naturalist without also being an atheist. I realize that the words "naturalist" and "naturalism" are used in many different ways. I'll use "naturalism" as a name of the view that there is no such person as God or anything like God. The young Hegel, perhaps, was an atheist; he didn't believe in God. But he was not a naturalist. The same goes for Plato, with his Idea of the Good, and for Aristotle, with his "unmoved mover" that thinks only about itself. This makes the notion of naturalism a bit vague, but it may still be workable for present purposes.

Why think that the reflective naturalist gets a defeater for R? For present purposes I'll also assume that a reflective naturalist will accept the current scientific theory of evolution. Of course, I realize that there are several theories of evolution, but most of the differences between these theories need not concern us here. Most of them hold that the variety of the biosphere has come to be in large part by way of natural selection operating on some source of genetic variation such as genetic mutation and/or genetic drift. The naturalist, as I'm thinking of him, believes that we, like other creatures, have come to be by way of natural selection winnowing genetic variation, and our cognitive faculties, like everything else about us, have also been crafted in this way. And, of course, the naturalist will think of natural selection as unguided by the hand of God or any other person.

Now the first thing to see is that natural selection is interested in behavior (taken broadly), not in belief, except insofar as belief contributes to behavior. Natural selection rewards adaptive behavior and penalizes maladaptive behavior. Creatures that engage in adaptive behavior will tend to survive and reproduce; creatures that engage in maladaptive behavior will display that pathetic but praiseworthy tendency to die before reproducing their kind. But natural selection doesn't care one way or the other about *belief*. As long as you behave in adaptive fashion, you can believe whatever you like.

Still, perhaps it is plausible to suppose that there is a connection between belief and behavior, a connection of such a sort that false belief will often result in maladaptive behavior. A 12-year-old who lives on the plains of the Serengeti and thinks lions are large, friendly pussycats who like nothing better than to be petted will probably not live long enough to reproduce. Cognitive faculties that produce false beliefs of that sort will likely be weeded out by natural selection. Natural selection will tend to select for belief-producing processes and faculties that produce true beliefs – at least about matters that relate to survival and reproduction. So it's not initially implausible to think that unguided natural selection could have produced creatures with cognitive faculties that are reliable about matters relevant to survival and reproduction.

But what about metaphysical beliefs, beliefs like determinism, or materialism, or theism, or atheism, or naturalism? Such beliefs have little or no bearing on behavior related to survival and reproduction, and unguided natural selection couldn't care less about them or their truth-value. So consider a metaphysical belief: atheism, for example. If your behavior is adaptive, it doesn't matter, for survival and reproduction, whether or not you have that belief, and it doesn't matter whether or not the belief is true. After all, it is only the occasional member of the Young Humanist Society whose reproductive prospects are enhanced by accepting atheism. Natural selection would probably not weed out cognitive faculties that produce false metaphysical beliefs. Natural selection would probably not mold our cognitive faculties in the direction of reliability with respect to such beliefs. And that means that the probability that my cognitive faculties are reliable with respect to metaphysical beliefs, given naturalism and evolution, is low. But, of course, naturalism is itself a metaphysical belief. So the devotee of naturalism who accepts evolution, and who also sees that this probability is low, has a defeater for any metaphysical belief she happens to have, including naturalism itself. Unless she has a defeater for that defeater, she can't rationally believe naturalism.

But consider an objection: couldn't reliability with respect to metaphysical beliefs be a spandrel, piggybacking on reliability with respect to beliefs relevant to behavior? Maybe so, maybe not. In any event, we can respond to this objection by taking the argument further. So far I've argued that a person who accepts naturalism and evolution and sees that the relevant probability of "R" is low, has a defeater for her metaphysical beliefs. But the argument can be extended to *all* beliefs, whether metaphysical or not. The reflective naturalist gets a defeater for all of her beliefs, and is thus committed to a deep skepticism – of her metaphysical beliefs, to be sure, but also of her scientific and commonsense beliefs. To facilitate brief statement of the argument, let "R" be the proposition that our cognitive faculties are reliable, "N" be naturalism, and "E" be the proposition that we and our cognitive faculties have come to be in the way specified in the contemporary scientific theory of evolution. The first and most important premise of my argument is:

(1) P(R/N&E) is low, i.e., the conditional probability of our cognitive faculties, given naturalism and given that our cognitive faculties have come to be by way of evolution, is low. The second premise is:

(2) Anyone who accepts N&E and sees that (1) is true has an undefeated defeater for R; the remaining premise is:

(3) Anyone who has an undefeated defeater for R has an undefeated defeater for any belief she holds; the conclusion is:

(4) Anyone who accepts N&E and sees that (1) is true has an undefeated defeater for N and hence can't rationally believe it.

The first premise is perhaps the most controversial, so I'll begin by explaining and arguing for this premise.

First, note that most if not all naturalists are *materialists* about human beings. That is, they hold that human beings are material objects. From this perspective, a human person is not (contrary to Descartes and Augustine) an immaterial substance or self that is connected with or joined to a material body. Nor is it the case that a human being is a composite that has an immaterial component, for on this view human beings do not have anything like an immaterial soul. I *am* my body (or maybe my brain, or its left hemisphere, or some other part of it, or some other part of my body) or possibly another material object composed of the matter that constitutes my body.

Now suppose you are a materialist, and also think that there are such things as beliefs. That is, there are cases of a person's believing a proposition. For example, you believe the proposition that Proust is subtler than Louis L'Amour. What kind of a thing *is* this belief – i.e., this act of believing that proposition? From a materialist perspective, it looks as if it would have to be something like a longstanding event or structure in your brain or nervous system. What else could it be? A belief will be a neuronal event or structure, composed of neurons connected with each other in various ways. Such a structure will have input from other parts of the nervous system and output to still other parts as well as to muscles and glands. And such a neuronal structure, if it is a belief, will have properties of two quite different sorts. On the one hand, it will have neurophysiological properties ("NP properties"): among these would be such properties as that of involving n neurons, and n^* connections between neurons, properties that specify which neurons are connected with which others, what the rates of fire in the various parts of the event are, how these rates of fire change in response to changes in input, and so on. On the other hand, if this structure is a belief, it will also have to have a *content*. That is, it will have to be the belief that p, for some proposition p. If it's the belief that Proust is a subtler writer than Louis L'Amour, then its content is the proposition "Proust is subtler than Louis L'Amour." It is in virtue of its content that a belief will be true or false. In other words, a belief is true just if its content, the proposition that is its content, is true.

Suppose we think next about belief and action. On the materialist view, what causes an action or a bit of behavior? Suppose I raise my arm. What causes my arm to go up? Well, there will be a chain of neuronal events, perhaps starting in my brain, involving the transmission of signals from the brain, via nerves or neuronal channels. The firing of the right nerves, finally, causes the relevant muscles in my arm to contract, and the arm goes up. Now suppose a belief is involved here; suppose a belief is a part-cause of a given bit of behavior. This belief, as we have seen, will be a neuronal structure or event of some kind. It will have both NP properties and a content. And clearly enough, on the materialist account, the belief can get involved in the causal chain leading to behavior. But from the point of view of materialism, it is by virtue of the NP properties of this structure – properties involving the firing of neurons, the connection between neurons, the connection of this structure with other structures, and the like, that the belief causes what it does. It is because this structure sends certain signals down certain nerve pathways that it is a cause of action.

So how does the content of the belief figure in? It doesn't. It looks like the content doesn't matter to the production of action or behavior. If the belief in question had had the same NP properties but a different content, it would have made the very same contribution with respect to behavior. It looks as if materialism is committed to what we might call "content epiphenomenalism": the content of a belief, as opposed to its NP properties, is not involved in the causal chain leading to behavior.

Now suppose this is true. Natural selection selects for adaptive action; it does not, as such, care about the truth of beliefs. Provided your behavior is adaptive, you can believe whatever you want as far as natural selection is concerned. But if content doesn't get into the causal chain leading to behavior, then content will be invisible to natural selection. Natural selection will presumably modify belief-producing faculties or processes in the direction of greater fitness. It will do so by weeding out those processes that produce maladaptive beliefs – that is, beliefs that cause maladaptive action. As we have seen, however, beliefs cause behavior only by virtue of their NP properties, not by virtue of their content properties. So natural selection will act on the NP properties of beliefs, but not on their contents. Natural selection can't be expected to weed out processes that produce false belief. That's because whether a belief is true or false doesn't matter to its adaptivity. So unguided natural selection can't be expected to move organisms capable of belief in the direction of having more true beliefs and fewer false beliefs. And that means that there is no reason to expect that creatures crafted by unguided natural selection will have mostly true beliefs. Consider any such creature, and any belief it has. The belief will be adaptive, no doubt, but no more likely to be true than to be false. We'd have to say that the probability, with respect to any particular belief that it is true, given N&E (E including materialism), will be about ½. But that means that the probability that the creature in question has reliable belief-producing faculties will be very low. If I have 100 independent beliefs and the probability of truth with respect to each is ½, the probability that, say, ¾ of these beliefs is true – certainly a conservative requirement for the reliability of my belief producing faculties – is very low indeed.

Consider an objection, however: don't materialists think there's a connection between content properties and NP properties? Content properties don't just sit there, wholly independent of NP properties. And if so, won't true content tend to go with adaptive NP properties? Surely, given materialism, there is a connection between content properties and NP properties; content is *determined by* NP properties, or *supervenes* on NP properties. A belief has the content it has by virtue of the NP properties it has.

Right. Still, how does that so much as slyly suggest that adaptive NP properties confer true content on a belief? Here's the picture: the NP properties of a belief are adaptive in that they cause adaptive behavior. Those NP properties also determine a content property. But as long as the NP properties are adaptive, it doesn't matter, for survival and reproduction, what content emerges from those NP properties. It could be true content; it could be false content. The point is that it doesn't matter. The fact that these creatures have survived and evolved, that their cognitive equipment was good enough to enable their ancestors to survive and reproduce – that fact would tell us nothing at all about the *truth* of their beliefs or the reliability of their cognitive faculties. It would tell us something about the *neurophysiological* properties of a given belief; it would tell us that by virtue of these properties that belief has played a role in the production of adaptive behavior. But it would tell us nothing about the *truth* of the *content* of that belief. Its content *might* be true, but might with equal probability be false. So shouldn't we suppose that the proposition in question has a probability of roughly 0.5? Shouldn't we estimate its probability, on the condition in question, as in the neighborhood of 0.5? If so, however, then once more it follows that P(R/N&E) is low.

Here is the most common objection to this argument. Isn't it just obvious that true beliefs will facilitate adaptive action? A gazelle who mistakenly believes that lions are friendly won't be long for this world. The same goes for a rock climber who believes that jumping from a 200 ft cliff will result in a pleasant and leisurely trip down with a soft landing. Isn't it obvious that true beliefs are much more likely to be adaptive than false beliefs? Isn't it obvious, more generally, that true beliefs are more likely to be successful than false beliefs? I want to go from New York to Boston: won't I be more likely to get there if I believe it's north of New York than if I believe it's to the south?

Yes, certainly. This is indeed true. But it is also irrelevant. We are not asking about how things *are*, but about *what things would be like if both evolution and naturalism (construed as including materialism) were true*. We are asking about P(R/N&E), not about P(R/the way things actually are). Like nearly everyone else, I believe that our cognitive faculties are for the most part reliable, and that true beliefs are more likely to issue in successful action than false. But that's not the question. The question is what things would be like if N&E were true; and in this context we can't just assume, of course, that if N&E (E including materialism) were true, then things would still be the way they are. And it's materialism that's crucial here. That is, we can't assume that if materialism were true, it would still be the case that true beliefs are more likely to cause successful action than false beliefs.

"What has materialism to do with this question?" Here's what. We ordinarily think true belief leads to successful action because we also think that beliefs cause (are among the causes of) actions, and do so *by virtue of their content*. I want a beer; I believe there is one in the fridge, and this belief is among the causes of my going over to the fridge. We think it is by virtue of the *content* of that belief that it causes me to go over to the fridge. It is because this belief has as content that there is a beer in the fridge that it causes me to go to the fridge rather than, say, the washing machine. More generally, we think it is by virtue of the content of a belief B that B causes the behavior that it does cause.

But now suppose materialism were true. Then, as we've seen, my belief will be a neural structure that has both NP properties and also a content.

It is by virtue of the NP properties, however, not that content, that the belief causes what it does cause. It is by virtue of *those* properties that the belief causes neural impulses to travel down the relevant efferent nerves to the relevant muscles, causing them to contract, and thus causing behavior. None of this occurs by virtue of the content of this belief, in other words, because the content of the belief is irrelevant to the causal power of the belief with respect to behavior. Going back to materialism and the content of belief, then, it is by virtue of the NP properties of a belief B, not by virtue of its content, that the belief causes the behavior it does cause. If the belief had had the same NP properties but different content, it would have had the same effect on behavior.

The response to this common objection, therefore, is that it assumes that if naturalism (including materialism) were true, our commonsense assumption that beliefs cause action by virtue of their contents would still be true. But that's false. If materialism were true, it would not be by virtue of content that beliefs cause what they do.

This concludes my defense of the first premise. I'll say just a bit about the remaining premises of the argument. According to the second premise, (2) one who accepts N&E and sees that (1) is true has an undefeated defeater for R, the belief or assumption that her faculties are reliable.

It's obvious, I think, that one who accepts N&E and sees that (1) is true has a *defeater* for R. But why think that defeater is itself undefeated? Well, what would a defeater for that defeater be like? Couldn't I go to the MIT cognitive-reliability laboratory for a checkup? And if they give me a clean bill of cognitive health, won't I have a defeater for that defeater?[7] Clearly not. That course would *presuppose* that my faculties are reliable; I'd be relying on the accuracy of my faculties in believing that there is such a thing as MIT, that I have in fact consulted its scientists, that they have given me a clean bill of cognitive health, and so on. The great Scottish philosopher Thomas Reid put it like this:

> If a man's honesty were called into question, it would be ridiculous to refer to the man's own word, whether he be honest or not. The same absurdity lies in attempting to prove, by any kind of reasoning, probable or demonstrative, that our reason is not fallacious, since the very point in question is, whether reasoning may be trusted.[8]

---

[7] Compare Paul Churchland, "Is Evolutionary Naturalism Epistemologically Self-Defeating?," *Philo* 12 (2009): 135–141. Aaron Segal and I have written a reply: "Response to Churchland," *Philo* 13 (2010): 201–207.

[8] Thomas Reid, *Inquiry and Essays*, eds. Ronald Beanblossom and Keith Lehrer (Indianapolis: Hackett Publishing Co., 1983), 276.

It looks as if any defeater defeater, here, will have to involve an argument of some sort. But any argument will have premises; and I will have the very same defeater for each of those premises that I have for R. I will also have the very same defeater for the belief that if the premises of that argument are true, then so is the conclusion. So it looks as if this defeater can't be defeated. Naturalistic evolution gives its adherents a reason for doubting that our cognitive faculties are reliable. If so, it won't help to *argue* that they are reliable. For the very reason for mistrusting our cognitive faculties *generally* will be a reason for mistrusting the faculties that produce belief in the goodness of that argument.

The final premise of the argument is: (3) Anyone who has an undefeated defeater for R has an undefeated defeater for all of her beliefs. Again, this premise is obvious. If you have a general reason for mistrusting your cognitive faculties, then, clearly enough, you will have a reason to mistrust any belief produced by those faculties.

Given the truth of these premises, the conclusion follows. One who accepts both naturalism and evolution has good reason to give up the assumption that our cognitive powers are reliable. This is not, of course, an argument for theism: another option is agnosticism. But what does follow is that a reflective naturalist can't rationally assume, with the rest of us, that our faculties are reliable. Naturalism is self-defeating, and hence irrational.

Suppose, as we have seen, that naturalism is self-defeating and irrational because it presumes an epistemic reliability that, in fact, is undermined by the very logic of naturalism. Suppose, further, that theism is rational by virtue of its undefeated assumption of a God that has equipped humans with reliable cognitive faculties. Supposing all this, what conclusions might we draw about human nature, the nature of religion, and ultimately, religious freedom?

As far back as Aristotle and the classical Greeks, efforts to comprehend and define human nature have often sought recourse to the notion of rationality. Above all else, Aristotle and many since have claimed that humans are *rational* animals, endowed with a unique capacity for reason that sets them apart from other earthly creatures. If humans are indeed defined by their capacity for reason, then the foundations of rationality are highly relevant not only to the pursuit of an authentic self-understanding but also to the norms, values, rules, and other organizing principles that flow from this understanding and that order the various social, political, legal, and moral aspects of collective life. With all this in mind, the proposition that theism, or belief in God, is foundational to rationality must be taken seriously.

If theism is rational, and stronger still, *foundational* to rationality, then religious belief is neither a cognitive malfunction that should be subordinated to "secular" reason, an extraneous oddity to brush aside, nor a vestige of our primitive history to overcome. Rather than grating against some perceived secular human nature, religious belief takes on a certain epistemic advisability if not necessity: deeply and organically rooted in human experience, it nicely coheres with natural and healthy human cognition. Accordingly, to deny the right to religious freedom – to attempt to suppress the capacity for religious belief and the actions to which it gives rise – is to do violence to our human nature. Protecting the right to religious *belief*, therefore, simply amounts to a recognition of the human condition, a condition in which human rationality coheres best with a "supernaturalist metaphysics" and a religiously grounded account of human cognition.[9] And protecting the right to religious *practices* – the actions motivated by religious beliefs, including those that spill into various aspects of "public" life – similarly recognizes that, just as our capacity for rationality cannot be turned off, our religiously- grounded actions and motivations cannot and should not be cordoned off or marginalized, except for very compelling reasons.[10]

---

[9] Alvin Plantinga, *Warrant and Proper Function* (Oxford: Oxford University Press, 1993), 237.

[10] Alvin Plantinga reviewed and fully endorsed these last three concluding paragraphs, but we (the volume's editors) were their original drafters, as we believed (and Plantinga agreed) that they serve to clarify the connections between the chapter and the overarching themes and issues of the volume.

6

Alvin Plantinga on Theism, Naturalism, and Rationality

Ernest Sosa

Alvin Plantinga's paper has two main parts. The first considers whether belief in God is rational. The second argues that atheist naturalism is self-defeating and hence irrational. My comments will begin with two corresponding parts. Two later parts will then reflect more broadly on the issues and the reasoning, with a special focus on the critique of naturalism.

CAN BELIEF IN GOD BE RATIONAL?

1. Natural theology has always faced the argument from evil. The evil around us is said to prove that there is no God. What is more, the order of the biosphere is explained at least as well by evolution as by theology. Divine design is hence threatened by the rival account due to Darwin.

Both of these attacks confront theology directly in either of two ways. One attack is by refutation: the evil we see leaves no room for an omnipotent, omniscient, fully benevolent God. The other targets rather the cogency of theology's rational support: if much of the most striking order around us is well enough explained by evolution, it no longer demands a Divine designer.

Although both attacks are "direct," the first is also frontal, since it contradicts outright the central claim of any theology. It concludes that there is no God from the fact that there is evil. The second, evolutionary attack is not frontal. It targets not the truth of theology but the cogency of its supporting rationale.

Nietzsche, Freud, and Marx launch an even less direct attack. They all pursue different versions of the same basic strategy. Their target is not the truth of religious beliefs, nor even the quality of their supporting arguments. Their target is rather the *sources* of religious belief. They point to deplorable factors, psychological or sociological, that originate or sustain such belief. For Nietzsche, religion is a way for the weak to gang up on the strong and keep them in line. For Freud, religion is wishful thinking that provides a comforting view of our situation and its prospects. For Marx, religion is opium used to distract the masses from their economic and social misery and keep them in chains.

For its enemies, the Christian religion has been misused in those and other ways throughout much of recorded history.

What makes a way of forming beliefs intellectually acceptable is, at a minimum, this: that it delivers truth reliably enough, that its deliverances are probably enough true. A belief that lacks reliable sources might serve the functions attributed to religious belief by Nietzsche, Freud, or Marx. But it could hardly be epistemically justified, much less could it be knowledge, even if by luck it happened to be true. If religious belief really originates only in the way claimed by the enemies of religion, then it might be comforting, or otherwise useful, but it could hardly amount to knowledge.

What response is open to the friends of religion? If they deny what their enemies say about sources, this requires empirical backing. Only through empirical research could we uncover actual sources. A full and credible account would need to draw on the psychology, history, and sociology of religion. Nietzsche, Freud, and Marx manage only some initial exploration of broad fields still under patient, disciplined cultivation. Of course, theists might well counter that the critique of the sources of religion must itself be empirically well based. But a further, more aggressive response is also available.

2. Plantinga delivers that further response from the comfort of his armchair. First, he defends the epistemic rationality of belief in God for average educated humans. Relative to the profiles of experience and belief shared generally by such humans,

... the deliverances of reason, with respect to a given profile of belief and experience, will be the beliefs that could be formed by a person occupying that profile whose cognitive faculties are (1) functioning properly, and (2) are also not overlaid or impeded by wish-fulfillment or pride or any other of these affections that sometimes skew the operation of our cognitive or rational faculties. In other words, there are two sides to cognitive proper function here: on the one hand, there must be no problem with the faculty itself; on the other, no factor like undue self-love (or self-hate) that interferes with the operation of the faculty in question.[1]

---

[1] Alvin Plantinga, "Theism, Naturalism, and Rationality," this volume, p. 124

As we have seen, indirect critics of religion appeal to such distorting factors in explaining why humans are so prone to host religious beliefs. Plantinga responds that perhaps it is atheists who are misled by epistemically unfortunate affection, such as inordinate pride or desire for autonomy. So he is led to ask who is right: is it the atheist or the theist? "Each thinks the other irrational; is there a way to decide between them?"

If theism is true, he answers, and

[o]ur cognitive faculties are such that there is this powerful tendency towards belief in God or something like God, ... [then] it's very likely that God has endowed us with faculties or cognitive processes that enable us to be aware of him and his presence ... [The] most likely scenario, given theism together with the vastly widespread belief in God or something like God, is that he has created us in such a way that we have cognitive or epistemic access to his existence and his presence to us.[2]

While distrusting my own ability to judge thus over the vast span of infinite time and space, except perhaps for certain general truths knowable *a priori* or scientifically, here I will shelve such general doubt in favor of a more specific problem.

Suppose our solution to the problem of evil requires some ignorance of God's ways. Correlatively, we might claim ignorance of how the ostensible evil we discern fits into the overall infinite value package. If so, then here's the implied problem: that defense against evil would seem to import a corresponding ignorance of how generous God may be epistemically. Even supposing he wanted us to know him, why think that this is a trumping value, given the potentially infinite number of conceivable trade-offs?

I mean to pose an issue of coherence for the theist who solves the problem of evil by invoking our ignorance. How can he coherently plead ignorance in defense against evil, while claiming knowledge or sufficiently justified belief when it comes to God's epistemic benevolence?[3]

Let "R" stand for the proposition that our cognitive faculties are reliable, "N" for naturalism, "Th" for theism, and "E" for the proposition that we and our cognitive faculties have developed in the way

---

[2] Ibid., 28–29.

[3] For a similar take on an earlier version of Plantinga's reasoning, see Blake Roeber, "Does the Theist Have an Epistemic Advantage Over the Atheist? Plantinga and Descartes on Theism, Atheism, and Skepticism," *The Journal of Philosophical Research* 34 (2009): 305–328.

specified by the contemporary scientific theory of evolution. The theist might then respond as follows:

T   Pr(R/E) is very low, and since Pr(E/N) is higher than Pr(E/Th), therefore Pr (R/N) will be lower than Pr(R/Th) *even if* worries arising from the problem of evil make Pr(R/Th) lower than we might have thought.

But this seems weak, given the content of the evil-based critique, which argues that there is a plausible parity between the following two claims:

V   God's preferences must be quite a mystery to us, given our ignorance of the infinite value package and the trade-offs and organic wholes that may be involved in it, so far as we know. Therefore, we cannot have any very good reason to claim that he just would not have permitted the seemingly pointless suffering that we know is plentiful out there, as with the little doe that burns to death in a forest fire.

E   God's preferences must be quite a mystery to us, given our ignorance of the infinite value package and the trade-offs and organic value wholes that may be involved in it, so far as we know. Therefore, we cannot have any very good reason to claim that he would have ensured that we would have epistemically reliable faculties.

But if V and E are on a par, then anyone who opts for the ignorance-based defense against the argument from evil cannot plausibly make the claims in T above. How can he be sure enough that he has a good enough handle on Pr(R/Th) to say any of the things he says about it in T?

What is more, I wonder if the plausible parity between V and E does not *also* lead to a line of thought more threatening yet for theists who both endorse a V-based defense against evil, and wish to argue as does Plantinga.

DT   Pr(R/Th) is at best approximately 50 percent or else inscrutable. And this gives us (relevant) theists a defeater for our belief in R. So now we need a defeater defeater. And how can we get it while avoiding vicious circularity?

The problem here for the theist is a very close match for the problem to be posed by Plantinga for the naturalist. The heart of the problem for both is that once one has a defeater for R, there's no apparent way to defeat that defeater while avoiding vicious circularity: that is to say, there is then no apparent way to defeat that defeater.

Let me point to a further worry. It is not quite clear to me how Plantinga's reasoning is meant to address the question he raises as follows: "Who is right when the atheist and the theist accuse each other of irrational belief?" The answer proposed is that the theist is rational if and only if his theism is true. But that will help only if we can take theism to be true, or to be false. In order to complete that answer, then, we would have to address the question of theism. So, I wonder: can we properly address that question by reasoning theologically, or just by flat-out assertion? Can we really do so even as we confront an atheist challenge to the rationality of our relevant beliefs and reasonings? These are baseless, after all, or improperly based, if we believe Freud, Marx, or Nietzsche. Again, I am not so much proposing an answer as raising a question, of a sort to which we shall return in due course below. But first we turn to the second theme in Plantinga's paper.

IS ATHEIST NATURALISM SELF-DEFEATING?

Now we turn to a very different defense of natural theology, a further imaginative and original turning of the tables. I mean the way in which Plantinga has turned the momentum of religion's enemies against them, using their own strategy to trip them onto their own sword. How is all this supposed to come about?

1. Plantinga's target is the "naturalist" – i.e., the atheist and materialist who denies that there is a God or anything like God and who believes in evolution.[4] Such naturalism is self-defeating because it imports a defeater for naturalists' belief in their own epistemic reliability. So, naturalists cannot coherently believe that our cognitive faculties (those that produce our beliefs) are reliable (proposition R above).

According to Plantinga, moreover, epistemic reliability is to be understood so that "our cognitive faculties are *reliable* if and only if they produce an appropriate preponderance of true beliefs in this and nearby possible worlds."[5]

---

[4] Note, though, that on Plantinga's view it is possible to be an atheist without being a naturalist, but, as he notes in his chapter in this volume, "you can't be a naturalist without also being an atheist." He adds: "I realize that the words 'naturalist' and 'naturalism' are used in many different ways. I'll use 'naturalism' as a name of the view that there is no such person as God or anything like God. The young Hegel, perhaps, was an atheist; he didn't believe in God. But he was not a naturalist. The same goes for Plato, with his Idea of the Good, and for Aristotle, with his 'unmoved mover' that thinks only about itself. This makes the notion of naturalism a bit vague, but it may still be workable for present purposes." Plantinga, "Theism, Naturalism, and Rationality," this volume, p. 131. However, I don't believe these distinctions matter for the response to Plantinga I lay out here.

[5] See footnote 6 in Plantinga, "Theism, Naturalism, and Rationality," this volume, p. 130 (emphasis original).

I will interpret both of the above-indented statements so as to have existential import (just to take care of a technicality). The first, for example, then says the following: "We do have cognitive faculties, which produce our beliefs," and they are reliable; and similarly for the second.

Plantinga adopts the abbreviations we have stipulated as follows: "R" for the proposition that our cognitive faculties are reliable, "N" for naturalism, and "E" for the proposition that we and our cognitive faculties have developed in the way specified by the contemporary scientific theory of evolution.

Given those stipulations, here is the argument:

(a) P(R/N&E) is low.
(b) Anyone who accepts N&E and sees that (a) is true has an undefeated defeater for R;
(c) Anyone who has an undefeated defeater for R has an undefeated defeater for any belief that she holds.

Therefore,

(d) Anyone who accepts N&E and sees that (a) is true has an undefeated defeater for (their belief of) N, and hence can't rationally believe it.

2. Because he takes (a) to be the most controversial premise, Plantinga gives it his fullest defense, as follows:

a. The naturalist is by definition a materialist.
b. What kind of thing is a belief, an act of believing? For a materialist, it would have to be something like a long-standing event or structure in your brain or nervous system.
c. Such a structure would have two sorts of properties: first, neurophysiological properties; second, propositional contents.
d. When true, beliefs are true in virtue of the truth of their contents.
e. Given b, beliefs will (even partially) cause actions only in virtue of their neurophysiological properties and not in virtue of their contents, or so a materialist would have to think.
f. Natural selection weeds out beliefs that are maladaptive.
g. However, natural selection can't be expected to weed out processes that produce false belief; that's because the truth value of a belief does not matter to its adaptivity. What matters is only the properties by virtue of which the belief enters the causal order, and these,

for the materialist, are only its neurophysiological properties, and not at all its content.

Plantinga concludes his reasoning with the following passage:

Natural selection can't be expected to weed out processes that produce false belief. That's because whether a belief is true or false doesn't matter to its adaptivity. So unguided natural selection can't be expected to move organisms capable of belief in the direction of having more true beliefs and fewer false beliefs. And that means that there is no reason to expect that creatures crafted by unguided natural selection will have mostly true beliefs. Consider any such creature, and any belief it has. The belief will be adaptive, no doubt, but no more likely to be true than to be false. We'd have to say that the probability, with respect to any particular belief that it is true, given N&E (E including materialism), will be about ½. But that means that the probability that the creature in question has reliable belief-producing faculties will be very low. If I have 100 independent beliefs and the probability of truth with respect to each is ½, the probability that, say, ¾ of these beliefs is true – certainly a conservative requirement for the reliability of my belief producing faculties – is very low indeed.[6]

PLANTINGA'S CRITIQUE OF NATURALISM

1. The critique Plantinga offers proceeds via two commitments of the naturalist: to evolution and to materialism. However, we can argue – more simply and no less cogently – that naturalism is self-defeating *without any reference to evolution*. The new argument runs as follows:

   a. Our cognitive faculties are *reliable* if and only if they produce an appropriate preponderance of true beliefs in this and nearby possible worlds.
   b. Our cognitive faculties will *produce* an appropriate preponderance of true beliefs in this *and nearby possible worlds* only if the truth and hence the content of our beliefs can enter the causal order – i.e., the dispositions that constitute our cognitive faculties must favor truth over falsity in their belief production, so they must be sensitive to the contents and indeed to the truth value of the beliefs produced.
   c. For a materialist, beliefs enter the causal order only in virtue of their neurophysiological properties and not at all in virtue of their contents.

---

[6] Plantinga, "Theism, Naturalism, and Rationality," this volume, p. 135.

Therefore,

> d. For a materialist, our cognitive faculties are *not* reliable. And hence, for a *naturalist*, our cognitive faculties are not reliable.

Recall Plantinga's argument (relabeled to fit the present context):

> (i) P(R/N&E) is low.
> (ii) Anyone who accepts N&E and sees that (i) is true has an undefeated defeater for R;
> (iii) Anyone who has an undefeated defeater for R has an undefeated defeater for any belief she holds.

Therefore,

> (iv) Anyone who accepts N&E and sees that (i) is true has an undefeated defeater for (their belief of) N and hence can't rationally believe it.

We have now seen how we retain an equally good (or bad) argument if we excise E.

2. However, not all naturalists are so radically reductive as Plantinga's materialist is supposed to be. There are of course various conflicting proposals for how we should understand mental causation and for how to address attendant problems such as that of exclusion. According to one attractive option, the social sciences host causal explanations that would be put in doubt by the same features that are said to make trouble for mental causation. Any premises that yield epiphenomenalism are thus reduced to absurdity. One might thus seek a more flexible account of causal explanation that will accommodate a causal role for the content of beliefs within less fundamental levels than that of physics or even biology. We need causation also in psychology and even in sociology, after all. Even with no such account in hand, why should we think that the only way to be a materialist is the radically reductive way? Good naturalists might find understanding not only in physics and biology, but also in psychology and other social sciences, and even in commonsense explanations.

Accordingly, only those on one side of the several-sided controversy over mental causation would be affected directly by Plantinga's anti-naturalist argument, which attributes to the naturalist a highly reductive commitment. Those of us who reject any such radical reduction, or who suspend judgment on the matter, need not worry just yet. *We* can contemplate the argument with equanimity, while noting that it may simply provide a further reason to be wary of radical reductionism. This radical view would indeed make trouble for trust in our own epistemic reliability. But we would be able to resist this radical view and its crippling consequences so long as we retain our commitment to a modest naturalism that avoids radical reduction.

3. One might try to save the argument from evolution by modifying Plantinga's argument in a different way. Suppose we excise not evolution but materialism. The resulting argument might then be acceptable to moderate naturalists. How might this new argument go? We would need to conclude that our belief-forming dispositions are unreliable without premising radical materialist reductionism. Although I cannot stop to consider in full detail how that might be done, I would like to suggest some preliminary worries.

In the first place, those of our beliefs bearing on our survival are likely to be reliably formed, given how the truth of such beliefs will matter. This is not to say that the truth of our beliefs *must* matter *with apodictic necessity* in any possible world. Our claim is more modest (but would still be telling if true): beliefs that bear on our survival are *likely* to be reliably formed.

But don't we still have a problem for our metaphysical and other general philosophical beliefs, since they seem *not* to bear on our survival? These now seem subject to defeat, since there is no reason to consider them reliable in light of evolution.

There is a problem, however, for this more restricted line of attack against metaphysical naturalism. The problem is how implausible it seems that there are relevantly distinctive ways of forming beliefs. Are there epistemic faculties that pertain to metaphysical beliefs and not at all to the more practical beliefs whereby we flourish as a species? More plausibly, surely, the faculties whereby we form such beliefs are the usual, including introspection, perception, memory, testimony, and inference of the familiar sorts: deductive, inductive, and abductive. These are the intellectual competencies whereby we flourish practically, and they seem essentially the same competencies whereby we flourish theoretically and philosophically. Only the subject matter is different, not our relevant epistemic competency.

4. Moreover, there is a further doubt about the argument from evolution. Consider the proposition that (at least in the realm of contingency) at one time there was just primordial muck (or undifferentiated chaos). Call this thesis "PM." The probability that an epistemically reliable humanity would be in place about now seems no higher conditional on PM than it would be conditional on E (unguided evolution). Given the considerations in 3, above, it seems less likely that we'd be here with our epistemic

competence conditional on PM than conditional on E. So, why not appeal to unguided derivation from primordial muck rather than to unguided evolution? I hazard that atheist naturalists would tend to agree that conditional on PM, it was quite improbable that we'd be here now with our epistemic endowments. Why is this not just as much a defeater as E, one whose truth naturalists are much less likely to dispute?

Suppose we argued as follows. Yes, it is very improbable we'd be here now with our epistemic competence, given the assumption of PM. So, our emergence from primordial muck with no benefit of guidance – our being now alive and competent with such origins – was not to be expected. How do we trump this low probability?

We might say in response that our belief in our own reliability is in fact reliably formed through proper child development, so that eventually this belief dawns on us along with our Moorean common sense. But how is *this* belief *about* our dawning beliefs properly formed? Well, we arrive at it through reflection on our own situation as we consider what we know about proper child development. Certain processes of belief formation plausibly lead us all not long after infancy to such a commonsense picture. And we take these processes to be reliable.

Alternatively, some may prefer the (supposedly) "Moorean" inference to the specific and general reliability of our faculty of vision from particular visual beliefs, as when we are able to see that here is a hand. So, on this view we just bootstrap to our belief in our general reliability.

According to a third alternative, finally, suppose we arrive at belief in the reliability of our visual perception by reasoning from data provided by our *other* senses, and so on for each sense, and for each faculty, more generally; so that, in the end, our trust in our general reliability properly derives from such coherent mutual support.

Whichever such approach we may take, here is a reply we might expect that is in line with Plantinga's critique of the naturalist.

You are giving me an account of how you can right now properly believe that you are well-endowed epistemically despite how improbable it was that you would come into being so endowed, as part of humanity's unguided rise from primordial muck. Our unpromising origin defeats the belief that humanity could now be in existence with its epistemic endowment. This was just too improbable conditional on PM; we who accept PM have a defeater for our belief that humanity is now in place with its impressive competence. And how can we possibly defeat that defeater? If we appeal to our Moorean commonsense, and we try to buttress this in any of the three ways floated, we appeal to the sort of competence that has been put in doubt by the improbability that we would enjoy it given our origins. This seems subject to Reidian ridicule: when a source has been put in doubt it would be ridiculous to use its own deliverances to defeat the doubt.

How, if at all, is this line of argument different from the Plantinga line? Our line replaces E with PM. Aside from that, the two seem parallel. So, are we to suppose that our belief in PM equally defeats all of our beliefs beyond redemption? In our attempt to defeat this defeater, are we denied appeal to common sense or to science? Is there no way to buttress such appeal, whether through dawning child development, or through "Moorean" bootstrapping, or through mutually supportive coherence? Will any such attempt encounter a charge of vicious circularity and of defending a source by reference to its own deliverances?

Once again, the appeal to evolution seems dispensable, this time in favor of an argument that appeals instead to our unguided rise from primordial muck or undifferentiated chaos. My point here is that Plantinga's argument falls short because there is an argument that replaces E with PM, and has the same effect with premises much more easily acceptable to the naturalist. Granted, this is not a fatal objection. It cuts nowhere near the heart of the theistic position nor even of its critique of naturalism.

My point about excising references to evolution in favor of simple materialism is a similar criticism. This one seems more consequential in helping us to see how the argument depends on a reduction that is quite radical and controversial (last I looked) in the philosophy of mind and the philosophy of science. So I think Plantinga's argument is only as strong as is one particular side in a several-sided and long-standing controversy. Ours is hence an argument for avoiding all of that problematic controversy in favor of the simpler, more defensible argument just in terms of PM.

PLANTINGEAN MEDITATIONS

1. Here in brief is the Plantinga-inspired argument we have been considering:

Naturalism eschews or rejects appeal to the supernatural, and traces our origins back to blind and uncaring forces. Relative to forces that are in that sense brute, however, the probability that our cognitive faculties are reliable must be too low, which defeats any trust we may have in their reliability. Absent such trust, finally, we are deprived also of epistemic justification for beliefs deriving from those faculties. But among these beliefs is the very belief in naturalism, which therefore defeats itself.

Naturalist reply: "Surely we naturalists know more about our origins than that! We know we come from evolutionary processes that ensure our fitness to do well in our environmental niche." In response, Plantinga invokes the epistemology of defeat. Consider the following proposition:

R   that one's faculties are reliable.

Any belief that one is at the epistemic mercy of a demon bent on mischief would defeat one's trust that R is true, and thereby defeat in turn the ostensible deliverances of these faculties. Similarly, once persuaded that brute forces have raised us from primordial muck, this belief also defeats one's trust in one's faculties, and in turn defeats their ostensible deliverances. Or so argues the anti-naturalist. How plausible is this?

2. Suppose a walk down by the riverside turns up a smooth, round stone. After noting that it would reliably roll down inclines, one muses: "That stone must have derived from brute forces, relative to which there is only a low probability that it be either round or a reliable roller." Have we now a defeater of the belief (call it S) that the stone is both round and a reliable roller?

We can plainly see and feel the stone's smooth roundness, and we know through much experience that such an object would roll reliably. The improbability of its having been rounded so smoothly, given its origin in brute forces, does not preclude our perceiving it to be smoothly round, and even a reliable roller, nor is our justification for so believing defeated by our belief that here the improbable has occurred. I trust everyone will readily agree with that much, and even find it obvious.

If that is an obviously correct response in the case of the round stone, why are we deprived of it when it comes to our own nature as reliable perceivers with eyes and ears through which we have reliable access to the colors, shapes, and sounds around us? Start first with someone else, a friend whom we believe to be a reliable perceiver of the colors and shapes of things seen in good light, etc. Can't we forestall or defeat the alleged defeater here again, as with the stone? Can't we know through experience that our friend is as described? Surely we can know this despite how improbable it must have been that brute forces would produce someone so endowed.

However, perhaps it is only in one's own case that we run into real trouble, and not if the belief concerns only some introspectible feature of one's mind or some perceptible feature of one's body. I can know that I now ache or that I have hands, no matter how improbable it may be that brute forces should produce someone aching or with hands, and despite my believing us to derive from such forces.

Is it then something specific to proposition R that might make one's belief of it susceptible to defeat? And what exactly could that be? What might be the basis for the conclusion or for the assumption that R specifically is thus susceptible? Here is a possibility.

One might suppose that acceptance of a faculty's deliverances is bound to rely implicitly on the reliability of the faculty, and that this reliance takes the form of an assumption playing the role of an implicit prior premise. Call this *the implicit premise thesis*. As soon as this implicit belief is put in question, then, one can hardly find support for it by appeal to the ostensible deliverances of that very faculty. Such appeal would after all require a prior trust in the reliability of the faculty, and we would be in a vicious circle.

Is it such reasoning that distinguishes belief that one is reliably a perceiver from belief that a smooth stone is reliably a roller, and even from belief in the cognitive reliability of someone else? In these other cases, one can rationally base one's belief on one's perceptions, memories, and reasonings, thus overcoming any doubts based on the fact that the entity derives from brute forces. By contrast it would be viciously circular to argue in parallel fashion from the deliverances of one's own perception, memory, and reason to the reliability of these faculties seated in oneself.

How defensible is *the implicit premise thesis*? Compare the following three theses:

R   That one's faculties are reliable.
S   That the stone by the riverside is rounded and reliably a roller.
F   That one's friend is a reliable perceiver of colors and shapes.

We are trying to understand what could possibly be epistemically distinctive of R, what might distinguish it relevantly within our present dialectic. If not on the basis of the implicit premise thesis, how might we support the required distinction between R, on the one hand, and the likes of S and F, on the other? How to support the claim that R is subject to defeat by brute origins, whereas S and F are exempt from such defeat? What accounts for this distinction if not *the implicit premise thesis*?

Something like the implicit premise thesis may be found in Thomas Reid, where it raises subtle and difficult issues. While unable to take up these issues in detail here, I elsewhere conclude that no vicious circularity need be involved.[7] As a consequence, I can see no way to support the required distinction between R, on the one hand, and S and F, on the

---

[7] I take the issues up in a discussion of Reid's epistemology in Ernest Sosa, *Reflective Knowledge: Apt Belief and Reflective Knowledge, Volume II* (Oxford: Oxford University Press, 2009). Although I lack the space for a detailed discussion in our main text, here is a sample of my relevant reasoning:

How can [any of Reid's First Principles] . . . be justified foundationally or immediately, as a "self-evident" universal or probabilistic truth? How can we sensibly allow ourselves justification for believing such a truth from the armchair, absent proper empirical inquiry into our actual contingent surroundings?

On behalf of Reid, I answer:

What would make us justified is that we proceed in an epistemically appropriate and desirable way, given the aims of systematic acquisition and retention of truth (especially truth that gives understanding), and that we do so not haphazardly but by our nature and in keeping with the nature of things, which makes us non-accidentally sensitive precisely to the "validity" of the inferential [reason-basing] patterns constitutive of those faculties and their bundled implicit commitments. Further pleasing explanatory coherence would derive from an explanation of how we are thus attuned by nature with how things stand around us. And this last could be detailed more specifically in various ways, the two main competing options involving respectively (a) Divine Providence, and (b) natural evolution; either one would serve present epistemological purposes. Reid clearly took the first (as did Descartes). But, however the story is detailed at that level, the fact remains: humans are a certain way by nature, a way that, given our normal environment, furthers our epistemic aims of attaining truth and understanding, and does so with non-accidental sensitivity to the truth, including the subjunctive truth constitutive of the validity of our inferential [reason-basing] patterns. . . The main point is now straightforward: namely, that the mechanisms in question might include, and according to Reid do include, taking our sense experience at face value, and gaining access to the states of mind of our neighbors through beliefs instinctively prompted by the external, behavioral signs of such states. Et cetera.

Thus may we attain justification for the use of our basic faculties, for our "belief" in or implicit commitment to the various "first principles" adherence to which in practice is constitutive of such faculties. And this justification would remain even for victims of a Cartesian evil demon. Reasoning from such implicit commitments may eventually yield conscious awareness of your faculties and subfaculties, of their nature and how they fit you for cognitive success in your relevant normal environment. To a greater or lesser extent this would constitute a worldview that underwrites, with coherent understanding, your use of those faculties. Moreover, such conscious awareness of your intellectual makeup (your nature and second nature) might also aid its gradual improvement, as when you no longer take the sun to be (strictly) rising, no longer take the oar to be bent, no longer take the Müller-Lyer lines to be incongruent, and so on. You might no longer accept deliverances which earlier, however briefly or long, had been admitted without question.

Is that vicious? No more so here than it was for Descartes. Who could object to the use of our faculties resulting in such a worldview with its attendant coherence and yield of understanding? How plausible, surely, that the individual component beliefs should also gain epistemically by now being part of a more comprehensively coherent and explanatory establishment. (pp. 79–80)

other. So, I do not believe that the foregoing line of argument can be successful. Only the implicit premise thesis offers hope of an epistemically important distinction, but the implicit premise thesis falls short. It does so either because we make no such assumption whenever we use our faculties, not even implicitly, or because even if we do make it in some sense, at least implicitly, doing so need not involve any *vicious* circularity.

3. That brings us to more promising reasoning in terms of *reflective* knowledge: how might the requirements for such knowledge offer better support for the case against naturalism?

Reflective knowledge requires underwriting the knower's belief through her own epistemic perspective. And now it can be argued that the naturalist, unlike the theist, is denied such a perspective, and is hence at an epistemic disadvantage. Is the naturalist ill-positioned to attain reflective knowledge? Is he in a self-defeating position?

I don't believe so. And how implausible this view of the naturalist's position is may be seen as follows.

As a supernaturalist one might use certain faculties (as does Descartes his faculties of *a priori* reflection) in devising an epistemically comforting view of one's universe, according to which one is so constituted, and so related to one's world, that one's faculties would be truth-conducive, not misleading. I take that to be Descartes's strategy.

What denies such a strategy to the naturalist? Why can't one as a naturalist develop a view of oneself and one's surroundings that shows one's situation to be epistemically propitious? Of course, one would need to be able to self-attribute ways of acquiring and retaining beliefs that would tend to yield beliefs that are true. As a naturalist, what precludes one's doing so by means of science, if the supernaturalist can do so by means of theology?

Here now is a key question about the Plantingean strategy under review: is there any proposition N integral to naturalism, whose inclusion in a view V would spoil V's prospects for constituting reflective knowledge? In other words, would any view V that contained N be precluded thereby from being coherently enriched so as to enable holders of the enriched V to become thereby reflective knowers?

I myself can see no bright prospect for showing that the following would be such a proposition N: *that we humans derive through brute forces from primordial muck*. That proposition is tenable compatibly with the following complex view: that we are good cognizers of our surroundings through our use of vision, hearing, etc.; that these faculties put us reliably enough in touch with the truth about empirical and contingent goings-on around us; and that we are thereby enabled to know about these goings-on. Issues of circularity do arise as to how we can rationally and knowledgeably adopt such a view about our own epistemic powers. But these problems of circularity are not exclusive to naturalism, as Descartes was soon to find out from his critics.

4. Consider any subject who faces the question whether her faculties are reliable, and realizes that if she does have reliable faculties, this is a contingent matter, and that she cannot just assume that she does and let it go at that. Given the contingency of the reliability of her faculties, what assures her that though they *might* have been unreliable, in fact they are reliable? Wouldn't the inability to give a rational, non-arbitrary answer to this question itself constitute a problem?

Compare your situation as a naturalist facing the fact that your faculties derive through brute forces from primordial muck. If you agree that you and your faculties are so derived, does this not defeat your belief in your cognitive reliability? Suppose you try through your faculties to attain a picture of yourself and the world around you offering assurance that your faculties are reliable despite their brute derivation. Is this to proceed circularly? Well, it is to proceed in a kind of circle. Will it be said that the circle is vicious? Yes, that has often been said, and no doubt will be repeated. But *such* a circle cannot possibly be avoided once we face so fundamental a question. How then can it really be "vicious"? That would presumably mean that to proceed accordingly is wrong, or faulty, or flawed. But once we face the question and try to answer it, the circle is unavoidable. Is it then wrong, or flawed, or faulty to so much as face the question, given the inevitable upshot of so doing?

5. How in sum should we respond to Plantinga's anti-naturalist meditations? If our faculties are brutely derived, their reliability does indeed seem low, relative to that fact. Even so, this defeats our belief in the reliability of our faculties only if we have no other basis for believing them to be reliable. We do have another basis, however, beyond anything we may believe about the etiology of our faculties. Their *own* deliverances, after all, provide such a basis. And what more specifically is this basis? Is it the mere fact that our faculties are self-supportive and yield belief in their own reliability? No, that cannot suffice on its own. Superstitious "faculties" might easily share *that* property with little epistemic effect. At a minimum our faculties must satisfy an additional condition. It is not only that they must be self-supportive – i.e., productive of a picture of the believer and his world according to which those very faculties are reliable. In addition, they must be *in fact* reliable.

Suppose, as argued earlier, that a theist who offers the ignorance defense against evil must then declare $Pr(R/Th)$ to be either low (perhaps around 0.5) or else inscrutable, which provides a defeater of our belief in R. Such a theist is then under pressure to avoid the coal pit of skepticism in some way other than simply through his theism. And he may thereby become more receptive to the notion that there are important *disanalogies*, where earlier he had seen only clear analogies. For the sort of disanalogy that I have in mind, consider the contrast between gauges and perceptual organs such as eyes and ears. We must (eventually, through infancy, adolescence, and later learning) *acquire through some sort of learning* our right to trust the various gauges we end up trusting. But it is hopeless to suppose that we must equally acquire a right to trust *our senses* through learning. It seems rather that there is some minimal set of basic faculties (involving perceptual organs and senses, memory, testimony, reasoning) such that we cannot acquire our right to trust the deliverances of any of them without (at least implicitly) trusting the others (at least concurrently, logically and/or temporally). In that minimal set, gauges would seem not to figure the way organs do. Their right to be trusted must be earned through proper ratiocinative learning.

Why so? What gives a faculty or an organ a place in that minimal set? Here is a start on an answer to that important question: our focus here is on *human knowledge and its limits*, and the minimal set is the set on which normal humans (already in the Stone Age) converge. Our communities have and need eyes, ears, testimony, memory, reasoning. Once we advance technologically, some of us will eventually exploit gauges, instruments more generally, etc. But our trust in these is acquired (in the history of the human race, and in the life of individual members) only through the use of the epistemic items in the restricted set, none of which has ever been absent entirely from our communities, and none of which (arguably) *could* have been so absent without epistemic disaster, given the contingencies of how we can collectively access the facts we need in order to flourish and even to survive.[8]

---

[8] Many thanks to Blake Roeber for helpful discussion, which raised my awareness of how Alvin Plantinga might be thinking at various junctures.

7

Research on Religion and Health

Time to Be Born Again?

Linda K. George

Research on the topic of religion and health has experienced incredible growth over the past thirty years or so. In the mid- and late 1980s, Jeff Levin published several foundational review articles summarizing what was known about the links between religion and health. Those articles were directly responsible for the resurrection of scientific interest in the links between religion and health. His contributions spurred interest in multiple disciplines, including public health, the medical sciences, and the social and behavioral sciences. As a simple exercise, I used the ISI Web of Science to search for articles using the keywords "religion and health" before and after 1986. This procedure yielded a total of 62 articles before 1986 and 5,032 articles from 1987 to the present. This is clearly not an accurate count because a substantial amount of earlier research that reported associations between religious participation and health did not focus on those relationships. Nonetheless, it seems obvious that the past few decades have yielded incredible growth in research on religion and health.

I have not been a core contributor to the field of religion and health, although I have had the privilege of collaborating with many of the key figures in the field. My former students and mentees, who include Chris Ellison, Jeff Levin, Harold Koenig, Keith Meador, and Mark Musick, are stellar scholars in the field. My major role, as both a collaborator in some studies and a reviewer of others, has been to integrate and critique findings in the field and to ask my collaborators and the field more generally questions along the lines of: "What about this?" "Have you thought about that?" And that is the approach taken here, addressing two primary themes. First, I will express the opinion that, over the last decade or more, and despite the steady volume of research on religion and health, the field has become largely stagnant – an opinion with which others may disagree. Second, I will describe aspects of religion and health that I believe merit increased attention and may have the potential to re-energize the field.

STATE OF THE SCIENCE

In 2000, the *Journal of Social and Clinical Psychology* devoted an issue to the topic of "Classical Sources of Human Strength." David Larson, Harold Koenig, Mike McCullough, and I had a paper in that issue titled, "Spirituality and Health: What We Know, What We Need to Know."[1] As the title implies, this article reviewed the state of the science with regard to the relationships between religion/spirituality and health, including the hypothesized mechanisms that might explain those relationships, and outlined some high priority issues for future research.

Quoting directly from the paper, we concluded that "although the effect sizes are moderate, there typically are links between religious practices and reduced onset of physical and mental illnesses, reduced mortality, and the likelihood of recovery from or adjustment to physical and mental illness."[2] We examined three hypothesized mechanisms that might account for the typically positive relationships between religion and health and that had received substantial investigation at the time of the review. The first hypothesis is that religious participation leads to larger or higher quality social support systems that, in turn, foster good health. The second hypothesis is that religious participation leads to better health behaviors that, in turn, promote health. The third hypothesis is that certain psychological resources such as self-esteem and sense of control mediate the relationships between religion and health. We concluded that both individually and as a set these proposed mechanisms explained relatively little of the religion–health relationship.

I submit to you that if we were to review the research on religion and health today, more than a decade and a half later, our conclusions would be largely the same. Certainly, there would be a larger base of research to review. And certainly, several new or expanded topics would be included.

---

[1] Linda George et al., "Spirituality and Health: What We Know, What We Need to Know," *Journal of Social and Clinical Psychology* 19 (2000): 102–116.
[2] Ibid., 102.

Among them is a small body of research that compares the effects of church-based and secular social support[3] and civic engagement;[4] another small body of research reporting that religious doubts and struggles are associated with poorer health;[5] and a growing body of research that links religious involvement with biological markers of risk for illness, including measures of immune and endocrine function.[6] Nonetheless, I believe that our conclusions would be essentially the same. Yes, there is evidence that multiple dimensions of religious or spiritual experience are related to favorable health outcomes. But we still know little about the whys and hows that account for those relationships.

What will it take to move the field from the rather stagnant position in which I believe it now rests? Rather than investing in several dozen more studies that examine social support and health behaviors as mediators of the links between religion and health, I contend that we need to develop and pursue both new and understudied aspects of those links. I will turn now to some of the directions that I think might yield important and interesting results. I will begin with the more obvious "spin-offs" of existing research and then move to increasingly novel issues about which little is known.

[3] Neal Krause, "Exploring the Stress-Buffering Effects of Church-Based and Secular Social Support on Self-Rated Health in Late Life," *Journal of Gerontology: Social Sciences* 61 (2006): S35–S43.

[4] G. A. Acevedo, C. G. Ellison, and X. Xu, "Is It Really Religion? Comparing the Main and Stress-Buffering Effects of Religious and Secular Civic Engagement on Psychological Distress," *Society and Mental Health* 4 (2014): 111–128.

[5] Kelly M. McConnell et al., "Examining the Links Between Spiritual Struggles and Symptoms of Psychopathology in a National Sample," *Journal of Clinical Psychology* 62 (2002): 1459–1484; Kenneth I. Pargament et al., "Religious Struggle as a Predictor of Mortality Among Medically Ill Elderly Patients," *Archives of Internal Medicine* 161 (2001): 1881–1885; H. Abu-Raiya, K. I. Pargament, and N. Krause, "Religion as Problem, Religion as Solution: Religious Buffers of the Links between Religious/Spiritual Struggles and Well-Being/Mental Health," *Quality of Life Research* 25 (2016): 1265–1274.

[6] Harold G. Koenig et al., "Attendance at Religious Services, Interleukin-6, and Other Biological Parameters of Immune Function in Older Adults," *International Journal of Psychiatry in Medicine* 27 (1997): 233–250; Susan K. Lutgendorf et al., "Religious Participation, Interleukin-6, and Mortality in Older Adults, *Health Psychology* 23 (2004): 465–475; T. D. Hill et al., "Religious Attendance and Biological Functioning: A Multiple Specification Approach," *Journal of Aging and Health* 26 (2014): 766–785; C. F. Hybels et al., "Inflammation and Coagulation as Mediators in the Relationships between Religious Attendance and Functional Limitations in Older Adults," *Journal of Aging and Health* 26 (2014): 679–697.

CONCEPTUALIZING RELIGIOUS INVOLVEMENT

The first spin-off concerns how we think about and measure religious involvement. It is a truism in the field that religious involvement is multi-dimensional and that specific dimensions may be differentially important for specific health outcomes. A related question is whether engaging in multiple dimensions of religious participation yields greater benefits than engaging in one or two. A large body of research has examined the effects of multiple dimensions of religious experience using regression analyses in which the dimensions compete with each other and the results estimate the effect of each dimension on health net of each other. The typical finding is that not all dimensions of religion remain significant and the ones that do are viewed as more relevant to the health outcome.[7] I understand the logic of this kind of analysis. Indeed, I coauthored several papers that take this approach. This analytic approach is congruent with the desire to identify just what it is about religious involvement that affects health. From another perspective, however, why would we want to study the extent to which dimensions of religious experience *compete* with each other? Do we really think that there are winners and losers here?

Some researchers create a summary measure of religious involvement, adding up the number of dimensions of religious experience that study participants report.[8] I am not aware of any studies that carefully compared results based on summary scales with those based on measuring separate dimensions of religious experience. My sense, however, is that both methods yield compatible findings, and neither approach explains substantially more variation in health outcomes than the other.

What if, however, participation in multiple dimensions of religion operates multiplicatively rather than additively? Perhaps participating in multiple dimensions of religious experience exponentially affects health. I know of one study by Parker and colleagues that tested interactions among three dimensions of religious involvement.[9] The results indicated that the religious dimensions had both main and interactive effects on

---

[7] Christopher G. Ellison et al., "Religious Involvement, Stress, and Mental Health: Findings from the 1995 Detroit Area Study," *Social Forces* 80 (2001): 215–249; Harold G. Koenig et al., "Religion, Spirituality, and Acute Care Hospitalization and Long-Term Care Use by Older Patients," *Archives of Internal Medicine* 164 (2004): 1579–1585.

[8] Giancarlo Lucchetti et al., "Religiousness Affects Mental Health, Pain, and Quality of Life in Older People in an Outpatient Rehabilitation Setting," *Journal of Rehabilitation Medicine* 43 (2011): 316–322.

[9] M. Parker et al., "Religiosity and Mental Health in Southern, Community-Dwelling Older Adults," *Aging and Mental Health* 7 (2003): 390–397.

depression. Relatively little was said about the interactions, however, beyond the fact that they "complicated" the results. This is an important finding that merits additional effort on other samples with various health outcomes. I also find it a more logical approach to understanding the joint effects of different dimensions of religious involvement than putting them in competition with each other.

CLOSE PERSONAL RELATIONSHIP WITH GOD

A second spin-off concerns what, following the lead of a classic study by Melvin Pollner,[10] I like to call "divine support" or what the literature generally refers to as a "personal relationship with God." As I reviewed my stacks and stacks of articles on religion and health for this chapter, I was impressed by the strong associations between reporting a close personal relationship with God and a variety of health outcomes. This association emerges vividly in several qualitative studies[11] and has been observed in survey-based research as well,[12] including a study by Jeff Levin.[13] Again, I don't think we should view dimensions of religious experience as competing against each other. For those who do, however, I will simply note that in the quantitative studies I've seen, reporting a close personal relationship with God is significantly associated with a variety of health outcomes, with other dimensions of religious involvement (albeit not an exhaustive set of dimensions) statistically controlled. Other studies find that a close personal relationship with God can compensate for loneliness and for insecure attachment styles that make human relationships difficult.[14] Nonetheless, only a small number of studies have

---

[10] Melvin Pollner, "Divine Relations, Social Relations, and Well-Being," *Journal of Health and Social Behavior* 30 (1989): 92–104.

[11] Helen K. Black, "Life as Gift: Spiritual Narratives of Elderly African American Women Living in Poverty," *Journal of Aging Studies* 13 (1999): 441–455; Elizabeth K. Mackenzie et al., "Spiritual Support and Psychological Well-Being: Older Adults' Perceptions of the Religion-Health Connection," *Therapies in Health and Medicine* 6 (2000): 37–45.

[12] Terry L. Gall, "Relationship with God and the Quality of Life of Prostate Cancer Survivors," *Quality of Life Research* 13 (2004): 1357–1368; Jacqueline S. Mattis et al., "Religion and Spirituality in the Meaning-Making and Coping Experiences of African American Women: A Qualitative Analysis," *Psychology of Women Quarterly* 26 (2002): 309–321.

[13] Jeff Levin, "Is Depressed Affect a Function of One's Relationship with God? Findings from a Study of Primary Care Patients," *International Journal of Psychiatry in Medicine* 32 (2002): 379–393.

[14] Lee A. Kirkpatrick, "A Longitudinal Study of Changes in Religious Belief and Behavior as a Function of Individual Differences in Adult Attachment Style," *Journal for the Scientific*

examined divine support or the sense that one has a close, personal relationship with God.

This dimension of religious experience merits additional inquiry and not only because research findings to date have been consistent and strong. It appears that humans can obtain meaningful support from a number of invisible sources. One example is the phenomenon of imaginary friends during childhood. Research evidence is mixed, with some studies finding no significant differences between children with and without imaginary friends, and other studies reporting that having imaginary friends is associated with increased optimism, self-confidence, and creativity.[15] Importantly, no study has observed negative effects from relationships with imaginary friends. Another example is referred to in the literature as talking to the dead or continuing bonds with the dead.[16] It is very common for bereaved individuals to talk to their departed loved ones. Again, research to date, although not plentiful, suggests that maintaining relationships with deceased significant others is meaningful and brings substantial comfort. Support from non-visible sources also dovetails with the well-established empirical fact that *perceiving* one has a high-quality support network is more strongly and consistently related to positive health outcomes than is the actual receipt of assistance from significant others.[17]

There is considerable discussion of transcendence in writings about spirituality. I generally get the impression that transcendence in these writings refers to an overarching cosmic experience in which the material world is replaced by – or encased in – a world that is beyond human limitations of time and place. Undoubtedly some individuals do have such far-reaching transcendental experiences. But it also is likely that there are

Study of Religion 36 (1997): 207–217; Lee A. Kirkpatrick, Daniel J. Shillito, and Susan L. Kellas, "Loneliness, Social Support, and Perceived Relationship with God," *Journal of Social and Personal Relationships* 16 (1999): 513–532.

[15] Tracy Gleason, "Social Provisions of Real and Imaginary Relationships in Early Childhood," *Developmental Psychology* 38 (2002): 979–992; Marjorie Taylor, *Imaginary Companions and the Children Who Create Them* (New York: Oxford University Press, 1999).

[16] Susan L. Datson and Samuel J. Marwit, "Personality Constructs and Perceived Presence of Deceased Loved Ones," *Death Studies* 21 (1997): 131–146; Nigel P. Field, Beryl Gao, and Lisa Paderna, "Continuing Bonds in Bereavement: An Attachment Theory Based Perspective," *Death Studies* 29 (2005): 277–299; Craig M. Klugman, "Dead Men Talking: Evidence of Post Death Contact and Continuing Bonds," *Omega* 53 (2006): 249–262.

[17] Peggy A. Thoits, "Stress, Coping, and Social Support Processes: Where Are We? What Next?" *Journal of Health and Social Behavior Extra Issue* (1995): 53–79.

smaller, more bounded forms of transcendence, and receiving support from invisible sources may be one of them. Thus, I strongly encourage further research on the experience of having a close personal relationship with God and its implications for health.

CONTEXTUAL EFFECTS

A final spin-off is what in my discipline is called *contextual effects*. Contextual effects research focuses on the extent to which, and on the ways in which, social, cultural, and geographic settings affect individual outcomes over and above the effects of individual-level predictors. Consider poverty as an example. We can measure poverty at the individual level, separating study participants into those who do and do not have incomes below the poverty level. But we also can identify poor neighborhoods – that is, areas where a large proportion of residents have incomes below the poverty line. We know that individuals whose incomes are at or below the poverty line are more likely to have poor health than those who have higher incomes. The crux of contextual effects research is to ask whether living in a poor neighborhood increases the likelihood of poor health over and above the effects of personal poverty. By and large, we can say that it does – that the combination of being poor and living in a poor neighborhood is associated with worse health than being poor and living in a neighborhood that is not predominantly poor.[18]

As applied to religion and health, the issue is whether religious contexts promote health over and above individuals' personal religious involvement. Religious contexts can include congregations, neighborhoods, cities or counties, and even societies – any of which might affect health. The research base on religious contextual effects is very small and most of it focuses on adolescents and the extent to which religious context affects rates of delinquency and other problem behaviors.[19] And, indeed, both the presence of religious schools and religiously homogeneous

[18] Iain A. Lang et al., "Neighborhood Deprivation and Incident Mobility Disability in Older Adults," *Age and Aging* 37 (2008): 403–410; Catherine A. Ross and John Mirowski, "Neighborhood Socioeconomic Status and Health: Context or Composition?" *City and Community* 7 (2008): 163–179; R. A. D. Ximenes et al., "Is It Better to Be Rich in a Poor Area or Poor in a Rich Area? A Multilevel Analysis of a Case-Control Study of Social Determinants of Tuberculosis," *International Journal of Epidemiology* 38 (2009): 1285–1294.

[19] Mark D. Regnerus, "Moral Communities and Adolescent Delinquency: Religious Contexts and Community Social Control," *Sociological Quarterly* 44 (2004): 523–554; Jeffrey T. Ulmer, Christopher Bader, and Martha Gault, "Do Moral Communities Play

neighborhoods appear to reduce rates of delinquency. Dena Jaffe and colleagues authored a study that I found especially well done.[20] They found that individuals living in religiously homogeneous neighborhoods had lower mortality rates than those living in religiously heterogeneous neighborhoods after controlling on a wide range of individual and other contextual variables.

The research base is far too small to determine whether religious contexts in general and religious homogeneity in particular affect health in significant ways. But the limited research to date suggests that this topic merits further investigation.

THE WHOLE MAY BE GREATER THAN THE SUM OF ITS PARTS

It is a fair statement, I think, to say that most research on religion and health has focused on disaggregation, including efforts to determine which dimension or dimensions of religious experience are responsible for the generally positive relationships between religion and health. As I stated earlier, I understand the logic of these efforts, which are compatible with the search for mechanisms. It also is possible, however, that these kinds of studies will not, and perhaps cannot, identify the specific pathways between religious or spiritual practices and health. That is, religious experience may be a "package" in which the whole is greater than the sum of its parts.

As an example, consider the fact that attending religious services has stronger associations with many health outcomes than other dimensions of religious experience.[21] Attending religious services is the dimension of religious involvement that is most public and that involves participation in a faith community. Thus, this finding has been music to sociologists' ears and is compatible with the hypothesis that social support is a primary pathway from religion to health. But there is clear evidence that social support per se is not a major pathway by which religion promotes

a Role in Criminal Sentencing: Evidence from Pennsylvania," *Sociological Quarterly* 49 (2008): 737–768.

[20] Dena H. Jaffe et al., "Does Living in a Religiously Affiliated Neighborhood Lower Mortality?" *Annals of Epidemiology* 15 (2005): 804–810.

[21] Ellison et al., "Religious Involvement, Stress, and Mental Health" 215–249, and Shanshan Li et al., "Association of Religious Service Attendance with Mortality Among Women," *JAMA Internal Medicine* 176 (2016): 777–785. For a review, see also Linda K. George et al., "Explaining the Relationships Between Religious Involvement and Health," *Psychological Inquiry* 13 (2002): 190–200.

health.[22] Some research has compared church-based support and so-called secular support, but that research has not shown that this distinction explains a large proportion of variance in health outcomes. The same pattern has been observed in research on religious and secular civic engagement, including volunteering.[23]

Church-based support differs from other sources of support in ways that have not been empirically investigated, however. I suggest that church-based support is distinctive beyond who provides assistance when it is needed. Church-based support is more permanent and more normatively governed than other sources of support. Most individuals have highly committed personal networks of family and friends. But those networks are at risk of being lost in ways that a community of faith is not. Some of us outlive or otherwise outlast our personal support networks. Communities of faith generally continue. Some of our most intimate relationships may be with congregation members, but even if they die or move away, the congregation itself continues. Helping norms also are relevant. Social support received from family and friends rests on norms about helping others that probably vary widely across relationships (e.g., friends versus spouses). Most congregations, at least those in Protestant churches, have strong norms emphasizing mutual support and helping church members in need. Committees are formed to visit the sick, tend to the bereaved, and perform other forms of assistance. "Am I my brother's keeper?" is a rhetorical question in most congregations, but is answered in multiple ways outside that context.

This is a simple example, but I trust that it illustrates the point that, after all, congregations are communities and religion is a social institution. Moreover, I believe that religion is a unique social institution that provides its participants with a variety of goods and services – to borrow economic terminology – that other institutions do not. Other major social institutions – including the economy, politics, education, and so forth – have critically important functions as well. They do not, however, fulfill the same functions that religion does. Spurred by Robert Putnam's *Bowling Alone*, both scholars and the public now realize that American communities do

[22] George et al., "Explaining the Relationships Between Religious Involvement and Health," 190–200.
[23] Krause, "Exploring Stress-Buffering Effects," S35–S43; Acevedo, Ellison, and Xu, "Is it Really Religion?" *Society and Mental Health* 4 (2014): 111–128.

not offer the integration and collective effort that they once did (or at least that people thought that they did).[24] Faith communities are arguably the closest thing to effective communities that exist in American society. Thus, I'm not convinced that we need to dissect religion to demonstrate its importance for health. A better way to understand the effects of religion may be to compare it to other institutions.

MEANING AND WORLDVIEWS

Like most disciplines, my own discipline, sociology, covers a lot of territory. One major branch of sociology is symbolic interactionism or SI. A core tenet of SI is that social life is based on meanings that are shared among individuals and within groups and cultures. SI scholars posit that interaction is an ongoing, never-ending search for meaning. SI theorists also distinguish between meaning-making and meaning-taking. Meaning-taking occurs when individuals use existing elements of their cultures – both material artifacts and intangible elements such as values and beliefs – to make sense of the world and how it operates. A large proportion of meaning-taking occurs through routine socialization in which individuals are taught the primary shared meanings of their society or subgroup.[25] Although we learn the most about shared social meanings during childhood, meaning-taking occurs throughout the life course as we are exposed to kinds of knowledge that are new-for-us but preexisting for our society or sub-group. Meaning-making occurs when we encounter novel situations or try to understand things about which the culture seems to offer little preexisting knowledge. In these situations, individuals or groups will create new meanings.[26]

[24] Robert D. Putnam, *Bowling Alone: The Collapse and Revival of American Community* (New York: Simon and Shuster, 2001).
[25] Bryce L. Jorgensen and Jyoti Savla, "Financial Literacy of Young Adults: The Importance of Parental Socialization," *Family Relations* 59 (2010): 465–478; Gill R. Musolf, "Interactionism and the Child: Cahill, Corsaro, and Denzin on Childhood Socialization," *Symbolic Interactionism* 19 (1996): 303–321.
[26] Mattis et al., "Religion and Spirituality in the Meaning-Making" 309–321; Shirley A. Murphy and L. Clark Johnson, "Finding Meaning in a Child's Violent Death: A Five-Year Prospective Analysis of Parents' Personal Narratives and Empirical Data," *Death Studies* 27 (2003): 381–404; Teria Shantall, "The Experience of Meaning in Suffering Among Holocaust Survivors," *Journal of Humanistic Psychology* 39 (1999): 96–124.

An assumption of sociology in general, and SI in particular, is that lack of meaning is cognitively, emotionally, and even physically uncomfortable. It is not an accident that the inability to find meaning in life is a symptom of clinical depression. Jim Morrison, lead singer for the Doors, a popular rock group in the late 60s and early 70s, was known in part for his proclamation that "Life's a bitch and then you die." Clearly, he had a crisis of meaning.

Humans find some issues more difficult to imbue with meaning than others. Questions such as why people die, why some people must suffer incredible physical pain or mental anguish, and even, for some, why we should get up in the morning can pose major challenges to meaning. Individuals who experience crises in meaning are generally not productive members of society. In addition, they suffer intensely. One of the functions of our social institutions is to provide meaning where it would otherwise be elusive or problematic.

Providing meaning about life's tragedies and other unanswerable questions is a key function of religion. And although secularization has eroded religious authority to some extent, I believe that no other social institution comes close to religion in providing meanings about important issues that otherwise seem meaningless.

Aaron Antonovsky, a medical sociologist, devoted his life to studying psychosocial factors that promote health and well-being rather than those that harm health.[27] Much of his research was performed in Israel and involved Holocaust survivors who had relocated there after World War II. He originated the concept of "sense of coherence," which he believed to be a critically important resource for health. In his formulation, the sense of coherence has three components.

The first is *comprehensibility*, which he defines as a belief that things happen in an orderly and predictable way and a sense that you can understand the events in your life. The second component is *manageability*, which is a belief that you have the skills, the support, and/or the resources necessary to take care of things – i.e., that things are largely in your control. The third component is *meaningfulness*, or the belief that life really is worth living and that there are good reasons to care about what happens to you and to others.

---

[27] Aaron Antonovsky, *Health, Stress, and Coping* (San Francisco: Jossey-Bass, 1979); Aaron Antonovsky, *Unraveling the Mystery of Health: How People Manage Stress and Stay Well* (San Francisco: Jossey-Bass, 1987).

According to Antonovsky, meaningfulness is the most important component.[28] If a person believes that there is no reason to persist, to confront challenges, and to survive – if they have no sense of meaning – they will have no motivation to comprehend and manage events. Antonovsky also developed a scale to measure sense of coherence, including subscales of the three components.

A rather large body of research, most of it performed in Europe rather than the US, reports that a sense of coherence is significantly related to positive health outcomes.[29] Not all research finds such relationships, however.[30]

Despite the characteristics of his research participants, Antonovsky made only passing references to the role that religion might play in fostering a sense of coherence. Other investigators report positive correlations between religious involvement and sense of coherence, but these relationships have not been explored in depth. I highly recommend additional research on the linkages among religion, sense of coherence, and health. I'd also like to see the field delve even further into constellations of beliefs that may be important for health.

As a segue to discussing constellations of belief, I'd like to mention a recent article by Jeff Levin titled, "How Faith Heals: A Theoretical Model."[31] I view this as one of the best papers on the links between religion and health published in the last decade. The paper is outstanding in that it integrates a very large body of research in an innovative and useful way. I was especially impressed with his integration of research on several psychological constructs that are related to both health and religious involvement. Those constructs include hope, learned optimism, positive illusions, and "opening up," or trust. These psychological

---

[28] Antonovsky, *Health, Stress, and Coping.*

[29] M. Cederblad et al., "Coping with Life Span Crises in a Group at Risk of Mental and Behavioral Disorders: From the Lundby Study," *Acta Psychiatrica Scandinavia* 91 (1995): 322–330; Kamel Gana, "Is Sense of Coherence a Mediator Between Adversity and Psychological Well-Being in Adults?" *Stress and Health* 17 (2001): 77–83; Mika Kivimäki et al., "Sense of Coherence and Health: Evidence from Two Cross-Lagged Longitudinal Samples," *Social Science and Medicine* 50 (2000): 583–597; Sakari Suominen, "Sense of Coherence as a Predictor of Subjective State of Health: Results of 4 Years of Follow-up of Adults," *Journal of Psychosomatic Research* 50 (2001): 77–86.

[30] For a review, see Monica Eriksson and Bengt Lindstrom, "Antonovsky's Sense of Coherence Scale and the Relation with Health: A Systematic Review," *Journal of Epidemiology and Community Health* 60 (2006): 376–381.

[31] Jeff Levin, "How Faith Heals: A Theoretical Model," *Explore* 5 (2009): 77–96.

constructs might well form the nucleus of a system of beliefs in which, again, the whole is greater than the sum of its parts.

I take issue to some degree, however, with part of Levin's magnificent paper. After reviewing the psychological constructs, Levin tackles the question of why and how they might explain the links between religion and health. He states, "Two related topics come into play here. The first of these is the familiar if mysterious idea of placebos. The second is the quickly emerging scientific field of psychoneuroimmunology or PNI."[32] Later in that paragraph, Levin says, "...if one does not wish to pursue a more earnest scientific investigation of putative faith–health or religion–health linkages, then the simplest course is to attribute the whole phenomenon to the placebo effect or to PNI, without further detail or explanation. Such an approach does not do this subject justice."[33] In the remainder of the paper, Levin develops a typology of mechanisms, the study of which might do this subject justice and pinpoint the mechanisms that link religion to health.

Thus, Levin argues that an important challenge for religion and health research is to go "down" to increasingly specific aspects of life that might be the pathways from religion to health. I have no problem with that as one area of scientific inquiry on religion and health. But I am more enthusiastic about us going "up" a few levels of abstraction. In particular, I recommend examining structures of belief or, more accurately, meta-theories about the nature of the world to understand the links between religion and health.

A term used in both scientific research and philosophical writings to refer to these systems of belief or meta-theories is worldviews. Daniel Rowley and colleagues describe worldviews or belief systems especially well:

Belief systems are not beliefs. Rather belief systems are more basic in the psychological thinking process. They are the patterns of thinking that form the basis for attitude formation, knowledge, interpretations, beliefs, and personality. These relatively unconscious methods of interpretation allow people to attribute meaning to phenomena ... and they help people form an understanding of the world around them.[34]

Although there is as yet no firm empirical evidence supporting it, I contend that religious participation tends to promote worldviews or

---

[32] Ibid., 87.   [33] Ibid., 87–88.
[34] Daniel J. Rowley, Joseph G. Rosse, and O. J. Harvey, "The Effects of Belief Systems on the Job-Related Satisfaction of Managers and Subordinates," *Journal of Applied Social Psychology* 22 (1992): 212–231.

belief structures that are conducive to health – that are, in fact, more conducive to health than many competing worldviews.

Sense of coherence may be a worldview or part of a larger belief structure that fosters health. Any viable worldview must encompass or apply to the wide range of phenomena that individuals encounter and to which they need to respond. The three components of sense of coherence – comprehensibility, manageability, and meaning – seem to meet that need. There may be additional elements that round out sense of coherence as a worldview, but Antonovsky may have identified a core belief system that promotes health.

Fascinating research conducted by Jonathan Haidt and his colleagues provides another example of what can be learned by studying belief systems. Haidt and his colleagues are interested in the links between politics and morality.[35] They conducted an in-depth study of the speeches and literature produced by hundreds of politicians during the 2004 and 2008 presidential elections. They extracted from these sources statements that had clear moral or ethical content and studied how they differed across both socioeconomic classes and political philosophies. They concluded that both liberals and conservatives are morally driven but that they inhabit different moral universes.[36]

After immersing themselves in thousands of pages of political rhetoric, Haidt et al. identified five moral principles into which all the political rhetoric seemed to fit. They are:

1. Harm/care: It is wrong to hurt people. It is good to relieve suffering.
2. Fairness/reciprocity: Justice and fairness are good. People have rights that need to be upheld by individuals and social institutions.
3. In-group loyalty: Allegiance, loyalty, and patriotism are good.
4. Authority/respect: Social order is necessary to human life and must be honored.
5. Purity/sanctity: Certain aspects of life are sacred and should be kept pure.

---

[35] Jesse Graham et al., "Mapping the Moral Domain," *Journal of Personality and Social Psychology* 101 (2011): 366–385; Jesse Graham and Jonathan Haidt, "When Morality Opposes Justice: Conservatives Have Moral Intuitions That Liberals May Not Recognize," *Social Justice Research* 20 (2007): 98–116.

[36] Jesse Graham, Jonathan Haidt, and Brian A. Nosek, "Liberals and Conservatives Rely on Different Sets of Moral Foundations," *Journal of Personality and Social Psychology* 96 (2009): 1029–1046.

Haidt et al. found that people from across the political spectrum endorsed all five categories of moral or ethical principles, but weighted the importance of the categories differently. Indeed, a moral profile can be constructed for any individual based on the weights that he or she assigns to the five moral principles. These profiles can be aggregated and compared across political and other groups.[37]

Not surprisingly, Haidt and colleagues found that liberals and conservatives differed greatly on the weight that they attributed to these moral principles. Quintessential liberals highly weight Harm/care and Fairness/reciprocity. They give almost no weight to Purity/Sanctity. They are not morally offended if individuals burn American flags, express disdain for the military, or advocate overthrowing the government. Conservatives, in contrast, weigh the last three moral principles much more heavily than the first two. They value social order and its authorities, even at the expense of individual rights. They certainly do not advocate wholesale trampling of individual rights, but they clearly prefer social order even if some societal members suffer as a result. The bumper sticker that reads "Dissent is the highest form of patriotism" is sacrilege to right-wing politicians. In a more recent study, Haidt and colleagues found that liberals, as well as conservatives, view some issues, especially protecting the environment, as sacred. And for both liberals and conservatives, defending sacred values is important in the formation of cohesive moral communities.[38]

For Haidt, who has a fascinating blog and a book on this topic,[39] the major problem in political debates is that neither liberals nor conservatives acknowledge that both sides are operating on moral or ethical grounds. Liberals typically view conservatives as out of touch with modern life at best and ignorant at worst. Conservatives view liberals as ungrounded, reckless, and willing to dismantle order for chaos.

Dan McAdams, a psychologist at Northwestern University, and colleagues performed in-depth interviews with members of different religious denominations. They asked questions about their moral principles, including the trade-offs they would make if those principles were in conflict. They used Haidt's typology of moral principles to organize

---

[37] Graham et al., "Mapping the Moral Domain," 366–385.

[38] J. A. Frimer, C. Tell, and J. Haidt, "Liberals Condemn Sacrilege Too: The Harmless Desecration of Cerro Torre," *Social Psychological and Personality Science* 6 (2015): 878–886.

[39] Jonathan Haidt, *The Righteous Mind: Why Good People Are Divided by Politics and Religion* (New York: Pantheon, 2012).

their responses and found strong and predictable differences in the moral profiles for individuals from different religious denominations.[40]

Although they don't use the term, it seems to me that Haidt and colleagues revealed worldviews – distinctive constellations of moral beliefs that differ across individuals and groups.[41] We know that these worldviews are related to political philosophy. These worldviews may or may not be related to health, but there is emerging evidence that they are related to religious affiliation.

I strongly encourage research that links worldviews or systems of belief both to religious involvement and to health. We already know that specific religious beliefs such as whether there is a heaven and a hell do not explain the effects of religion on health. But my guess is that beliefs that are sufficiently integrated to provide a sense of coherence, as well as other beliefs such as the degree to which one sees the world as benevolent, are foundational in the religion–health relationship.[42]

The final issue I will address is even more abstract than worldviews. There is no definitive phrase for the phenomenon I will describe, so I will use the term "cultural ethos," which is one of many relevant terms in the literature. Cultural ethos is by its nature diffuse and abstract, but at heart it refers to the underlying paradigm by which people understand the world around them.[43] Scholars from a wide range of academic disciplines have participated in the challenge to identify the core paradigms of various points in history.

In general, scholars discuss the cultural ethos characteristic of three large periods of time: the premodern world, the modern world, and the

---

[40] Kathrin J. Hanek, Bradley D. Olson, and Dan P. McAdams, "Political Orientation and the Psychology of Christian Prayer: How Conservatives and Liberals Pray," *International Journal for the Psychology of Religion* 21 (2011): 30–42.

[41] Duncan R. Babbage and Kevin R. Ronan, "Philosophical Worldview and Personality Factors in Traditional and Social Scientists: Studying the World in Our Own Image," *Personality and Individual Differences* 28 (2000): 405–420; Mark S. Chapell and Masami Takahashi, "Differences in Worldviews of Japanese and Americans in Young, Middle-Aged, and Older Cohorts," *Psychological Reports* 83 (1998): 659–665.

[42] Abbott L. Ferriss, "Religion and the Quality of Life," *Journal of Happiness Studies* 3 (2002): 199–215; Michael Poulin and Roxane Cohen Silver, "World Benevolence Beliefs and Well-Being Across the Life Span," *Psychology and Aging* 23 (2008): 13–23.

[43] Shinobu Kitayama and Dov Cohen, *Handbook of Cultural Psychology* (New York: Guilford Press, 2010); M. M. Thomas, "Modernisation of Traditional Societies and the Struggle for New Cultural Ethos," *The Ecumenical Review* 18 (1966): 426–439.

postmodern world.[44] There are no hard and fast definitions of these eras, although a majority of authors would not quarrel with defining the premodern world as the fourteenth to eighteenth centuries, the modern world as the nineteenth and most of the twentieth centuries, and the postmodern world as the late twentieth and the twenty-first century. Scholars also largely agree on the cultural ethos associated with each period.[45] The overarching cultural ethos of the premodern world was provided by religion. The counterpart in the modern world was science and technology. For the postmodern world, scholars argue that there is no unified cultural paradigm because humankind has come to understand that there are no universals – that knowledge is constructed, not discovered, and that there is no reality that is not constructed and contextually situated.

Postmodernist thinkers believe that science will cease to be the defining or dominant source of knowledge in the world. Science will certainly exist, but it will sit amid many other systems for obtaining knowledge. Indeed, many postmodernist scholars believe that science has already lost much of its respect, and there is some evidence for this. For example, a 1995 survey of high school students in the US, Great Britain, and Australia included a series of statements about science. Students were asked to rate the extent to which they agreed or disagreed with each. Sixty-three percent of the students agreed that science is a tool used to concentrate wealth, power, and privilege among the elite rather than to help humankind more broadly. Seventy-six percent endorsed a statement that government primarily uses science to monitor and control people rather than to strengthen and empower people.[46] Similarly, a 2003 Gallup poll asked a random sample of American adults which of two priorities is more important – encouraging belief in God or encouraging scientific discovery and progress. Seventy-eight percent of the sample chose encouraging belief in God. This is twenty-three percent higher than when Americans were asked the same question in 1973.[47]

---

[44] Steve Bruce, "The Pervasive Worldview: Religion in Pre-Modern Britain," *British Journal of Sociology* 48 (1997): 667–680; Yves Lambert, "Religion in Modernity as a New Axial Age: Secularization of New Religious Forms?" *Sociology of Religion* 60 (1999): 303–333.

[45] Bruce, "The Pervasive Worldview" 667–680; Lambert, "Religion in Modernity" 303–333.

[46] Reported in Richard Eckersley, *Well and Good* (Melbourne: Text Publishing, 2005), 216.

[47] Ibid., 218.

Perhaps we should not be surprised if science loses its luster. The great German historian and philosopher Oswald Spengler foresaw the loss of faith in science in his influential study, *The Decline of the West*, first published in two volumes in 1918 and 1922.[48] Spengler predicted that by the end of the twentieth century, science would lose its role as the primary source of cultural knowledge and a resurgence of irrationality would become the dominant cultural paradigm. It took me about fifty pages of this book to realize that, for Spengler, irrationality was a synonym for religion.

One of my favorite authors on this topic is Richard Eckersley, a professor at Australian National University.[49] He is troubled by the assumptions of postmodernists and sees both religion and science as important social institutions. But he also thinks that each of them must serve humankind better than they do now. Here is what he says about science:

Scientific knowledge does transcend its cultural context; science does "advance" in a way that is unique. But scientific knowledge is never the whole truth or an absolute, immutable truth ... Science must be changed. While remaining rigorous, science must become intellectually less arrogant and culturally better integrated. Science must become more tolerant of other forms of reality, other ways of seeing the world.[50]

Eckersley believes that transformations of religion are needed as well. He is not very specific about what form these transformations should take, but does say: "The new religions would transcend, rather than confront the powerful individualising [sic] and fragmenting forces of post-modernity,"[51] and adds,

At the most fundamental, transcendent level is spiritual meaning: a sense of having a place in the universe. Religion offers something more. It represents the broadest and deepest form of connectedness. It is the subtlest, and therefore most easily corrupted, yet perhaps the most powerful. It is the only form of meaning that transcends our personal circumstances, social situation, and the material world, and so can sustain us through the trouble and strife of moral existence.[52]

---

[48] Oswald Spengler, *The Decline of the West* (New York: Oxford University Press, 1991).

[49] See Richard Eckersley, "Postmodern Science: The Decline or Liberation of Science?" in *Science Communication in Theory and Practice*, ed. S. M. Stocklmayer, M. M. Gore, and C. R. Bryant (Dordrecht: Kluwer, 2001), 83–94; and Eckersley, *Well and Good*.

[50] Eckersley, *Well and Good*, 216.   [51] Ibid., 225.   [52] Ibid., 222.

Does cultural ethos, in all its abstraction and fuzziness, affect health? I believe it does, although I cannot provide empirical support for that conclusion. Consider two quotations from so-called hard scientists who seem to epitomize the dichotomy in postmodern thinking. The first is from Richard Dawkins, the well-known British biologist and fervent atheist:

In a universe of electrons and selfish genes, blind physical forces and genetic replication, some people are going to be hurt; other people are going to get lucky, and you won't find any rhyme or reason in it, nor any justice. The universe that we observe has precisely the properties we should expect if there is, at bottom, no design, no purpose, no evil and no good, nothing but a pitiless indifference.[53]

Yikes! There is a guy that I would not want to chat with for very long. Now consider a quote from Paul Davies, an Australian physicist:

The true miracle of nature is to be found in the ingenious and unswerving lawfulness of the cosmos, a lawfulness that permits complex order to emerge from chaos, life to emerge from inanimate matter, and consciousness to emerge from life ... [The universe is] a coherent, rational, elegant, and harmonious expression of a deep and purposeful meaning.[54]

Now there is a man with whom I would love to have a conversation. Both of these worldviews exist in our postmodern world. It's not that their adherents go through life expressing themselves in these terms. It's that these perspectives act as filters through which everything that they see, feel, and experience passes. I also believe that they affect health. If I internalized Richard Dawkins' philosophy, I would see no reason to get out of bed in the morning. I would feel helpless. My only hope would be that randomness made me one of the lucky ones. And if I experienced good fortune, how could I take any pleasure in it?

In contrast, Davies' perspective makes me want to preserve, nurture, and celebrate life. It makes me want to be a part of and contribute to the miraculous entity that we call the universe. It excites and energizes me. It makes me want to take care of myself and others. At the same time that it empowers me, it assures me that I exist in a universe that is benevolent and purposeful.

---

[53] Richard Dawkins, *River Out of Eden: A Darwinian View of Life* (New York: Basic Books, 1995), 133.

[54] Paul Davies, "Physics and the Mind of God: The Templeton Prize Address," 1995, www .firstthings.com/article/1995/08/003-physics-and-the-mind-of-god-the-templeton-prize -address-24.

I believe that religion, more than any other social institution, encourages worldviews which claim that the universe is benevolent and purposeful; that life does have meaning, even when we suffer; and that life and health are to be celebrated, respected, and received with gratitude. Religion may not be the only route to that worldview or cultural ethos, but at minimum it is a major pathway to it.

As articulated throughout this volume, there are many reasons to sustain, protect, and celebrate religious freedom. Although imperfectly understood, the well-documented links between religion and human health are surely one of those reasons. At many times and places – and certainly now – shameful atrocities in which humans are killed and maimed have been pursued in the name of religion. I am frequently asked if these atrocities aren't evidence that religion can savagely harm health and survival. They are not. These barbaric acts need to be understood as *attacks on* religious freedom – not *acts of* religious freedom. Attacks on religious freedom harm legions. Religious freedom promotes human health and well-being.

Measuring worldviews and performing research that links them to health will not be easy or straightforward. The challenges are not only methodological. We also lack theories to guide us in conceptualizing alternate worldviews and identifying their boundaries. Once the scientific community has at least minimally adequate ways of measuring worldviews and estimating their relationships to health, many other tasks will remain, including identifying the sources of worldviews (e.g., religious socialization, individual experience, political philosophies) and determining the extent to which worldviews are malleable. I certainly do not have all – or even many of – the answers about how we might usefully go about identifying worldviews and their consequences. But I believe that efforts to do so would make a vital contribution to our understanding of the links between religion and health at a level of reality that does full justice to the power and ultimate grace of the human spirit.

8

Religion, Health, and Happiness: An Epidemiologist's Perspective

Jeff Levin*

As reflected in the title and description of the standing seminar series for which this chapter was prepared, religion is indeed intrinsic to human experience. It "intersects with questions of individual and collective identity, ethics, and action," including regarding its instrumentality as a force for human well-being, defined here as health and happiness. This intrinsic and instrumental relevance of religion, both personally and institutionally, for well-being parallels its salience for social, economic, and political development. Religious freedom, as an idea and a necessity, matters for the kinds of issues that occupy legislators and policymakers: military preparedness, global governance, legislative priorities, diplomatic strategies. But the free expression of religion also matters for the physical and mental health, quality of life, and flourishing of people throughout the world. Where this freedom is impeded, people suffer, not just in material ways but also in their bodies and psyches. For religious freedom, the epidemiologic component of this discussion may be as meaningful to unpack as the sociocultural and political–economic dimensions.

This chapter is a write-up and elaboration of remarks presented in response to Linda George's outstanding presentation at the event on religion, health, and happiness organized by the Religious Freedom Project at Georgetown in December 2011.[1] In the interest of honest disclosure, I have known Dr. George ever since my good fortune to be

* The author would like to thank Buster G. Smith, PhD, for his assistance in analyzing data from the Gallup World Poll.
[1] Linda K. George, "Research on Religion and Health: Time to Be Born Again?" this volume, pp. 157–176.

a student of hers in an undergraduate seminar course in sociology at Duke University, in 1980. Dr. George is a world-class scholar, her presentation was brilliant and provocative, and, to cut to the chase, it is hard to identify anything in her remarks that might merit disagreement. Stating this here may undermine the concept of my serving as a responder – there are only glowing words of approval in this chapter – but it is valuable to set the tone for what follows.

Using a book metaphor, this chapter begins with a prologue, restating Dr. George's key points. This is followed by the main text, containing a response to Dr. George and a reconstruction of this subject in epidemiologic context. This chapter concludes with an epilogue, laying out an agenda for future research. Unlike in most journal articles, however, this agenda is not a perfunctory list of possibilities for follow-up papers, but rather a detailed discussion of conceptual, theoretical, and methodological issues that require consideration, as well as policy-relevant questions that researchers need to begin asking. This is an important task as we map and project the global impact of religion in the twenty-first century. Accordingly, the epilogue is the lengthiest section of this chapter.

PROLOGUE: RESTATEMENT OF LINDA GEORGE'S KEY POINTS

In her presentation, Dr. George addressed the current state of research on religion, health, and happiness. Her remarks were cleverly, and very aptly, subtitled, "Time to Be Born Again?" Her principal critique can be distilled to these two points: (a) this research field has become stagnant, and (b) new topics can energize the field. As someone who has conducted research on this subject for over 35 years, it is hard for me to imagine anyone familiar with this field disagreeing with Dr. George's main points.

A paper that I wrote several years ago with Linda Chatters showed that the research questions that animate empirical studies today and show up on various lists promising an "agenda for future research" are the very same questions that were posited on such lists as long ago as the 1960s.[2] These include, for example, agenda items urging (a) research on the psychosocial mechanisms by which religiousness influences health, (b) study of predictors of change in religiousness over the life course, (c) use of measures of private religiousness in lieu of the overemphasis on public

---

[2] See Jeff Levin and Linda M. Chatters, "Religion, Aging, and Health: Historical Perspectives, Current Trends, and Future Directions," *Journal of Religion, Spirituality and Aging* 20 (2008): 153–172.

religious behavior, and (d) greater use of longitudinal designs. I am not suggesting that these recommendations are unworthy – quite the opposite. What I am suggesting is that they have been offered and responded to, repeatedly, in study after study for decades. More to the point, they are no longer the most pressing or vital questions that could and should be asked. As a result, while research on religion, health, and well-being has become more accepted and less marginal in recent years, the field as a whole has become stagnant and detached from the sorts of interesting and important issues that animate discourse on religion in larger intellectual circles and in the public square. I agree with Neal Krause whose recent essay characterized the literature on this topic as "disheveled."[3] He makes several thoughtful recommendations, including a more careful consideration of the role of theory in identifying significant research questions. Perhaps most importantly, he recommends attention to new conceptual approaches for understanding how religion may influence well-being, focused on things like self-transcendence, control, sociality, and meaning.

One of Dr. George's key suggestions is to build outward from a very fundamental premise: religion, as a domain of personal qualities and characteristics, comprises multiple facets and dimensions, and these exert differential impacts on the various dimensions and domains of physical and psychological well-being, yet we do not fully know how or why. She suggests all sorts of fascinating spin-offs of existing research. For example: (a) re-conceptualizing religious participation, including multiplicatively; (b) assessing and investigating impacts of a close personal relationship with God, such as through measures of "divine support"; and (c) examining contextual effects, whether social, cultural, or geographic. These are the kinds of reasonable conceptual elaborations of existing research that would be familiar to any social scientist whose focus is religion, but for those of us involved in the study of religion and health these are, sadly, far outside the norm of what is usually considered.

Besides these suggestions, Dr. George also raises a couple of more novel issues. First, there is a need to consider communal dimensions or expressions of religiousness – after all, religion is a collectively and communally experienced phenomenon, and religiousness or religiosity is not something easily done in isolation. For an epidemiologist, accustomed to exploring impacts of putative determinants on population-wide indicators of health or illness, the possibility of a directional association between

---

[3] Neal Krause, "Religion and Health: Making Sense of a Disheveled Literature," *Journal of Religion and Health* 50 (2011): 20–35.

"population religion" and population health is fascinating and challenging, both theoretically and methodologically.

Second, Dr. George also recommends moving beyond the usual forms of religious assessment (as in measures of religious behaviors, beliefs, attitudes, emotions, etc.) to consideration of issues of religious meaning and worldview. The first thing that springs to mind here, as it does for Dr. George, is Aaron Antonovsky's rich vein of writing on "salutogenesis" (a term he coined to focus research attention on those factors that contribute to the healing process) and a sense of coherence.[4] The interface of these constructs with personal and communal expressions of religiousness, and accounting for the contextual effects that Dr. George describes, would seem to map out a visionary program of research for social and psychosocial epidemiologists seeking to understand how and why some folks are healthy and happy and some are not, and what the unhealthy and unhappy can do to change their status.

TEXT: RESPONSE AND RECONSTRUCTION

Responding to Linda George

As noted earlier, this section is more elaboration than critique. Not much in the way of disagreement separates Dr. George's remarks and the material presented here.

The points of greatest agreement include these: (a) the religion and health field is stagnant; (b) new topics and directions are needed; (c) more of a focus is required on the "how" and "why" of a religion–health or religion–happiness association, not just on the "what"; (d) broader and more creative efforts are needed to assess the fullness of spirituality and human spiritual life; (e) a closer look should be paid to conceptualizing, describing, and assessing one's relationship with God or the divine or sacred; (f) greater attention is needed to contextual variables and to communal aspects and expressions of religiousness; and (g) the impact of religious meaning and worldview, as described by Antonovsky, is an important frontier for this field. I not only wholeheartedly agree with these points, but have commented on these and similar subjects in research

---

[4] See Aaron Antonovsky, *Health, Stress, and Coping: New Perspectives on Mental and Physical Well Being* (San Francisco: Jossey-Bass, 1979) and Aaron Antonovsky, *Unraveling the Mystery of Health: How People Manage Stress and Stay Well* (San Francisco: Jossey-Bass, 1987).

papers or reviews dating to the 1980s. I gladly and thankfully second each of Dr. George's main points.

Most of all, Dr. George lucidly and methodically makes the case for a broad rethinking of the main questions with which religion and health researchers concern themselves. In answer to the question that she poses in her subtitle, yes, it is time for this field to become "born again." Her remarks also stimulated further ideas that came to mind as I digested what she had to say. These are my elaborations of her list.

First, we ought to focus more on religious experience, including phenomena such as transcendent states of consciousness and feelings of divine love. For each of these, preliminary evidence suggests an association with physical or mental health outcomes, psychophysiological indicators, or general well-being.[5] One's relationship with the Source of Being, however defined, would seem to tap into something more profoundly reflective of one's intrinsic spirituality and determinative of other facets of psychosocial adjustment than the simple counts of discrete religious behaviors that dominate spiritual assessment in studies of health and well-being.

Second, we ought to extend our consideration beyond the various Christian communions to the other monotheistic faith traditions, to non-Western and non-theistic traditions, and to esoteric and new religious movements. It is unjustified to presume that the pattern, polarity, and salience of religion's impact in the lives of Western Christians is recapitulated in the lives of people of other faith traditions, other cultures, and other nationalities.[6] There is not much evidence that there are substantial commonalities among empirical findings even within the narrow range of populations that we tend to study, other than the most general finding – namely, that greater religiousness or faith, on average, tends to be salutary. Why then should we not expect diversity in religion's influence on health and happiness when taking into account the diversity of faith traditions in the world and the circumstances of their expression in different settings? Are not our government's highest officials, military and intelligence leaders, and diplomatic corps receiving daily reinforcement of the sad truth that our presumptions about faith traditions

---

[5] See Jeff Levin, "God, Love, and Health: Findings from a Clinical Study," *Review of Religious Research* 42 (2001): 277–293; also see Jeff Levin and Lea Steele, "The Transcendent Experience: Conceptual, Theoretical, and Epidemiologic Perspectives," *EXPLORE: The Journal of Science and Healing* 1 (2005): 89–101.

[6] See C. Meister, ed., *The Oxford Handbook of Religious Diversity* (New York: Oxford University Press, 2011).

outside of our comfortable Western Judeo-Christian orbit, and about their influence on human institutions and the conduct of human lives, are deeply flawed?

Third, on a very different note, we ought to examine religion's influence on outcomes taken from across the natural history of disease. Typically, epidemiologists focus their investigations on identifying determinants or predictors of population rates of disease or death that emerge over time in well populations. That is, we are in the business of identifying factors associated with elevated risk (risk factors) or diminished risk (protective factors) for subsequent adverse health-related events. The emphasis here is on preventing morbidity and mortality. Most published research on religion and health falls into this category. By contrast, clinical research is about identifying factors that promote salutogenesis, to return to Antonovsky's concept, particularly the healing of existing cases of disease. Relatively minimal research on religion has emphasized healing, as opposed to prevention.[7] Much of the clinical research on religion comes from Duke University, under the direction of Harold Koenig, and Linda George has been a part of many of the studies that have emerged.[8] The idea of a healing power of faith or spirituality is an attractive idea but one that remains only minimally validated relative to the well-vetted primary-preventive effects of religious participation. In what is probably the 180-degree reverse of popular perception, far more is known about the population-wide impact of religion on health and well-being (in selected populations) than on the personal effects of expressions of faith on sick people. A systematic effort to conduct research on the putative salutary functions of religious identity, belief, and practice for patients in the clinical setting, including the physiological and psychophysiological correlates or religiousness,[9] is highly recommended. This could be part of a larger effort to map out a salutogenically oriented "natural history of health"[10] as a counterpart to existing pathogenically oriented models of the natural history of disease, as a way to guide research on healing.

[7] See Jeff Levin, "'And Let Us Make Us a Name': Reflections on the Future of the Religion and Health Field," *Journal of Religion and Health* 48 (2009): 125–145.
[8] See H. G. Koenig, *The Healing Power of Faith: Sciences Explores Medicine's Last Great Frontier* (New York: Simon & Schuster, 2001).
[9] See H. G. Koenig and H. J. Cohen, eds., *The Link Between Religion and Health: Psychoneuroimmunology and the Faith Factor* (New York: Oxford University Press, 2002).
[10] Jeff Levin, "Integrating Positive Psychology Into Epidemiologic Theory: Reflections on Love, Salutogenesis, and Determinants of Population Health," in *Altruism and Health:*

Besides these broad points, stimulated by Dr. George's remarks, I also have learned from her earlier insights. In remarks at the annual meeting of the Gerontological Society of America in 1995, she advised that social scientists who research the impact of religion on health begin to engage real epidemiologic concepts.[11] Specifically, this implies that we ought to pay better attention to what epidemiologists term exposure assessment, in this instance a reconstituted effort to assess religious participation according to the parameters used in assessing other exposure variables (e.g., entry point, mode of transmission, latency period, intensity, duration), and not simply default to the static snapshots of current religious status that are the norm for this field. She also reiterated a call for greater emphasis on longitudinal epidemiologic designs. This would mean more prospective cohort studies, case-control studies, and ambidirectional studies, entailing estimation of risk or odds, besides the usual panel studies familiar to sociologists.

Dr. George's comments in 1995 influenced my own thinking, and I subsequently drew on her ideas in crafting detailed theoretical statements regarding the study of religious determinants of morbidity,[12] of personal prayer as a determinant of population health outcomes,[13] and of positive psychological constructs as factors in population health, disease, and morbidity.[14] Each of these papers sought to make a case for greater attention to (a) the conceptual nuances of religion and related constructs, and their assessment, and (b) the theoretical implications of such constructs for health and, concomitantly, how these can and cannot be teased out depending on assumptions underlying certain methodological approaches. Accordingly, my main programmatic approach to this subject could be summarized as "putting the 'epidemiology' into the epidemiology of religion." This includes, more recently, encouraging a focus on its public health relevance.

Perspectives from Empirical Research, ed. Stephen G. Post (New York: Oxford University Press, 2007), 189–218.

[11] Linda K. George, "Discussant's Comments" (presentation, Symposium on What Six Large Studies Tell Us About Religion and Health, 48th Annual Scientific Meeting of the Gerontological Society of America, Los Angeles, November 15–19, 1995).

[12] Jeff Levin, "How Religion Influences Morbidity and Health: Reflections on Natural History, Salutogenesis and Host Resistance," *Social Science and Medicine* 43 (1996): 849–864.

[13] Jeff Levin, "Prayer, Love, and Transcendence: An Epidemiologic Perspective," in *Religious Influences on Health and Well-Being in the Elderly*, eds. K. Warner Schaie, Neal Krause, and Alan Booth (New York: Springer Publishing, 2004), 69–95.

[14] Levin, "Integrating Positive Psychology into Epidemiologic Theory," 189–218.

An Epidemiologic Reconstruction

For an epidemiologist – as opposed to, say, a medical sociologist or a health psychologist or a physician–researcher – there is a characteristic way to unpack a putative exposure–outcome relationship involving psychosocial constructs or variables. This involves the posing of a series of sequential questions, each pertaining to a respective research-related task. This is not just the manner of social or psychosocial epidemiologists, like me. Even those who investigate outbreaks of infectious disease – the bread and butter of the profession for two centuries – will implicitly recognize this approach.

So, what would a distinctly epidemiologic approach look like in reconstructing this issue?

First, we would ask the *what* question. This is a matter of *exposure assessment*. Religion (and religiousness) is a name for a class of phenomena with multiple (a) dimensions, (b) inclusionary and exclusionary criteria, and (c) innate characteristics (e.g., onset, history, duration of exposure). An epidemiologist's approach to religion would be to treat it like any other exposure (i.e., independent variable), precisely as Dr. George recommended almost 20 years ago.[15]

Second, there are the *who, where,* and *when* questions. Providing answers constitutes the task of *descriptive epidemiology*. The aim here would be to calculate the population-wide incidence and prevalence of expressions of religion, and of health and happiness, as well as their distribution by categories of person (e.g., age, gender, ethnicity, religious affiliation), place (e.g., nationality), and time (i.e., to identify any longitudinal changes, such as due to secular cohort or period effects). We are often so anxious to build sophisticated research programs around some facet of religion and well-being that we skip over this step entirely. This is a key contributor to the contextual errors and theoretical misspecification that plague this field.

Third, there is the *how* question. Answering this question is the function of *analytic epidemiology*. This involves two discrete tasks: (a) identification of *trajectories* (i.e., prospective changes in levels of health or happiness due to religion) through dynamic analyses, rather than the usual static snapshot of most research studies; and (b) investigation of *mechanisms* (i.e., potential "active ingredients" in religion that are responsible for changes in levels of health or happiness). These hypothetical functions,

---

[15] Linda K. George, "Discussant's Comments."

expressions, or manifestations of being religious or spiritual or of "doing religion" include items such as practicing healthy lifestyle behaviors, being integrated into networks providing socially supportive tangible and emotional resources, having an outlet for expressing positive and cathartic feelings, affirming beliefs and attitudes expressive of hope and optimism, and even providing a gateway into soothing and perhaps transcendent states of consciousness with possible physiological and psychophysiological sequelae.[16] Granted, validation of such mechanisms may be well beyond the scope of the average epidemiologic study. Nonetheless, each of these things offers a hypothetical explanation of salutary religious effects, and respective studies can at least attempt to tease out possible mediating or moderating effects where associated measures are present.

EPILOGUE: AGENDA FOR RESEARCH

Based on this reconstruction of the manner in which a religion–health/ happiness relationship might be investigated, how would an epidemiologist's characteristically systematic approach play out? To answer this question, I take inspiration from my earliest epidemiologic mentor, the late Bert Kaplan, whose own important contributions to the study of religion and health reflected his belief that an indispensable way to respond to a research question is to propose a litany of additional questions that unpack conceptual, theoretical, and methodological fine points that may otherwise be skipped over.[17] In order to describe, analyze, and explain the relationship between religion and health in the most effective way possible, I believe that the following questions or issues should be posed.

First, there are *conceptual* questions. For example: what is health? How do we assess it? What is happiness? How do we assess it? Are these unidimensional or multidimensional constructs?

These questions matter: without being clear on what we mean by health or happiness, and without characterizing these constructs reliably and validly, any subsequent empirical findings will be of little use. It is easy to presume that "everybody knows" what health is or what happiness is,

---

[16] See Jeff Levin, *God, Faith, and Health: Exploring the Spirituality-Healing Connection* (New York: John Wiley & Sons, 2001).

[17] See, for example, B. H. Kaplan, "A Note on Religious Beliefs and Coronary Artery Disease," *Journal of the South Carolina Medical Association* 15, num. 5 (suppl.) (1976): 60–64.

and thus it must be a simple matter to measure these phenomena. But when one begins to delve into the scholarly literature on these subjects it is quickly apparent that the assessment of health and well-being, and its many domains and dimensions, is a seriously complex matter One is reminded of Duane Alwin's characterization of quality-of-life assessment as characterized by a "prevailing chaos of conceptualization" resulting in "a variety of scales that purport to measure a variety of ambiguous and poorly differentiated concepts."[18] Dr. George herself wrote on this topic in 1981, summarizing work dating to the 1950s, and concluded that in this literature the "first and foremost issue is the need for conceptual clarity."[19] Over 35 years later, this conclusion still holds.

Second, there are *theoretical* questions. These include: how and why should religion influence health or happiness? What constructs mediate these relationships? Do other constructs serve as effect-modifiers (i.e., moderators)? Do these "causal" models themselves differ by categories of some other construct(s)? Is there variation in religious effects by religious affiliation or categories of other religious constructs? Are there population-level or cross-national effects?

This latter question is especially interesting. As an aside, I would like to interject some interesting findings that were obtained using data collected through the Gallup World Poll (GWP) in 2009. The GWP is a continual cross-sectional survey of the adult population of over 160 countries using randomly selected, nationally representative samples.[20] Most GWP samples contain 1,000 respondents per nation per round, and use a standard set of core questions. Surveys have been conducted annually for over a decade. Among the hundreds of variables and scales in the GWP are a two-item religiosity index and multi-item personal health, positive experience, and negative experience indices. The latter are akin to what are sometimes called positive and negative well-being (or positive affect and negative or depressed affect).

Very simply, Pearson (r) correlations of the religiosity index with the other three scales were calculated for every nation in the GWP, and the scores were arrayed from highest to lowest. That is, they were listed from

[18] Duane F. Alwin, "Structural Equation Models in Research on Human Development and Aging," in *Methodological Issues in Aging Research*, eds. K. Warner Schaie et al. (New York: Springer, 1988), 120.

[19] Linda K. George, "Subjective Well-Being: Conceptual and Methodological Issues," *Annual Review of Gerontology and Geriatrics* 2 (1988): 375.

[20] See Gallup, Inc., "Worldwide Research Methodology and Codebook," *Gallup*, Washington, April 2011.

TABLE 8.1 *Correlation Between Religiosity and Well-Being Outcomes,
by Nation, in 2009 Gallup World Poll*

Health		Positive Well-Being		Negative Well-Being	
Kenya	.13	Kenya	.21	Moldova	.17
Tanzania	.11	Ghana	.18	Belarus	.16
Congo Kinshasa	.09	Nigeria	.17	Latvia	.14
Senegal	.08	Mali	.15	Slovenia	.14
Uganda	.08	Niger	.15	Ukraine	.13
Ghana	.08	Rwanda	.14	Lithuania	.13
Burundi	.06	Ivory Coast	.14	Albania	.12
Nigeria	.06	Zimbabwe	.11	Estonia	.11
Rwanda	.05	Congo Kinshasa	.11	Romania	.10
Chad	.05	Uganda	.10	Russia	.10
Slovenia	-.11	Chad	.10	Somaliland	-.05
Latvia	-.12	Senegal	.10	Uganda	-.05
Ukraine	-.13	Tanzania	.10	Rwanda	-.05
Romania	-.14	Tajikistan	-.01	Niger	-.06
Bulgaria	-.15	Estonia	-.02	Senegal	-.07
Albania	-.15	Ukraine	-.03	Tunisia	-.08
Russia	-.17	Albania	-.03	Burundi	-.08
Estonia	-.20	Russia	-.04	Congo Kinshasa	-.09
Moldova	-.21	Slovenia	-.06	Tanzania	-.10
Belarus	-.24	Romania	-.07	Ghana	-.10
Lithuania	-.24	Azerbaijan	-.07	Kenya	-.14
		Latvia	-.08		
		Belarus	-.12		
		Lithuania	-.12		
		Moldova	-.16		

the greatest positive associations to the greatest negative associations, with zero (i.e., no association) in the middle. When this was done, something very intriguing emerged (see selected findings from these analyses in Table 8.1).

Out of the sample of 160 nations, of the 14 countries with
a correlation ≥.05 between religiosity and health, 10 of these were
from rapidly Christianizing parts of Africa, primarily central Africa.
Of the 26 nations with a correlation ≥.10 between religiosity and positive well-being, 13 were from the same group. Among the 25 nations
with a correlation ≤ –.05 between religiosity and negative well-being, 11
were from this group, as well. It is among these nations, on the whole,
that one is most likely to observe religiosity associated with more salutary (i.e., health-promotive) outcomes. In the language of epidemiology,
religiosity seems to exhibit a protective or risk-reducing effect.

By contrast, again out of the whole sample of 160 nations, of the 19
countries with a correlation ≤ –.10 between religiosity and health, 11 of
these were from former Soviet-bloc countries. Of the 24 nations with
a correlation ≤ 0 between religiosity and positive well-being, 12 were
from this group. Among the 15 nations with a correlation ≥.10 between
religiosity and negative well-being, 10 were also from this group. It is
among these countries, on the whole, that one is most likely to observe
religiosity associated with more deleterious (i.e., health-damaging) outcomes. In the language of epidemiology, religiosity seems to exhibit a risk-
elevating effect.

What stands out most of all here is that salutary associations were
observed primarily in nations undergoing rapid Christian evangelization,
mostly in Africa. Deleterious associations, by contrast, were observed
primarily in nations of Eastern Europe associated with the former communist bloc. For the former nations, religion perhaps is identified as
a source of hope, thereby functioning as a personal and social resource,
and thus is a force for positive psychosocial adjustment. For the latter
nations, religion may elicit memories of persecution and be a source of
psychological stress or discomfort, and thus be associated with greater
physical and psychological distress. Of course, none of this is provable;
entirely different dynamics and causal relationships may be operative
here. Further, one must always be careful to avoid the famous
Durkheimian fallacy of misinterpreting ecologic-level data.[21] Moreover,
this is a very general finding, with exceptions present (unreported in the
table), not a one-to-one correspondence, and results were not adjusted for
age, socioeconomic status, or any other variable. Whatever is actually
going on, these findings are interjected here not as a definitive empirical

[21] Émile Durkheim, *Suicide: A Study in Sociology*, trans. J. A. Spaulding and G. Simpson
(1897; New York: The Free Press, 1951).

statement as to the global utility of religion for well-being, but simply to exemplify how fascinating and provocative (and, no doubt, confusing) the study of such cross-national effects can be when it comes to religion and well-being. There is much grist for the mill. But investigators must first affirm the value in exploring data such as these.

Third, besides conceptual and theoretical questions, a number of *methodological* issues demand exploration. Longitudinal designs are especially important so that secular trends may be tracked, as well as other forms of dynamic variation in how religion influences well-being. Throughout this literature, many useful strategies have been employed, including panel analysis, aging–period–cohort analysis, event history analysis, Cox proportional hazards modeling, and analysis of trajectories. Some of the most sophisticated studies of religion and health include a spate of analyses of mortality rates and longevity that have appeared since the 1990s.[22] In general, longitudinal analyses enable us to track more accurately the impact of religious identity and participation on outcomes in question, thus facilitating any future projections. Without longitudinal analysis, future projections are more often than not informed by extrapolations of data from only a single, static cross-sectional sample. The forthcoming transition of the GWP from an annual to a quarterly survey holds out promise that the global monitoring of religious impacts on health and well-being may someday be able to make use of sophisticated time-series analyses in tracking and mapping these relationships.

A separate methodological issue is the pressing need for study designs that enable evaluation of policy-relevant questions. Religious participation may be linked, on average, to psychologically better adjusted and happier people, across some populations. But how is this bit of information useful to the folks who make policies, laws, and decisions governing matters of real-world importance within and among nations? The policy issue here could be thought of as a different octave of the larger religion-and-well-being discussion, one that has been largely neglected, except perhaps for some recent statements about the intersection of the faith-based and public health sectors.[23]

[22] For example, R. A. Hummer et al., "Religious Involvement and U.S. Adult Mortality," *Demography* 36 (1999): 273–285; H. G. Koenig et al., "Does Religious Attendance Prolong Survival?: A Six-Year Follow-Up Study of 3,968 Older Adults," *Journal of Gerontology: Medical Sciences* 54A (1999): M370–M376; and W. J. Strawbridge et al., "Frequent Attendance at Religious Services and Mortality Over 28 Years," *American Journal of Public Health* 87 (1997): 957–961.

[23] For example, G. R. Gunderson and J. R. Cochrane, *Religion and the Health of the Public: Shifting the Paradigm* (New York: Palgrave Macmillan, 2012); Jeff Levin, "Engaging the

In light of existing studies of religion's influence on health and happiness, in the USA and globally, several policy-relevant questions might be posed. Each of these could evolve into distinct applied research projects that promise to advance our understanding of the instrumental value of religion, ideally, for social well-being and human progress. These include the following questions:

1. Does religious participation influence well-being through decreasing the health risks of or mitigating the health consequences of *deviant behavior*? Deviance is referenced here in the sociological sense, as non-normative behavior, especially behavior surrounded by taboos, negative sanctions, or some form of restrictive social control. The word deviance is used in this context simply as a social construction, without attaching any moral judgment. Examples may include illegal or rule-breaking activities, unusual sexual practices or identities, history of incarceration, forbidden or discouraged mental ideations or political beliefs or worldviews, and general "otherness" or outsider status. In theory, religious resources – psychological and social – may moderate the otherwise deleterious impact of such characteristics on mood disorders such as depression – an idea proposed over 20 years ago,[24] but one that remains an underexplored topic of research. If true, personal faith and institutional religion may constitute important resources for preventing the stresses associated with deviance from triggering episodes of mental illness, self-harm, or harm of others.

2. Can religious institutions provide health-promoting social and personal resources in times of *public resource scarcity*? This is a timely issue, given the present state of the economy and the ongoing public discourse on healthcare reform in the USA. Faith-based organizations, denominations, and philanthropies, and other voluntary institutions of civil society, have functioned historically as mediators between the individual and the state, including in the healthcare arena. They have a valuable role to play through "midstream" partnerships and initiatives that may contribute to the health of the

Faith Community for Public Health Advocacy: An Agenda for the Surgeon General," *Journal of Religion and Health* 52 (2013): 368–385.

[24] C. G. Ellison, "Religion, the Life Stress Paradigm, and the Study of Depression," in *Religion in Aging and Health: Theoretical Foundations and Methodological Frontiers*, ed. Jeff Levin (Thousand Oaks: Sage Publications, 1994), 78–121.

population,[25] such as through efforts to inform the public, raise risk awareness, and change behavior; to identify public health needs and eliminate health disparities in underserved populations; to deliver preventive healthcare; to strengthen the national resolve to bolster the public health infrastructure; and to help meet the nation's global health responsibilities.[26] Religious institutions may provide tangible resources and services that can complement or extend the mission and functions of government.

3. Should religious beliefs and worldviews inform ethical stances and responses regarding *healthcare as a common good*? Between 2008 and 2010, during the intense national conversation on healthcare reform – or, more accurately, on medical care expenditure reimbursement reform[27] – mainline religious denominations and associated organizations weighed in with considerable lobbying force in favor of various features of the proposed legislation. These included statements by the Roman Catholic bishops, by United Methodists, and by groups across the Jewish spectrum.[28] Such statements were consistent with the historic prophetic role of religion as an institution divinely charged with calling citizenry and governments out of their complacency, disobedience, and sin regarding issues of social justice and mercy. Institutional religion played an influential role in advocating for a legislative remedy for population health disparities that was grounded in bioethical principles derived from the sacred writings of Western faith traditions. Additionally, faith-based organizations continue to have an indispensable role to play in disease prevention and health promotion efforts at the national and local levels.[29]

4. Is religious faith or spiritual development a necessary or sufficient *feature of a good life*? There is a larger existing conversation emerging on religion in relation to human flourishing and *eudaimonia*. Global and cross-national research on happiness and quality of life

---

[25] Jeff Levin, "Engaging the Faith Community for Public Health Advocacy," 368–385.

[26] Jeff Levin and Jay F. Hein, "A Faith-Based Prescription for the Surgeon General: Challenges and Recommendation," *Journal of Religion and Health* 51 (2012): 57–71.

[27] Jeff Levin, "An Antipoverty Agenda for Public Health: Background and Recommendations," *Public Health Reports* 132 (2017): 431–435.

[28] See Jeff Levin, "Jewish Ethical Themes that Should Inform the National Healthcare Discussion: A Prolegomenon," *Journal of Religion and Health* 51 (2012): 589–600.

[29] See R. G. Bennett and W. D. Hale, *Building Healthy Communities through Medical-Religious Partnerships*, 2nd ed. (Baltimore: Johns Hopkins University Press, 2009); Gunderson and Cochrane, *Religion and the Health of the Public.*

has been enabled by several large-scale programs of multinational survey research: example, the Gallup World Poll, utilized above, as well as the World Values Survey; the International Social Survey Programme; the European Social Survey; and the Survey of Health, Ageing and Retirement in Europe. Each of these data sources collects information on religion and on facets of psychological or physical well-being, alongside various social indicators assessing societal, economic, and political attitudes and statuses. Investigators have begun to identify religious impacts on these indicators within and among nations.[30]

5. Could the faith-based sector play a role in US efforts to export (democratic) values in order *to enhance global security*? This is a difficult issue, surely, for an epidemiologist to address. Whether such a role is advisable is outside my bailiwick – or, as former President Obama once famously remarked, above my pay grade. The most prudent course of action is for decision-makers, whomever they may be, to be well informed by accurate and up-to-date information about respective faith traditions, their social and cultural and political concomitants, and the consequences of adherents' beliefs and practices for general well-being, physical or psychological or social. As noted, private and public expressions of religiosity can be sources of distress and social upheaval, on the one hand, but also forces for psychological adjustment and social equilibrium. For the most part, yes, religion seems to be a force for salutary outcomes among people and populations, but this conclusion is always mediated by the particularities of context – i.e., it is invariably a function of a particular religion, a particular society, a particular political context, and so on. Like a lot of generalizations that are possible regarding religion and that are tempting to make, the truth instead is that *it depends*. Rather than making tacit and not fully informed presumptions about the consequences and salience of religion, those in power ought to draw on the collected wisdom of those who study the phenomenon and ought to solicit

---

[30] For example, Ronald Inglehart et al., "Development, Freedom, and Rising Happiness: A Global Perspective (1981–2007)," *Perspectives on Psychological Science* 3 (2008): 264–285; A. Nicholson, R. Rose, and M. Bobak, "Association Between Attendance at Religious Services and Self-Reported Health in 22 European Countries," *Social Science and Medicine* 69 (2009): 519–528; and A. Deaton, "Aging, Religion, and Health," in *Explorations in the Economics of Aging*, ed. D. A. Wise (Chicago: University of Chicago Press, 2011), 237–262.

their ideas in the "strategic calculation"[31] that goes into deriving political and policy-related agendas from the observed prominence of religion in public life. This is hardly an outrageous request.

To conclude, three take-home points can be derived from these remarks. These correspond to the respective downstream, upstream, and midstream levels of focus for public health action plans identified by David Satcher, former US Surgeon General.

First, *for individuals*, religion matters for health and happiness in a variety of ways. Among those who value the personal and social resources that religion can provide, religious beliefs and worldviews are a source of faith that can sustain people in the face of life challenges, that can repair brokenness, and that can enhance life, providing a pathway to wellness and high-level flourishing. Many people may feel that religion is not for them, but for those who do embrace it, their faith may be an indispensable contributor to wellness and wholeness of body, mind, and soul. For others, it may become a source of anxiety and distress, even motivating acts of harm toward others. Either way, for good or for bad, empirical evidence shows that religion matters.[32]

Second, *across populations*, there appears to be a generally salutary and protective effect of religious involvement, on average and regardless of one's religion. Populations characterized by behavioral codes of living with clear prescriptions and proscriptions – for example, Latter-Day Saints and Seventh-day Adventists – have healthier and longer-lived epidemiologic profiles than secular or moderately religious counterparts. For psychiatric outcomes and psychological well-being, the evidence is more nuanced: for the most part, religious populations, communities, and groups have less psychiatric morbidity, but extreme or fanatical expressions of religiosity may be associated with psychopathology. This depends on the specific religion, form of expression, particular diagnosis, and other contextual factors related to culture, politics, and personality. But, again, at the population level as much as for individual people, religion matters.[33]

---

[31] R. B. Fowler et al., *Religion and Politics in America: Faith, Culture, and Strategic Choices* (Boulder: Westview Press, 2010), xvi.

[32] See H. G. Koenig, D. E. King, and V. B. Carson, eds., *Handbook of Religion and Health*, 2nd ed. (New York: Oxford University Press, 2012).

[33] See Jeff Levin, "The Epidemiology of Religion," in *Religion and the Social Sciences: Basic and Applied Research Perspectives*, ed. Jeff Levin (West Conshohocken: Templeton Press, forthcoming).

Third, *institutionally*, with respect to health status, healthcare, and health policy, religious denominations and organizations can be forces for great good or for neglect; generalizations beyond that are not simple.[34] As a force for good, institutional religion in the US has been a major player in health promotion and disease prevention programming, in establishing healthcare institutions and providing primary care services, in sponsoring medical and public health missions, in organizing community-based outreach to at-risk populations, and in advocating for healthcare reform. These functions have been performed by religions and religious denominations from across the spectrum of faith traditions, and for many decades.[35]

Social and health policymakers are not served by superficial religious research that is conceptually, theoretically, and methodologically inadequate. By extension, one might add, neither are legislators, diplomats, military and intelligence leaders, and political economists. The sorts of research questions that animate current empirical research on religion, health, and happiness do not for the most part provide the information required to answer the policy-related questions that confront us as we map and project the global impact of religion in the twenty-first century. We have our work cut out for us.

It is fitting that I close with a quotation from Dr. George. She wisely recognizes the limitations of our current understandings of the utility of religion for human health and well-being, while at the same time acknowledging the importance of efforts to remedy this lacuna:

I certainly do not have all – or even many of – the answers about how we might usefully go about identifying worldviews and their consequences. But I believe that efforts to do so would make a vital contribution to our understanding of the links between religion and health at a level of reality that does full justice to the power and ultimate grace of the human spirit.[36]

---

[34] J. F. Hein, *The Quiet Revolution: An Active Faith that Transforms Lives and Communities* (New York: Waterfall Press, 2014); M. Rogers and E. J. Dionne Jr., "Serving People in Need, Safeguarding Religious Freedom: Recommendations for the New Administration on Partnerships with Faith-Based Organizations," Brookings Institution, Washington, December 2008, www.brookings.edu/wp-content/uploads/20 16/06/12_religion_dionne.pdf.

[35] See Jeff Levin, "Faith-Based Partnerships for Population Health: Challenges, Initiatives, and Prospects," *Public Health Reports* 129 (2014): 127–131.

[36] Linda K. George, "Research on Religion and Health: Time to Be Born Again?" this volume, p. 176.

9

Why There Is a Natural Right to Religious Freedom

Nicholas Wolterstorff

In this essay, at the request of volume's editors, I address the foundations and character of religious freedom as a normative principle as well as the integral importance of religious liberty for liberal democracy. This is a daunting task: to discuss the nature of religious freedom, the foundations of religious freedom, and the importance of religious freedom for liberal democracy. Though I can treat only a few aspects of these topics, I hope that the aspects I have selected, and what I have to say about them, will prove interesting and worthwhile.

THE HISTORICAL ORIGIN OF THE RELIGION
CLAUSES IN THE US BILL OF RIGHTS

In a letter of 494 to the emperor Anastasius, Pope Gelasius I declared that "two [powers] there are, august Emperor, by which this world is ruled: the consecrated authority of priests and the royal power." The idea that Gelasius here expresses is that pope and emperor, church and state, are distinct authority structures whose essential difference is that they have jurisdiction over two distinct domains of human activity.

In his tract of two years later, *On the Bond of Anathema*, Gelasius elaborated his idea. Church and empire each have a distinct "sphere of competence," a distinct "jurisdiction." Christ himself, says Gelasius, "made a distinction between the two rules, assigning each its sphere of operation and its due respect." The emperor has governance over "human" or "secular" affairs. The pope, along with his bishops and priests, has governance over "divine affairs," over "spiritual activity."[1]

The doctrine that Gelasius articulated in these passages came to be known as the "two-rules" doctrine. From the time he wrote his letter until a century or so after the Protestant Reformation, this doctrine was almost always the framework employed in the West for discussing the relation of the state to religion and the church.[2] The doctrine assumed that the church in a given area was unified and that its membership was very nearly identical with the body of those who were subjects of whatever was the government in that area. What differentiated church and state was not a difference in those they govern but a difference in the activities that fall under their governance. Jews were an exception; they were subjects of the government but not members of the church. Their anomalous position put them at risk.[3]

The traditional separation of church and state was a crucial part of the context within which freedom of religion emerged in the West. There can be a certain degree of freedom of religion in a society that has a single unified governance structure with authority over the lives of the subjects as a whole, including their religion; but it will take a significantly different form from the form it has taken in the West. It may take the form, for example, of the Ottoman millet system for non-Muslims.

Though the separation of church and state presupposed by the two-rules doctrine was an important part of the context within which free-dom of religion emerged in the West, those who thought in terms of the

---

[1] My quotations from Gelasius are all from the translations to be found in Oliver O'Donovan and Joan Lockwood O'Donovan, eds., *From Irenaeus to Grotius: A Sourcebook in Christian Political Thought: 100–1625* (Grand Rapids: Wm. B. Eerdmans Publ. Co., 1999), 178–179.

[2] I realize that speaking of the governmental structures of the time as *states* is anachronistic.

[3] Though Jews were not members of the church, it is important to note that the medieval church nonetheless claimed a certain amount of authority over the Jews and their internal affairs. Ian Christopher Levy, in an illuminating essay, notes that Pope Innocent IV (1243–54) declared that "the pope can judge the Jews if they act against the law in moral matters (*contra legem in moralibus*) and their own leaders fail to punish them; likewise, if they are found to be fostering heresies against their own law." At the same time, the medieval church exercised a kind of guardianship over the Jews, defending them against coerced conversion both in order to safeguard the principle that authentic faith in Christ must be voluntary and to preserve their existence as a witness to the Old Covenant. As such, Levy observes that European Jews periodically "appealed to the papacy to secure their right to live and practice their religion in peace." See Ian Christopher Levy, "Liberty of Conscience and Freedom of Religion in the Medieval Canonists and Theologians," in *Christianity and Freedom: Volume 1, Historical Perspectives*, eds. Timothy Samuel Shah and Allen Hertzke (New York: Cambridge University Press, 2016), 149–175.

doctrine seldom affirmed freedom of religion, the reason being that they almost always assumed a perfectionist view of the state, as they did of the church: state and church together aim at perfecting the people in virtue and piety. This assumption remained implicit in Gelasius' letter and tract; in numerous later writings it was stated explicitly. From the many passages that could be quoted on the matter, let me select one from John Calvin. Calvin is emphatic in his insistence on the importance of distinguishing the two rules. "These two, as we have divided them, must always be examined separately; and while one is being considered, we must call away and turn aside the mind from thinking about the other. There are in man, so to speak, two worlds, over which different kings and different laws have authority."[4] As to the task of government, this is what Calvin says:

[Government] does not merely see to it ... that men breathe, eat, drink, and are kept warm, even though it surely embraces all these activities when it provides for their living together. It does not, I repeat, look to this only, but also prevents idolatry, sacrilege against God's name, blasphemies against his truth, and other public offenses against religion from arising and spreading among the people; it prevents the public peace from being disturbed, it provides that each man may keep his property safe and sound, that men may carry on blameless intercourse among themselves, that honesty and modesty may be preserved among men. In short, it provides that a public manifestation of religion may exist among Christians, and that humanity be maintained among men.[5]

In 1579, twenty years after the fourth and final edition of Calvin's *Institutes*, there appeared a tract with the title, in English translation, *A Discourse upon the Permission of Freedom of Religion, called Religions-Vrede in the Netherlands*. Though the author presents himself as Catholic, the predominance of scholarly opinion nowadays is that he was the prominent Huguenot, Philip du Plessis Mornay. Here is what the author says in one place:

I ask those who do not want to admit the two religions in this country how they now intend to abolish one of them ... It goes without saying that you cannot abolish any religious practice without using force and taking up arms, and going to war against each other instead of taking up arms in unison against Don John and his adherents and delivering us from the insupportable tyranny of the foreigners. If we intend to ruin the Protestants we will ruin ourselves, as the French did. The conclusion to be drawn from this is that it would be better to live in peace with

---

[4] John Calvin, *Institutes of the Christian Religion*, ed. John T. McNeill, trans. Ford Lewis Battles (Philadelphia: Westminster Press, 1960), bk. 3, chap. 19, sec. 15.
[5] Calvin, *Institutes*, bk. 4, chap. 20, sec. 3.

them, rather than ruin ourselves by internal discord and carry on a hazardous, disastrous, long and difficult war or rather a perpetual and impossible one. Taking everything into consideration, we can choose between two things: we can either allow them to live in peace with us or we can all die together; we can either let them be or, desiring to destroy them, be ourselves destroyed by their ruin ... As we cannot forbid these people to practice their religion without starting a war and cannot destroy them by that war without being destroyed ourselves let us conclude that we must let them live in peace and grant them liberty...[6]

The argument is eloquent and poignant. The situation in The Lowlands is that the religious unity that once prevailed is gone. Many have left the Catholic Church and become Protestant. Any attempt to recover the hegemony of the Catholic Church by force of arms would require appalling bloodshed, devastating the Catholic population as well as the Protestant and leaving both at the mercy of the Spaniards. The only option is for the state to give up its perfectionist attempt to enforce religious conformity; Protestants as well as Catholics should have a civil right to practice their religion. Catholics should tolerate and live at peace with the Protestants so that together they can fight Don Juan.

Du Plessis Mornay's argument was prescient. The impossibility of undoing the religious fission caused by the emergence of Protestantism forced Europeans to consider an alternative to the two-rules doctrine and the perfectionist view of the state. Initially they played with the idea of mini-Christendoms, each political unit enforcing its own preferred religion, be that Catholic or some version of Protestantism: *cuius regio, eius religio*. But within a relatively short time even that proved impossible. What then slowly took place, among Western European political thinkers and actors, was a fundamental rethinking of the task of the state and of the relation of the state to its citizens, not just to the religions of its citizens but to its citizens more generally.

The idea of natural rights had been current ever since the twelfth century among canon lawyers and, to a lesser extent, among philosophers, theologians, and other theorists.[7] That idea was now employed to replace the perfectionist idea of the state with what might be called the *protectionist* idea: the state is to protect citizens against violations of their

---

[6] *Discours sur la Permission de Liberte de Religion, Dicte Religions-Vrede au Pays-Bas [1559]*, translation taken from E. H. Kossman and A. F. Mellink, eds., *Texts Concerning the Revolt of the Netherlands* (Cambridge: Cambridge University Press, 1974), 163.

[7] On this see especially Brian Tierney, *The Idea of Natural Rights* (Grand Rapids: Wm. B. Eerdmans, 1997).

natural rights by their fellow citizens, and citizens are in turn to be protected against violation of their natural rights by the state.

The former of these two ideas, the idea of the state as a rights-protecting institution, received canonical formulation in the US Declaration of Independence: "We hold these truths to be self-evident that all men are ... endowed by their Creator with certain inalienable rights, that among these are life, liberty, and the pursuit of happiness. That, to secure these rights, governments are instituted among men."[8]

The latter of these two ideas, the idea of the state as a rights-honoring institution, received canonical expression in the first ten amendments to the US Constitution, known as the Bill of Rights, the aim of which was declared to be to "prevent misconstruction or abuse of [the federal government's] powers."[9] The First Amendment famously paired religious freedom with non-establishment by declaring, in its first sixteen words, "Congress shall make no law respecting an establishment of religion, or prohibiting the free exercise thereof."[10] This represents a stunning rejection of the perfectionism that went hand-in-hand with the two-rules doctrine: instead of the state being enjoined, in conjunction with the church, to seek the perfection of the citizens with respect to religion, this first article protects the people against the state with respect to the exercise of their religion.

The Bill does not explicitly declare that freedom of religious exercise and freedom from establishment are to be civil rights because they are natural rights. However, as we shall see later, there is considerable evidence for the conclusion that that is how many, if not all, of its authors were thinking.

The reference to non-establishment can seem baffling in this connection: why would it be thought that there is a natural right to freedom from establishment, if indeed that is how the authors were thinking? It helps, then, to remind ourselves of how people at the time thought of this right; subsequent jurisprudence has led us to think of it quite differently. Here is how the Pennsylvania Constitution of 1776 put it: "[N]o man ought or of right can be compelled to attend any religious worship, or erect or support

---

[8] "A Century of Lawmaking for a New Nation: U.S. Congressional Documents and Debates, 1774–1875," *Journals of the Continental Congress, Vol. 5,* found in Library of Congress, http://memory.loc.gov/cgi-bin/ampage?collId=lljc&fileName=005/lljc005 .db&recNum=94.

[9] Preamble to the *United States Bill of Rights,* 1791.

[10] First Amendment, *United States Bill of Rights,* 1791.

any place of worship, or maintain any ministry, contrary to or against, his own free will and consent."[11]

Let me summarize what I have said thus far. The religion provisions of the US Bill of Rights declare that citizens are to have the civil right to freedom of religious exercise and to freedom from establishment. The emergence of that conviction was the result of the contingent confluence of three factors: (1) the traditional understanding of church and state as two distinct institutions with different jurisdictions; (2) the breakup of the religious unity of Europe and the subsequent abandonment of the perfectionist view of the state; and (3) the employment of the idea of natural rights, long common among canon lawyers, to think of the state as a rights-protecting and rights-honoring institution, with religious freedom and non-establishment prominent among the natural rights to be honored.

THE NATURE OF RELIGIOUS FREEDOM

I now turn to the nature of religious freedom from a somewhat oblique angle. In modern liberal democracies Protestants and Catholics are not killing each other, as they were when the author of *A Discourse upon the Permission of Freedom of Religion* wrote his tract. But the relation of the state to the religions of its citizens remains the site of controversy in our liberal democracy as it does in all others. These controversies assume forms quite different from the ones they assumed previously. In former days, the controversies were almost always jurisdictional controversies between church and state; now and then, in the USA, controversies of that sort still erupt in the form of legal cases involving the so-called *ministerial exception.*[12] For the most part, however, our controversies are not jurisdictional disputes between church and state. Nonetheless, religion remains a problem for the liberal democratic state. One sometimes hears someone from the West talking to the rest of the world as if, in liberal

---

[11] *Constitution of Pennsylvania*, Article II, September 28, 1776. Until roughly twenty-five years ago, the US Supreme Court quite consistently interpreted the no-establishment clause as meaning no governmental support for any religion. It appears to me that in recent years it has been moving in the direction of interpreting it as equal treatment: the state is not to favor anyone, or discriminate against anyone, on account of his or her religion.

[12] The most recent example is the US Supreme Court case, *Hosanna-Tabor Evangelical Lutheran Church and School v. EEOC*, 565 U.S. 171 (2012).

democracies, religion no longer poses problems to the state. The truth is quite otherwise.

The question whose answer I wish to pursue for a time is: what is it about religion, and what is it about the liberal democratic state, that results in religion continuing to pose quandaries to the state, with those quandaries, and the state's handling of them, in turn causing controversies in public life? To get at this question, I will use the USA as my example. The outcome of our discussion will be an understanding of why the civil right to religious freedom has taken the particular form it has in the USA. Once we understand that, we will also realize that we must expect it to take different forms in other countries. Considerations of space require me to focus exclusively on free exercise and to say next to nothing about non-establishment. That is unfortunate because the form that the civil right to religious freedom has taken in the USA is due, in good measure, to its close connection with the proscription of establishment.

Some of the quandaries presented by religion to the liberal democratic state are definitional controversies. Is this act on the part of these citizens an exercise of their religion or is it not? If it is, does this law or policy on the part of government constitute an infringement on their free exercise of their religion? (The term that the Bill of Rights uses is not "infringing on" but "prohibiting.") Sometimes these definitional questions have no clear answer, with the result that reasonable people disagree on the answer, or prefer to give no answer.

In her contribution to an online forum on "The Politics of Religious Freedom," sponsored in 2012 by the blog, *The Immanent Frame*, Winifred Fallers Sullivan wrote:

It is a commonplace in the academic study of religion to observe that the word religion is manifestly conditioned by the history of its use and that it is deeply problematic, epistemologically and politically, to generalize across the very wide range of human cultural goings-on that are now included in this capacious term . . . It is also common to note the very specific difficulty of definition that faces interpreters and enforcers of legal instruments purporting to protect and regulate the freedom of religion.[13]

I understand Sullivan to be suggesting, though not quite saying, that the term "religion" is too vague for "freedom of religion" to pick out anything definite. We should cease and desist from talking about freedom of religion.[14]

---

[13] Winifred Fallers Sullivan, "The World That *Smith* Made," *The Immanent Frame* (blog), March 7, 2012, http://blogs.ssrc.org/tif/2012/03/07/the-world-that-smith-made/.

[14] Sullivan has a book titled *The Impossibility of Religious Freedom* (Princeton: Princeton University Press, 2007).

It is true, of course, that the term "religion" is not what might be called a "natural kind" term. It is more like the term "game" that Ludwig Wittgenstein famously discussed at length in *Philosophical Investigations*. Games, he argued, are united not by some shared essence but by family resemblances.[15] The term *religio* was used by the ancient Romans to group together certain activities whose similarities they found it important, for the purposes at hand, to take note of. The same is true for our term "religion." Though a much-used item in our English vocabulary, Sullivan holds that the term is, nonetheless, "deeply problematic" because it is "manifestly conditioned by the history of its use" and because it generalizes across a "very wide range of human cultural goings-on." Others argue that it is problematic because there are borderline cases in which we're not sure whether to call some activity a religion or not.

I do not find these arguments for the proposition that the term "religion" is deeply problematic to be compelling. In particular, I am not persuaded by the argument that we should give up talking about freedom of religion because the concept of religion is too "problematic." All terms are conditioned by the history of their use. And many terms generalize across a wide range of phenomena. The term "heavenly body" generalizes across a wide range of phenomena; that does not make its use particularly problematic. And as to the suggestion that there are borderline cases in which we're not sure whether to apply the term "religion" or not, it is certainly true that there are borderline cases, or hard cases, or grey areas. But the fact is that many if not most terms are like that – the term "raining," for example. That does not make such terms too problematic to be of any use. The term "raining" is very useful.

As to jurisprudence concerning the free exercise clause, the issue to consider here is whether there are so many cases in which it is unclear whether something is or is not a religion that the term has become useless for the purposes of the law. I judge that that is definitely not the case. In a great many cases it is perfectly obvious that something is a religion and perfectly obvious that it is being exercised. Most of these cases do not find their way into the courts precisely because they are obvious. It is the borderline cases that are likely to turn up on the dockets of courts and catch our attention. In such cases, judges have to make a judgment call that reasonable people can disagree on. You and I, unlike judges, can say, "In a way it's a religion and in a way it's not," and let it go at that. And

---

[15] Ludwig Wittgenstein, *Philosophical Investigations* [*Philosophische Untersuchungen*] (Malden: Wiley-Blackwell, 2009 [1953]).

unlike judges we can say, "In a way it's an exercise of religion and in a way it's not." Still, despite all of this, I take it to be highly significant that – contra Winifred Sullivan – distinguished legal scholar Andrew Koppelman recently observed that "American courts have had little difficulty determining which claims are religious, and the question is rarely even litigated. [Religion] has a (mostly) settled semantic meaning."[16]

If the definitional quandaries surrounding the civil right of Americans to freedom of religion turn out to be relatively insignificant, other kinds of controversies and challenges are plentiful. There may be little doubt that some law or policy on the part of government is an example of infringing on someone's exercise of his or her religion; nonetheless, it may be a point of controversy as to whether or not it is permissible. Let's see why this is.

Most of the religions present in Western liberal democracies are exercised by religious adherents who participate in communal religious rituals and engage in acts of private religious devotion. One would think that such forms of exercise would pose few quandaries to the liberal democratic state. It's easy to see that these activities count as an exercise of the religion in question, and usually it's easy to tell whether or not some law or policy infringes on their free exercise.[17] But things prove not to be as simple as one would have expected.

Here's why. The religion provisions in the First Amendment in the US Bill of Rights have the rhetorical flavor of articulating absolutes: Congress shall make *no* law respecting an establishment of religion and

---

[16] The wider context of Koppelman's observation is most illuminating and instructive. According to him, "for law's purposes, [religion's] bluntness has its advantages." He continues: "Although 'religion' is a term that resists definition, American courts have had little difficulty determining which claims are religious, and the question is rarely even litigated. It has a (mostly) settled semantic meaning." In accordance with my own invocation of Wittgenstein just now, Koppelman goes on to say that "[t]he best accounts of this meaning have held that this denotes a set of activities united only by a family resemblance, with no necessary or sufficient conditions demarcating the boundaries of the set. Timothy Macklem objects that the question of what 'religion' conventionally means is a semantic one, but the question of what beliefs are entitled to special treatment is a moral one, and it requires a moral rather than a semantic answer. But in certain contexts, 'religion' may be the most workable proxy for Integrity, which is not directly detectable by the state. All laws are bounded by the semantic meaning of their terms, which only imperfectly capture real moral salience." Just so. See Andrew Koppelman, "How Could Religious Liberty Be a Human Right?" unpublished paper presented at the Fourth International Center for Law and Religion Studies Conference on "Freedom of/for/from/within Religion: Differing Dimensions of a Common Right?" St. Hugh's College, Oxford University, September 2016.

[17] It's not always easy; it may be clear that a law places a burden on the free exercise by some people of their religion but not clear whether that burden rises to the level of infringement.

no law prohibiting the free exercise thereof. But that is not how the courts have interpreted these clauses. They have interpreted them as articulating *prima facie* rather than absolute, *ultima facie*, prohibitions on governmental action – or to view it from the other end, as articulating *prima facie* rights of citizens vis-à-vis the government rather than absolute, *ultima facie*, rights. One's *prima facie* right to the free exercise of one's religion can be outweighed by other, more weighty, *prima facie* rights. The currently operative formula, as I understand it, is that the government may substantially burden a person's exercise of his or her religion only if it can demonstrate a compelling interest in doing so and only if it uses the least restrictive means available.

Whether or not a person's *prima facie* right to free exercise is in fact outweighed in a given instance by other rights is very much a judgment call on the part of the courts. These judgment calls are invariably controversial; and liberal democracies differ considerably in how they make them. To know what the American government is actually prohibited from doing by the two religion clauses, and hence to know what our civil right to religious freedom actually comes to, one cannot just exegete the language of the clauses; one has to look at the long and complex series of often-convoluted court decisions as to which infringements on free exercise and which violations of no-establishment are permissible and which are not.

Suppose that the members of some religion have come to the conviction that they are called by God to offer the occasional child sacrifice in their communal rituals; should they be permitted to do so? It's obvious that they should not be so permitted; no liberal democracy would permit them to do so. But suppose that it is the long-established practice of some group to use certain mind-altering drugs when performing their rituals; and suppose that the government passes a law that has the effect of making this illegal in the interest of public health. Would this infringement on free exercise be permissible? The answer in this case is not obvious. In a famous case, *Employment Division v. Smith* (1990), the US Supreme Court declared that this is permissible.[18] Again, suppose that the government passes a general law forbidding alcohol in prisons whose effect is to make it impossible for prisoners to receive the wine of the Eucharist. Would this infringement on free exercise be permissible? The answer is not obvious.

[18] *Employment Division v. Smith*, 494 U.S. 872 (1990).

The quandaries posed to the government by the communal rituals and private devotions of the religions present in society pale before the quandaries posed by the fact that seldom is the exercise of a religion limited to such activities. Almost always the exercise of a religion spreads out into everyday life, sometimes in surprising ways. In order to exercise their religion as they believe it should be exercised, groups establish faith-based hospitals, adoption agencies, educational institutions, relief agencies, development agencies, housing agencies, social justice organizations, and so forth. To exercise their religion as they believe it should be exercised, they do such things as pray and wear religious garb in public and post the Ten Commandments in public places. To exercise their religion as they believe it should be exercised, they resist doing such things as serving in the military, getting vaccinated, educating their children beyond elementary school, working on Saturdays or Sundays, or employing members of other religions or of same-sex couples in their businesses and organizations.

It's easy to see that such forms of religious exercise will regularly pose quandaries to the government. Suppose the government decides that recitation by school children of the Pledge of Allegiance enhances national unity, and that such unity is important. Is it then permitted to require recitation of the Pledge by all school children even though reciting the Pledge would violate the religious convictions of Jehovah Witnesses? When the US Supreme Court was faced with this question, it determined that this was not permissible.[19]

We do not have to dredge the past for cases of this sort. The recent debates over the restrictions on free exercise of religion implicit in the Affordable Care Act in its present form provide another example of the point.

It's worth noting that the civil right to free exercise of one's religion is not unique in being a *prima facie* rather than an absolute right. The same is true, for example, of the civil right of Americans to free speech and their right to bear arms. Those opposed to one and another form of gun control sometimes talk as if any restriction on the right to bear arms is a violation of the Bill of Rights: "they're trying to take our guns away." In this case the US Supreme Court has explicitly stated that the right is not absolute.[20] The issue to be debated concerning any proposed restriction is always whether the restriction is wise and is justified all things considered.

[19] *West Virginia State Board of Education v. Barnette*, 319 U.S. 624 (1943).
[20] See, for example, *District of Columbia v. Heller*, 554 U.S. 570 (2008).

One of the lessons I want to draw from these observations is that the precise contour of the civil right of Americans to freedom of religion depends on how the courts resolve disputes over borderline applications of the terms "religion" and "free exercise" and on how they resolve disputes over when the *prima facie* right to free exercise is outweighed by other, more weighty, rights.[21] Each decision on these matters slightly alters the contour from what it was before, so that the contour is constantly changing. A second lesson I wish to draw is that we must expect that the precise contour of the civil right to freedom of religion will differ from one liberal democracy to another, as indeed it does. The contour of the civil right to freedom of religion in the United States is significantly different from the contour of the civil right to freedom of religion in France, for example.

What follows? Does it follow that there is the present-day American civil right to freedom of religion, the present-day French civil right to freedom of religion, and so forth, and that that's the end of the matter? Does it follow that there is no such thing as the natural right to free exercise of one's religion? When the US Congress passed the International Religious Freedom Act in 1998, requiring the State department to report annually on the state of religious freedom around the world and, in various ways, to promote religious freedom, was it, at bottom, just engaging in an attempt at cultural domination? Was the passage of the act nothing but power masquerading as high principle?

I understand it to be the view of some of those who posted contributions to the online forum on "the politics of religious freedom," sponsored by *The Immanent Frame*, and of a later edited volume with the same title, that these things do follow.[22] In a review essay, Daniel Philpott and Timothy Shah call these "the new critics of religious freedom." They summarize their position as follows: "Far from being universal … religious freedom is the product and the agenda of one culture in one historical period: the modern West. And in the West it should stay – and be kept under strict surveillance."[23]

---

[21] It also depends on how courts resolve disputes over the sorts of entities that are deemed to bear the right; *cf. Citizens United v. Federal Election Commission* 558 U.S. 310 (2010).

[22] The forum is titled "The Politics of Religious Freedom" and appears on the *Immanent Frame* blog, available at: http://blogs.ssrc.org/tif/the-politics-of-religious-freedom/. The contributions to the forum were later assembled and published as an edited volume: Winifred Fallers Sullivan et al., eds., *The Politics of Religious Freedom* (Chicago: University of Chicago Press, 2015).

[23] Daniel Philpott and Timothy Samuel Shah, "In Defense of Religious Freedom: New Critics of a Beleaguered Human Right," *Journal of Law and Religion* 31, no. 3 (2016): 381.

Let's assume that the Philpott and Shah interpretation is correct: there are what might be called "the new critics of religious freedom," and they affirm the position Philpott and Shah attribute to them. I would argue that the position of the "new critics" does not follow from the fact that the particular contour of the civil right to religious freedom differs from society to society and from time to time within a given society. In denying that religious freedom is a universally valid principle, the new critics presumably mean to deny that there is a natural right to religious freedom. But from the fact that certain persons have a civil right to so-and-so, nothing follows, one way or the other, as to whether or not they also have a natural right to so-and-so. Some civil rights are grounded in natural rights; some are grounded in consequentialist considerations. So too, from the fact that certain persons do not have a civil right to so-and-so nothing follows, one way or the other, as to whether or not they also lack a natural right to so-and-so.

A natural response to this observation is that, though formally correct, it's irrelevant to the topic at hand. If there is no such thing as *the* civil right to freedom of religion, but only the civil right in 2018 of Americans to freedom of religion, the civil right in 1918 of Americans to freedom of religion, the civil right in 2018 of the French to freedom of religion, and so forth, then how can these diverse civil rights all be grounded in something referred to as "*the* natural right to freedom of religion?"

Assume, for the moment, that there is a natural right to freedom of religion. My answer to the question posed is that the various contours of the civil right to freedom of religion are all to be understood as *positivizings* – to use a term that seems to have fallen out of the vocabulary of political theorists – of the natural right to freedom of religion. Each particular contour of the civil right to freedom of religion is the articulated inscription into law, the positivizing, of the natural right to freedom of religion.

There is nothing peculiar here about religion. The points I make here about freedom of religion also apply to freedom of speech. The contour of the civil right of Americans to free speech is slightly different in 2015 from what it was in 1915, and significantly different from that of the right of the English to free speech in 2015. Assuming that there is a natural right to free speech, these distinct contours of the civil right to free speech are all to be seen as positivizings of the natural right.

I have emphasized that the civil right of Americans to religious freedom arose out of a unique confluence of historical factors; from this it does not follow that a civil right to religious freedom cannot emerge from a very different set of historical factors – witness the Ottoman millet system.[24] I have likewise emphasized that the civil right of Americans to religious freedom has its own unique contours; from this it does not follow that when I, an American, urge some other government to grant religious freedom to its citizens, I am implicitly urging them to imitate the American contour. I may be doing that; if so, I am rightly to be charged with an attempt at cultural imperialism. But rather than urging them to imitate the American contour, I may simply be urging them to positivize the natural right to religious freedom in whatever way they judge best for their society.

THE FOUNDATIONS OF RELIGIOUS LIBERTY

Now we get to what the volume's editors, in the assignment they gave me, called "the foundations of religious freedom as a normative principle." Before I present my own proposal, I think it will be helpful if we take note of views about religious freedom's foundations that were in the air at the time of the American founding.

Talal Asad has argued that an important part of what happened in sixteenth- and seventeenth-century Europe as a result of the emergence and spread of Protestantism was that religion came to be identified with *belief*, and that it was widely held that what one believes is in one's own hands; it cannot be coerced by laws and sanctions or any other outside forces.[25] On the contrary, it is my own reading of the intellectual history of the time that a good many philosophers and other intellectuals not only held that belief cannot be determined by outside forces but also that it is not a product of the believer's will; it was commonly said to be determined by "evidence." That was the view of John Locke, for example, and, as we shall see, of Thomas Jefferson and James Madison.[26] But if religion is

---

[24] It appears to me that the substantial difference between the Ottoman millet system for religious freedom and the American system is that freedom of religion is paired in the US with the proscription on establishment, this now being interpreted by the courts, roughly speaking, as no preference and no discrimination by the government among citizens on the basis of their religion (or lack thereof).

[25] For my knowledge of Asad's position I am indebted to the contribution on the *Immanent Frame* blog by Elizabeth Shakman Hurd, "The Politics of Religious Freedom: Believing in Religious Freedom," *The Immanent Frame* (blog), March 1, 2012, http://blogs.ssrc.org /tif/2012/03/01/believing-in-religious-freedom/.

[26] For an elaboration of my own views about John Locke on matters of belief and episte-mology, including as they pertain to religion, see my *John Locke and the Ethics of Belief* (Cambridge and New York: Cambridge University Press, 1996).

a matter of belief, and if what one believes cannot be determined by laws and sanctions, then it is futile to pass laws aimed at prohibiting one and another form of religion. Rather than securing true religion, such laws will only encourage hypocrisy.

Speaking now as a Protestant who knows something about the relevant history, I myself doubt that very many, if any, Protestants thought that their religion consisted just of beliefs. Rather, it involved religious practices as well: participation in the public liturgy, public proclamation of the Word, reading of Scripture, private devotions. What is true is that Protestantism gave considerably more salience to beliefs than did traditional Catholicism; what they believed was, for Protestants, an important component of their religion, though never more than a component. The fact that it was an important component of their religion was enough, however, for them to argue for religious freedom on the ground of the futility of trying to control religion by law. At the same time, in an observation of Immanuel Kant I quote at length below, the philosopher astutely notes that when Protestants and others protested against their persecution during the ages of the European religious wars, they did not do so merely or primarily out of a concern to defend the integrity of their religious beliefs. "[T]he oppressed" in these conflicts, Kant rightly pointed out, "have complained not that they were hindered from adhering to their religion (for no external power can do this) *but that they were not permitted publicly to observe their ecclesiastical faith.*"[27] If the Protestants (and other religious sects) of this period thought that adherence to their religion were only a matter of interior belief and not public observance, then Kant's observation would be nonsense. While I do not often agree with Kant, in this case his observation was right on. Contrary to what Asad claims, for Protestants as well as other Christians of sixteenth- and seventeenth-century Europe, religion, and the freedom they sought for religion, was much more than a matter of mere belief.

In his "Bill for Establishing Religious Freedom," introduced to the Virginia House of Delegates on June 12, 1779, Thomas Jefferson wrote: "Well aware that the opinions and beliefs of men depend not on their own will, but follow involuntarily the evidence proposed to their minds, that Almighty God hath created the mind free and manifested his Supreme will that free it shall remain, by making it altogether insusceptible of restraint: That all attempts to influence it by temporal punishments or burthens or

---

[27] Immanuel Kant, *Religion Within the Bounds of Reason Alone*, trans. T. M. Greene and H. H. Hudson (New York: Harper & Brothers, 1960): 99–100. The emphasis is mine.

by civil incapacitations, tend only to beget habits of hypocrisy and meanness."[28] And James Madison, in his "Memorial and Remonstrance against Religious Assessments" of June 20, 1785, begins his argument for religious freedom by quoting from the Virginia Declaration of 1776, Article 16: "Religion or the duty which we owe to our Creator and the manner of discharging it, can be directed only by reason and conviction, not by force or violence." He then continues as follows: "The Religion then of everyman must be left to the conviction and conscience of every man; and it is the right of every man to exercise it as these may dictate."[29]

It is worth underscoring three points about these passages. The first is that it is remarkable how strongly Jefferson and Madison emphasized that the religious beliefs and opinions of individuals are not subject to external coercion but also – contrary to Asad again – not subject even to their own direct control. Such opinions and beliefs, in the clear words of Jefferson's Act, "depend not on their own will, but follow involuntarily the evidence proposed to their minds." For Madison, similarly, it is conviction and conscience that "dictate" the manner of religion's exercise, clearly indicating that it is not a matter of the believer's will.

Second, Jefferson and Madison were here repeating, in their own way, a line of argument that runs deep in Christian tradition, from the church fathers to the Reformers. Tertullian, the late second-century and early third-century father of Latin Christianity (*ca.* 155–*ca.* 240), thundered that Roman religious persecution was a grave crime because authentic religion cannot be coerced: "See that you do not give a reason for impious religious practice by taking away religious liberty (*libertatem religionis*) and prohibiting choice (*optione*) in divine matters, so that I may not worship as I wish (*velim*), but am forced to worship what I do not wish. No one, not even a man, will wish to receive reluctant worship."[30] In about 212, in *Ad Scapulam*, an audacious letter to a Roman official, Tertullian made the even more sweeping claim that "it is a human right (*humani iuris*) and a natural privilege (*naturalis potestatis*) that one should worship whatever

---

[28] Thomas Jefferson, "A Bill for Establishing Religious Freedom," June 12, 1779, available at: http://press-pubs.uchicago.edu/founders/documents/amendI_religions37.html.

[29] James Madison, "Memorial and Remonstrance against Religious Assessments," June 20, 1785, available at http://press-pubs.uchicago.edu/founders/documents/amendI_religion s43.html.

[30] Tertullian, *Apologeticus*, 24.6–10. For discussion of this passage and of the nature and significance of Tertullian's arguments for religious liberty more generally, see Timothy Samuel Shah, "The Roots of Religious Freedom in Early Christian Thought," in *Christianity and Freedom: Volume 1, Historical Perspectives*, 33–61.

he intends (*quod putaverit colere*); the religious practice of one person neither harms nor helps another."[31] A later church father, Lactantius (*ca.* 240–*ca.* 320), taking for granted that true devotion cannot be legislated, echoed Tertullian as well as the Hebrew prophets in arguing that God has no interest in ritual behavior that is not the expression of true devotion. "[N]othing is so much a matter of free will as religion. The worship of God . . . requires full commitment [*maximum devotionem*] and faith. For how will God love the worshipper if He Himself is not loved by him, or grant to the petitioner whatever he asks when he draws near and offers his prayer without sincerity [*ex animo*] or reverence. But they [the pagans], when they come to offer sacrifice, offer to their gods nothing from within, nothing of themselves, no innocence of mind, no reverence, no awe."[32] And in characteristically vivid language, Luther insisted to his fellow Christians that though it would be a good thing if heresy were restrained, laws and sanctions are useless for the purpose:

You say: "The temporal power is not forcing men to believe; it is simply seeing to it externally that no one deceives the people by false doctrine; but how could heretics otherwise be restrained?" Answer: This the bishops should do; it is a function entrusted to them and not to the princes. Heresy can never be restrained by force. One will have to tackle the problem in some other way, for heresy must be opposed and dealt with otherwise than with the sword. Here God's word must do the fighting. If it does not succeed, certainly the temporal power will not succeed either, even if it were to drench the world in blood. Heresy is a spiritual matter which you cannot hack to pieces with iron, consume with fire, or drown in water.[33]

Third, we have reason to believe that Jefferson and probably Madison were aware that their arguments for religious freedom were not Enlightenment or Protestant inventions but had deep roots in the Christian tradition. Timothy Shah points out that Jefferson's discussion of religious freedom in Query XVII in his *Notes on the State of Virginia* included a handwritten reference to Tertullian's early third-century text, *Ad*

---

[31] Tertullian, *Ad Scapulam*, chap. II, 1–2. Again, for discussion, see Shah, "Roots of Religious Freedom in Early Christian Thought," 33–61.

[32] Lactantius, *Divine Institutes*, v.20. I thank Robert Wilken for the translation. For an alternate translation, see Lactantius, "Of the Vanity and Crimes, Impious Superstitions, and of the Tortures of the Christians," *Divine Institutes*, Chap. XX, *Christian Classics Ethereal Library*, www.ccel.org/ccel/schaff/anf07.iii.ii.v.xx.html.

[33] Martin Luther, "Temporal Authority: To What Extent It Should Be Obeyed," in *From Irenaeus to Grotius: A Sourcebook in Christian Political Thought: 100–1625*, eds. Oliver O'Donovan and Joan Lockwood O'Donovan (Grand Rapids: Wm. B. Eerdmans, 1999), 502–503. The tract comes from early in Luther's career. In later writings he affirmed the traditional two-rules doctrine.

Scapulam, which, as I just noted, contains a sweeping argument for religious freedom.[34] It is in Query XVII that Jefferson offers the famous declaration: "Our rulers can have authority over such natural rights only as we have submitted to them. The rights of conscience we never submitted, we could not submit. We are answerable for them to our God. The legitimate powers of government extend to such acts only as are injurious to others. But it does me no injury for my neighbor to say there are twenty gods, or no god. It neither picks my pocket nor breaks my leg." Shah observes that at this very point in his own private copy of the *Notes* Jefferson includes a handwritten annotation: the remarkable passage from *Ad Scapulam* declaring that religious freedom is a matter of "human right" and "natural power" and that one person's religious practice "neither harms nor helps another."[35] We do not know precisely when Jefferson became aware of the Tertullian passage, but whenever he did the early church father's striking anticipations of some of Jefferson's own liberal assertions about religious freedom must have astounded him.[36]

Let's move on now to all those who had a hand in drafting, redrafting, and ratifying the US Bill of Rights. Why did this large group, spread across the original thirteen states, hold that in the newly formed United States of America there should be a constitutionally defined and protected civil right to the free exercise of religion? In the Bill itself they don't say. Evidently they thought it wasn't necessary to say. Perhaps some of them were thinking along the same lines as Luther, Jefferson, and Madison; Madison, after all, was the original drafter of the Bill of Rights, drawing heavily on the Virginia Declaration of Rights.[37] I think it almost certain, however, that most of them, if not all of them, had another argument in mind as well, namely, a natural rights argument. Notice that Jefferson, in Query XVII in his 1782 *Notes on the State of Virginia*, speaks of "rights of conscience" as "natural rights." Natural rights language also appears in Jefferson's 1779 "Act for Establishing Religious Freedom" and Madison's 1785 "Memorial and Remonstrance," and there is even a hint of a natural

---

[34] Shah, "The Roots of Religious Freedom in Early Christian Thought," 57.

[35] Thomas Jefferson, *Notes on the State of Virginia*, ed. Frank Shuffleton (New York: Penguin Books, 1999), Query XVII, p. 165. Jefferson's annotation referencing Tertullian is noted and discussed on p. 321, n. 193. Also see Shah, "The Roots of Religious Freedom in Early Christian Thought," 57.

[36] For discussion of Jefferson's use of the Tertullian passage, see Shah, "Roots of Religious Freedom in Early Christian Thought," 33–61.

[37] I exclude Lactantius at this point, since what he says can only be a matter of "free will" is not belief but full devotion and faith; I judge that by "full devotion and faith" Lactantius did not have in mind just belief.

rights argument in Tertullian's *Ad Scapulam* (which must be part of why Jefferson found that text so arresting).[38] At the same time, Luther does not explicitly frame his argument for the civil right to religious freedom in terms of a natural rights argument, nor was du Plessis Mornay's argument a natural rights argument. Nonetheless, I think it almost certain that, whatever other considerations those who had a hand in drafting and ratifying the religion provisions of the First Amendment may have had in mind, most if not all of them believed that there should be a civil right to free exercise of religion because there is a natural right to free exercise of religion. I base my inference that this is how they were thinking on the fact that this line of thought was very much in the air at the time, even apart from the writings of Jefferson and Madison.

For example, after the issuing of the Declaration of Independence from England in 1776, all of the newly formed states composed constitutions in which citizens were declared to have a civil right to free exercise of their religion. With the exception of the New York State constitution, all of these constitutions base that declaration more or less explicitly on the claim or assumption that there is a natural right to the free exercise of religion. The most explicit and elaborate of these declarations is that of the Pennsylvania Constitution of 1776. I have already quoted part of it; let me now quote it in its entirety:

That all men have a natural and unalienable right to worship Almighty God according to the dictates of their own consciences and understanding. And that no man ought or of right can be compelled to attend any religious worship, or erect or support any place of worship, or maintain any ministry, contrary to, or against, his own free will and consent: Nor can any man, who acknowledges the being of a God, be justly deprived or abridged of any civil right as a citizen, on account of his religious sentiments or peculiar mode of religious worship: And that no authority can or ought to be vested in, or assumed by any power whatever, that shall in any case interfere with, or in any manner control, the right of conscience in the free exercise of religious worship.[39]

---

[38] Jefferson's "Bill for Establishing Religious Freedom" concludes that "we are free to declare, and do declare, that the rights hereby asserted are of the natural rights of mankind, and that if any act shall be hereafter passed to repeal the present, or to narrow its operation, such act will be an infringement of natural right." Madison's "Memorial and Remonstrance" concludes that the equal right of the free exercise of religion is "held by the same tenure with all our other rights," and that "[i]f we recur to its origin, it is equally the gift of nature..." (para. 15).

[39] *Pennsylvania Constitution 1776*, Article II. I discuss the religion clauses in these various state constitutions in some detail in Nicholas Wolterstorff, *Understanding Liberal Democracy: Essays in Political Philosophy*, ed. Terence Cuneo (Oxford: Oxford University Press, 2012), 333–341. I believe my view that natural rights arguments played an important role in the early American decision to give religious freedom constitutional

In our day and age, we who believe that the civil right to religious freedom is of fundamental importance can obviously not restrict ourselves to reciting these words from the Pennsylvania Constitution in defense of our conviction. Many of our fellow citizens hold that there are no natural rights, only rights bestowed by laws, social practices, and speech actions. Of those who agree that there are natural rights, many hold that there is no god, almighty or otherwise; and so, of course, there is no natural right to worship almighty God. Some of those who hold that there is no god regard religion as a menacing relic of irrational primitive ways of thinking, and see no more reason to think that there is a natural right to the free exercise of one's religion than there is a natural right, say, to the practice of quack medicine. Yet others hold that it is a mistake to single out religion for special treatment. The right to religious *belief* should be treated as a species of the right to liberty of conscience, and the right to religious *exercise* should be treated as a species, say, of the right to freedom of speech and assembly.

IN DEFENSE OF THE CLAIM THAT THERE IS A NATURAL RIGHT TO FREE EXERCISE OF ONE'S RELIGION

I come now to the hard part, namely, my own attempt to defend the claim that there is a natural right to free exercise of one's religion. Looking back over previous writings of mine I notice, to my surprise, that this is something I have never hitherto attempted.[40]

It's worth noting, before we set out, that the right to free exercise of one's religion is, strictly speaking, a permission-right rather than a claim-right. That is, it is the right to be permitted to do something rather than the right to be treated a certain way by others. Of course, corresponding to the permission-right to exercise one's religion freely is the claim-right, with respect to others, that they not interfere with one's exercise of one's religion.[41]

To establish that there is a natural right to religious freedom it is not sufficient to argue, as does John Finnis in *Natural Law and Natural*

---

protection is consistent with the story told in John Witte and Joel A. Nichols, *Religion and the American Constitutional Experiment* (New York: Oxford University Press, 2016).

[40] This isn't quite true. I gave a very brief formulation of a Christian case for religious freedom in Timothy Samuel Shah, *Religious Freedom: Why Now? Defending an Embattled Human Right* (Princeton: Witherspoon Institute, 2012).

[41] I distinguish between permission-rights and claim-rights in *Justice: Rights and Wrongs* (Princeton: Princeton University Press, 2010), 137–139.

Rights, that religion is a great good in our lives.[42] For one thing, if religion is just a great good in our lives, then it's possible that situations would arise in which a society would judge that the form religious exercise has taken in that society is so destructive of the common good that it should be severely restricted. More important for our purposes here is the fact that one cannot pull the rabbit of rights out of a hat that contains only life-goods. It would be a great good in my life if the Rijksmuseum in Amsterdam gave me Rembrandt's *The Jewish Bride* to hang on my living room wall, along with a round-the-clock security force to stand guard. But I don't have a right to their doing that; the Rijksmuseum is not wronging me by not doing that. On the other hand, the brusque reply to my inquiry, by the receptionist in the health service, is but a small harm in my life. Nonetheless, I have a right to her not answering me in that way. There are some great life-goods to which one has no right and some small life-goods to which one does have a right.

To account for why it is that we have a right to certain life-goods and not to others we have to introduce into the picture something other than life-goods.[43] I hold that that something is the worth or dignity of the rights-holder. You have a right to the life-good of my treating you a certain way just in case I would not treat you as befits your worth or dignity.

On this occasion let me assume, without argument, that rights are indeed grounded in the worth or dignity of the rights-holder. Let me also assume, without argument, that there are natural rights, that is, rights not conferred on rights-holders by laws, social practices, or speech actions. I know, of course, that both of these assumptions are highly

---

[42] John Finnis, *Natural Law and Natural Rights* (New York: Oxford University Press, 1980).

[43] Finnis and others introduce the idea of *basicness*, and hold that what differentiates between those goods to which one has a right and those to which one does not is that the former are basic. Those who think along these lines typically say that aesthetic delight is a basic good. I hold that no matter how much aesthetic delight my having a Rembrandt hanging on my living room wall would give me, I do not have a right to the Rijksmuseum offering me one of their Rembrandts. In his contribution to this volume, Christopher Tollefsen takes issue with my line of argument against the natural-law and basic-goods approach of Finnis and other natural law theorists. He objects to my *Jewish Bride* example by observing that the Rijksmuseum has ownership rights to *The Jewish Bride*. True. But that doesn't gainsay the fact that I don't have a right to the great good of their giving me the painting; it just explains it. I also do not have a right to the great good of my well-to-do neighbor offering me a new car to replace my old one.

controversial. I have defended them at length elsewhere;[44] if I did so here, we would never get to the topic at hand.

I invite those readers who are dubious about these two assumptions to adopt a hypothetical attitude toward the argument that follows. Suppose there are natural rights, and suppose they are grounded in the worth or dignity of the rights-bearer. What reason might there be for holding that among our natural rights there is a natural right to free exercise of one's religion?

For my purposes here, I need some account of religion. Rather than devising and offering my own account, let me adapt the account Thomas Nagel offers of what he calls "the religious temperament" in his essay, "Secular Philosophy and the Religious Temperament."[45]

The religious temperament, says Nagel, is the belief "that there is some kind of all-encompassing mind or spiritual principle in addition to the minds of individual human beings and other creatures – and that this mind or spirit is the foundation of the existence of the universe, of the natural order, of value, and of our existence, nature, and purpose." The religious temperament is the "belief in such a conception of the universe, and the incorporation of that belief into one's conception of oneself and one's life." The religious temperament addresses "the question of how a human individual can live in harmony with the universe."[46]

Nagel identifies the religious temperament with belief of a certain sort. That seems to me a mistake; there's more to the religious temperament than belief. More important for my purposes here, however, is that, however we analyze the religious temperament, a person's religion should not be identified with her religious temperament; her religion is her religious temperament along with her way of giving expression to that temperament in her way of living, including her religious practices. A person's religion is her particular way of living "in harmony with the universe." The beliefs comprised within her religious temperament will often be implicit within her way of living and within her religious practices, rather than consciously entertained.

I judge that everything covered by this account would naturally be called a religion; whether it is also the case that everything that would

---

[44] See Wolterstorff, *Justice.*

[45] Thomas Nagel, "Secular Philosophy and the Religious Temperament," in *Secular Philosophy and the Religious Temperament* (Oxford: Oxford University Press, 2010), 3–18.

[46] Nagel, "Secular Philosophy and the Religious Temperament," 5.

naturally be called a religion is covered by this account is perhaps less clear. But whatever one concludes on that matter will not make a difference to my argument. Opponents of religion often speak as if religion were some quirky add-on to what science and common sense tell us, a relic of the childhood of the human race. On Nagel's description, and according to many of the contributions to this volume, religion is anything but that. Our question now is whether, and in what way, depriving a person of the freedom to practice her religion constitutes treating her in a way that does not befit her worth.

Most present-day thinkers who hold both that there are natural rights and that these are grounded in the worth or dignity of those who possess the rights are of the view that what imparts to the rights-holder the relevant dignity is the capacity for rational agency – that is, the capacity to act for reasons and not just from causes. Some hold the more specific view that the dignity in question is grounded in the capacity for *normative* agency – that is, in the capacity to perform an action for the reason that one judges it to be a good or obligatory thing for one to do. This is the view defended, for example, by James Griffin in his book, *On Human Rights*; he urges his readers to "see human rights as protections of our normative agency."[47]

I have argued in a number of places that this account of the dignity that grounds natural rights is inadequate.[48] Obviously it does not account for the dignity of those human beings who are not capable of functioning as persons and who, accordingly, lack the capacity for normative agency – infants, for example, and those in a permanent coma or suffering from the final stages of Alzheimer's disease. More relevant to our purposes here, it also fails to account for many of the rights possessed by those who are capable of fully functioning as persons. It does not account for the right not to have one's privacy invaded. Even if the person who invades one's privacy does nothing with what he learns other than enjoy it at home, thus in no way impairing one's agency, one has nonetheless been wronged. Neither does it account, in my judgment, for the right not to be raped or castrated. Rape and castration do indeed constitute an impairment of one's normative agency; but I find it grotesque to suggest that this is what is fundamentally wrong with rape and castration. Rape and castration are gross violations of a person's bodily integrity.

---

[47] James Griffin, *On Human Rights* (Oxford: Oxford University Press, 2008), 33.
[48] See, in particular, Wolterstorff, *Justice*.

Rational and normative agency do indeed give to those creatures who possess such agency great worth and dignity. But what is indicated by the examples I have given, along with a good many others, is that what gives to those human beings who are capable of functioning as persons the full panoply of their natural rights has to be more than just the capacity for rational and normative agency. To account for their natural rights we need a richer account of what it is to be a human person.[49]

Here is not the place to present an account of the human person rich enough to account for the dignity that grounds the full panoply of natural rights.[50] Let me confine myself to singling out two aspects of the human person, beyond the capacities for rational and normative agency, that seem to me directly relevant to the natural right to free exercise of one's religion.[51]

1. To be a full-fledged human person is to have *the capacity to interpret reality and one's place therein*. Some of these interpretations happen naturally, as in perception and introspection. I just naturally interpret what is presented to me as the sun rising above the horizon. In our capacity for such interpretations we are similar to some of the animals. But to be a human person is also to have the capacity for interpretations that are not given with our nature and that go far beyond perceptual and introspective interpretation. We interpret what is happening as the gods being angry, as the far-flung effects of the Big Bang, as the dire effects of libertarianism spreading among the populace, and so forth. Interpretations such as these go vastly beyond the sorts of perceptual and introspective interpretation that are built into our nature.

As for myself, I cannot imagine what it would be like not to have the capacity for such interpretations of reality and of my place therein; it is a pervasive and fundamental part of my life, so pervasive and fundamental that I hardly ever take note of it. I take it for granted. But when I do stand back and take note of it, I find it remarkable, amazing. If any of the non-human animals have this capacity, or something like it, they have it only to a minimal degree.

---

[49] The bearers of the natural right to religious freedom are those human beings who are capable of functioning as persons. A human being in a permanent coma cannot exercise her religion; accordingly, the issue of whether she has the permission-right to do so freely does not arise.

[50] I have attempted that in Chapter 8 of *Understanding Liberal Democracy*, 201–226.

[51] The thought comes to mind that perhaps these two aspects should be incorporated into a more comprehensive understanding of rational and normative agency. I think not. Neither one is, strictly speaking, a capacity for agency.

2. To be a full-fledged human person is to have *the capacity to form what I shall call a valorized identity*. What I mean by the "valorized identity" of a person consists of the relative importance that the person assigns to the states and events in her own life: to her various beliefs, her various commitments, her plans for action, her memories, her attachments to persons, animals, and objects, and so forth. We say such things as, "This commitment is more important to me than any other; I cannot imagine giving it up. It is fundamental to who I am." Thereby one is verbalizing one aspect of one's valorized identity. One's valorized identity consists not of the importance one assigns to things outside oneself but, to repeat, to the various states and events in one's own life.

As for myself, I cannot imagine what it would be like not to have the capacity to form my own valorized identity; it, too, is a pervasive and fundamental part of my life, so much so that I hardly ever take note of it. I take it for granted. But when I do stand back and take note of it, I find it remarkable, amazing. If any of the non-human animals have this capacity, or something like it, they have it only to a minimal degree.

I have stressed that these capacities are amazing. On account of possessing these capacities, in addition to those of rational and normative agency, and yet others that I have not mentioned, human persons are remarkable, amazing. So far as we know, no other creatures that dwell on earth possess these capacities to anywhere near the same degree, if, indeed, they possess them at all. But not only are human persons remarkable on account of possessing these capacities; they have great worth on account of possessing these capacities. On account of possessing these capacities human persons are precious. They have multifaceted dignity. They are to be prized. Something of great worth is lost when these capacities are destroyed or lost.

Religions represent a remarkable exercise of these two capacities, along, of course, with the capacities for rational and normative agency. To see this, recall Nagel's description of the religious temperament. The religious temperament is the belief "that there is some kind of all-encompassing mind or spiritual principle in addition to the minds of individual human beings and other creatures – and that this mind or spirit is the foundation of the existence of the universe, of the natural order, of value, and of our existence, nature, and purpose." It is the "belief in such a conception of the universe and the incorporation of that belief into one's conception of oneself and one's life." I suggested that the religious temperament includes such a belief but more, and that, in turn, a person's religion includes more than her religious temperament. It includes the expression of her religious temperament in her way of life.

It's obvious that religion, so understood, is a manifestation of the two capacities I identified, along with those of rational and moral agency. The belief that there is some kind of all-encompassing mind or spirit that is the foundation of the existence of the universe, of value, and of our own existence, nature, and purpose, is obviously an exercise of the remarkable and precious capacity for interpretation that I took note of above. And giving expression to that belief in one's life and practice is perforce an exercise of the remarkable and precious capacity for forming a valorized identity.

If one holds, as I do, that these two remarkable and precious capacities give to those creatures who possess them great worth, as do the capacities for rational and normative agency, then one will have a *prima facie* reason to refrain from stifling or restraining the exercise of these capacities and for resisting the attempt of others to do so. That *prima facie* reason will be especially weighty when we are dealing with interpretations and valorizations as deep and fundamental as those of religion. Forbidding the religious person the free exercise of his or her religion is a deep violation of their personhood.

Now consider Richard Dawkins, Daniel Dennett, and others of their sort: people who embrace a secular alternative to religion that is a manifestation of the same capacities of which religion is a manifestation and to which they are as ardently attached as is any religious adherent to his or her religion. The argument I have given leads to the conclusion that their embrace and exercise of that alternative should receive the same protection in law as does the free exercise of religion. I dare say that some will regard this implication as a *reductio ad absurdum* of my argument. I regard it as an implication that should be embraced. Making it illegal for Dennett to express and practice his secular alternative to religion would be a violation of his personhood in the same way that making it illegal for me to express and practice my religion would be a violation of my personhood.

ADDITIONAL SHAPING UP?

Rather often one hears it said that a fundamental principle of liberal democracy is that the state is to be neutral between one religion and another and between religion and non-religion. It is debatable whether this is true, strictly speaking, even for the religions embraced by the citizenry of some liberal democracy. But certainly it is not true for religions in general. Earlier I noted that the religious fracturing of Europe and the subsequent wars of religion eventually forced the emergence in the West of a new form of state, liberal democracy; the old familiar perfectionist form of state was no longer possible. But the fracturing of religion also required a certain kind of religion. There had to be mutual accommodation: accommodation of the state to religion and accommodation of religion to the state. Richard Rorty remarks in one place that the "happy, Jeffersonian compromise that the Enlightenment reached with the religious ... consists in privatizing religion – keeping it out of" the public square.[52] That is clearly not correct; religion in liberal democracies has not, in general, been privatized. But the larger point, that certain forms of religion are incompatible with the liberal democratic state, is undeniable. Were I to develop this point, I would look at the version of Islam that Sayyid Qutb propounded in the commentary that he wrote on the Koran titled *In the Shade of the Koran*.[53] In good measure, Qutb shaped his view of Islam in conscious opposition to the "hideous schizophrenia" between religion and life that he saw as characteristic of Western liberal democracies.[54]

But rather than developing that point, let me bring this essay to a close by calling attention to the presence in liberal democracies of voices that find the structural accommodations of religion to liberal democracy inadequate. These voices hold that religions endanger peace, justice, and the stability of liberal democracy even if they have accommodated themselves to the structural principles of liberal democracy and even if religious people do accept those infringements on the free exercise of religion that the courts judge permissible. These voices call for a further shaping up on the part of religion. They do not propose that laws be enacted to bring about this further shaping up; they hope that moral suasion and intellectual argumentation will do the work. Let me order these voices, starting with those that call for the most limited form of shaping up and concluding with those that call for the most radical form.

John Rawls and his followers hold that it is acceptable for citizens to employ reasons drawn from their own particular religion when debating significant political issues in public and when making decisions on those issues; but if they do, they must "stand ready" to offer reasons for their

---

[52] Richard Rorty, *Philosophy and Social Hope* (London: Penguin Books, 1999), 169.

[53] Qutb was an Egyptian intellectual who spent some time as a student in the United States, in Greeley, Colorado, and then returned to Egypt. After being imprisoned for more than ten years by the Egyptian government, he was executed in 1966.

[54] Paul Berman, "The Philosopher of Islamic Terror," *New York Times*, March 23, 2003, www.nytimes.com/2003/03/23/magazine/the-philosopher-of-islamic-terror.html.

favored policy positions that are drawn from what Rawls calls "public reason." What exactly Rawls means by "public reason" is the subject of a literature that is by now vast; for our purposes here it will be sufficient to say that public reason, as Rawls understands it, consists of principles, drawn from the governing idea of liberal democracy, for the just distribution of benefits and burdens, civil rights and duties, by the state and other public institutions. Rawls holds that those who affirm liberal democracy, rather than merely putting up with it, implicitly embrace such principles, whatever might be their religious disagreements. Accordingly, appealing to such principles when debating and deciding significant political issues enhances the stability of a liberal democratic society; resting content with employing our diverse religious reasons endangers that stability.

In all liberal democratic societies there are religious people who affirm liberal democracy but are not in the habit of debating and deciding political issues on the basis of reasons drawn from public reason. It is their habit to debate and decide political issues on the basis of reasons drawn from their own particular religion. For some, this is not just a habit; they believe that this is what they *ought* to do. Many of those who are in the habit of debating and deciding political issues on the basis of reasons drawn from their own particular religion are not familiar with any other way of debating and deciding such issues; this is the way they learned in their families and in their religious institutions. They don't know how to appeal to public reason. Satisfying the Rawlsian injunction requires of them that they shape up by acquiring the ability and the willingness to debate and decide significant political issues on the basis of reasons drawn from public reason.

Richard Rorty urges a more stringent form of shaping up. In an unpublished essay consisting of remarks he made upon receiving the Eckhart Prize and titled "Religion after Onto-Theology: Reflections on Vattimo's *Belief*," he asserts that ecclesiastical institutions, "despite all the good they do – despite all the comfort they provide to those in need or in despair – are dangerous to the health of democratic societies, so that it would be best for them eventually to wither away." The dangers posed to democracy by institutionalized religion are "particularly evident," he says, in present-day United States, where "Christian fundamentalists whose support has become indispensable to right-wing American politicians are undermining the secularist, Jeffersonian, tradition in American culture."[55] The danger

---

[55] Richard Rorty, "Religion After Onto-Theology: Reflections on Vattimo's *Belief*" (unpublished draft of remarks to be given upon receiving the Meister Eckhart Prize in Berlin, November 9, 2001).

fundamentalists pose to our liberal democracy is not that they are threatening to overthrow the US government; the danger they pose is their support of legislation restricting behavior that other groups in society regard as completely acceptable – abortion and homosexual activity, for example.

The danger can only be averted by religion shaping up so that it becomes entirely personal and private. The religion of one's inner life can be of whatever form and intensity one wishes; no harm there. It is when religion leaves the sanctuary of the inner life and tries to influence the state and other social institutions in accord with its convictions that it endangers liberal democracy. To repeat the passage from Rorty quoted earlier: the happy "Jeffersonian compromise that the Enlightenment reached with the religious … consists in privatizing religion – keeping it out of" the public square.

From the discussions of John Hick and his allies on religious pluralism, one finds a yet more radical proposal for the shaping up of religion. Both Rawls and Rorty propose setting bounds to religion as we find it: religion must shape up so that it no longer appeals exclusively to its own resources when debating and deciding significant political issues, or so that it no longer speaks on institutional matters in general. Within those bounds, religion is free to take whatever form it wishes. In his well-known book, *Interpretation of Religion*,[56] John Hick argues that particularist religions, rather than learning to live within bounds, should reinterpret their particularisms so that they are no longer exclusivist.

Hick holds that any "axial" or "post axial" religion that does not accord equal religious significance to all other such religions perforce harbors within itself the threat of coercion and violence, thereby being a menace to peace.[57] To cite just one example: as long as Christianity harbors a supersessionist attitude toward Judaism, there can be no enduring peace between the two religions. The solution is for each axial and post-axial religion to regard all such religions as alternative ways of engaging The Real, with none of them giving us the literal truth of the matter, and for each to concede that all are equally successful in achieving salvation for their adherents.

---

[56] John Hick, *Interpretation of Religion* (London: Palgrave Macmillan, 2004).

[57] The period extending from 800 to 200 BCE has come be to called "the axial age" in world religious history. Axial religions are those that emerged during that period, for example, Judaism, Buddhism, and Confucianism. Christianity, and Islam are post-axial religions. Hick regards pre-axial religions as inferior to axial and post-axial religions.

A fourth, and yet more radical, version of the line of thought that I am delineating says that particular religion, whatever its form, content, or self-understanding, poses a danger to the liberal democratic society. It must wither away. Rather than shaping up by living within the bounds of public reason, by living within the bounds of the inner life, or by interpreting its particularism in non-exclusivist fashion, particularist religions, on this fourth view, must shape up by transmuting themselves into non-particularist religion.

This is what Jacques Derrida proposed in some of his late writings. In his reflections on "the return of religion" that he sensed to be occurring at the time, Derrida undertook "a program of analysis for the forms of evil perpetrated in the four corners of the world 'in the name of religion.'"[58] His analysis led him to the conclusion that violence is the inevitable consequence of what he calls "determinate" religion. The violence may or may not be what those of us would call "violence" who are less given to hyperbole than was Derrida; it might just be what we would call "coercion."

The solution is for determinate religion to be transmuted into "religion without religion." Take an example. A structural feature typical of the religions that interested Derrida is the messianic structure: adherents of the religion look forward to a day when justice and peace shall reign. "Religion without religion" would be religion in which all determinate content has been abstracted from such messianic anticipation, leaving only the pure structure. Such religion would be "structural messianism," "messianism without content," or simply, "the messianic." A condition of the elimination of political "violence" is the transmutation of present-day religions into a religion in which messianism is purely structural; determinate messianisms necessarily harbor the threat of "war."[59]

The great grey eminence behind this way of thinking is Immanuel Kant, though it must at once be added that the religion Kant proposed was by no means a religion of pure structure and no content; it was a *determinate* religion without being a *particular* religion. Kant explicitly shared with the other thinkers we have canvassed here the conviction that particular religion is a danger to peace, justice, and the stability of liberal democracy. If "eternal peace" is to arrive, particularist religion must wither away.

---

[58] James K. A. Smith, "Determined Violence: Derrida's Structural Religion," *The Journal of Religion* 78 (1998): 197. The quoted phrases that follow are all taken from Smith's article.

[59] Smith, "Determined Violence," 197–212.

Kant did not consider whether reining it in would be sufficient, nor did he consider the possibility of religions reinterpreting their particularisms so that they were no longer exclusivist. Since what Kant says about the menace of particularist religion is as vivid as Kant's writing ever gets, let me quote him at some length:

> The so-called religious wars which have so often shaken the world and bespattered it with blood, have never been anything but wrangles over ecclesiastical faith; and the oppressed have complained not that they were hindered from adhering to their religion (for no external power can do this) but that they were not permitted publicly to observe their ecclesiastical faith.
>
> Now when, as usually happens, a church proclaims itself to be the one church universal (even though it is based upon faith in a special revelation, which, being historical, can never be required of everyone), he who refuses to acknowledge its (peculiar) ecclesiastical faith is called by it an *unbeliever* and is hated wholeheartedly; he who diverges therefrom only in part (in non-essentials) is called *heterodox* and is at least shunned as a source of infection. But he who avows [allegiance to] this church and yet diverges from it on essentials of its faith (namely, regarding the practices connected with it), is called, especially if he spreads abroad his false belief, a *heretic*, and, as a rebel, such a man is held more culpable than a foreign foe, is expelled from the church with an anathema ... and is given over to all the gods of hell. The exclusive correctness of belief in matters of ecclesiastical faith claimed by the church's teachers or heads is called *orthodoxy*.[60]

The solution to these evils of religion is the withering away of "positive" religions and their replacement with a purely rational religion, that is, a religion whose content is grounded in reason alone and not in the particularities of revelation, mania, or tradition. As humankind progresses toward full rationality, this is the religion that it will increasingly embrace. Such religion, though determinate in content, will nonetheless not be a *particular* religion, since it will enjoy universal acceptance; it will therefore not be a danger to peace and justice. The coming of such religion, shared by all on account of their common rationality, will finally bring about "the world of an eternal peace."[61]

RESPONSE

The line of thought that I have just now been highlighting runs deep in the mentality of modernity. Religions pose a danger to peace, justice, and the

---

[60] Kant, *Religion Within the Bounds of Reason Alone*, 99–100.
[61] Kant, *Religion Within the Bounds of Reason Alone*, 76.

stability of the liberal democratic polity. They must, accordingly, shape up in ways that go beyond what is required for living within the structure of liberal democracy and beyond acceptance of those infringements on free exercise that the courts judge permissible.

My response is that I see no prospect whatsoever of religion in general disappearing, nor of all determinate religions disappearing to be replaced by some religion of pure structure, nor of all particular religions disappearing to be replaced by a single determinate religion, nor of all particular and determinate religions reinterpreting themselves so that they are no longer exclusivist, nor of all particular and determinate religions becoming privatized. That religion is often a danger to peace, justice, and the stability of our liberal democratic society is beyond doubt. I think we have no choice but to deal with those dangers in *ad hoc* fashion when and where they arise. There is no prospect of averting them all in advance.

In the above list of what I saw no prospect of happening, I did not mention that I saw no prospect of all adherents of particular and determinate religions appealing to Rawlsian public reason in debating and deciding political issues, not even if it be in addition to appealing to the resources of their own particular religion. One of the best statements of the present state of the public reason debate is a recent essay by my commentator in this volume, Stephen Macedo, titled "Why Public Reason? Citizens' Reasons and the Constitution of the Public Sphere." In his opening paragraph, Macedo observes that among the objections to the public reason position launched by critics is, "In a deeply religious and pluralistic society the proposed norm seems unlikely to be accepted."[62] As Macedo well knows, I am one of the critics of the public reason proposal; and I do indeed see no chance of citizens in general conforming to the Rawlsian norm.

But rather than pressing that point farther, I want to close this essay by posing an objection to the public reason proposal that flows directly from my defense of there being a natural right to religious freedom. It's an objection that I have raised in previous writings; in the literature on these matters it has come to be called "the integralist objection."[63]

---

[62] Stephen Macedo, "Why Public Reason? Citizens' Reasons and the Constitution of the Public Sphere," published electronically August 23, 2010, doi:10.2139/ssrn.1664085.

[63] Apparently Nancy L. Rosenblum and Philip L. Quinn were the first to use the term "integralist" for this objection and they did so independently of each other. See Quinn's article, "Can Good Christians Be Good Liberals?" in *God and the Ethics of*

Consider a religious person of the following sort. He favors liberal democracy. He endorses, to quote Rawls, the "ideas of citizens as free and equal persons and of society as a fair system of cooperation over time." He has different views than Rawls does as to the implications of those ideas; but he affirms the ideas as stated. He is willing to offer reasons for the policies he favors, and he is willing to listen with open mind to criticisms of those reasons coming from others.

As to the reasons he offers, he regards himself as obligated to ground his political reflections and arguments on the resources of his own religion (plus relevant non-normative factual knowledge) *and on those resources alone* – when these speak to the matter at hand. The conviction that he is so obligated belongs to his religion; he sees fidelity to God as requiring this of him. To use Rawls' language: a component in his comprehensive religious doctrine is that he uses the resources of his comprehensive doctrine *and only those resources* in deliberating, debating, and voting on some political issue (plus the relevant non-normative factual knowledge). Acting in accord with that conviction is an important part of exercising his particular form of religion.[64] Given the understanding of religion that I adopted from Nagel, an understanding according to which religion is a comprehensive interpretation of reality rather than some sort of add-on, we should not be surprised that there would be religious people of this sort.

If the person in question is a Christian, he believes that his thinking about political issues should be shaped by the Old Testament prophets and by the teachings of Jesus – not by some political conception of justice, be it that which Rawls favors or some other. He recognizes that he and the Rawlsian are likely to agree on a fairly large number of policies. He's happy about that convergence whenever it occurs. He's even willing to inhabit the mind of the other person sufficiently to point out to him or her unnoticed implications of their way of thinking, especially when those implications coincide with his own convictions. But he himself is not going to think about political issues in Rawlsian terms. For him, thinking that way is unfaithful to God; and fidelity to God overrides all other considerations.

Belief, eds. Andrew Dole and Andrew Chignell (Cambridge: Cambridge University Press, 2005): 274, n. 12.

[64] In Christopher Eberle, *Religious Conviction in Liberal Politics* (Cambridge: Cambridge University Press, 2002). Eberle poses the integralist objection with a somewhat different type of religious believer in mind.

He knows that lots of people in his society, including a good many of his co-religionists, regard him as deeply misguided. They call him a "fundamentalist."[65] Whenever people go beyond referring to him with this pejorative language and give him a reason for thinking that he is deeply misguided, he listens carefully and with open mind to what they say. So far, he has not been convinced. Having listened carefully and openly to their objections without being convinced, he is now entitled to his convictions; there's nothing more that can be asked of him. It can't be asked of him that he decide to change his views. Nobody can do that.

Let's give this sort of religious person a name. Let's call him a barthian – lower case "b."[66] The attitude of the barthian toward employing public reason in thinking and talking about political issues is very much like the attitude of the Kantian toward thinking about moral and political issues along utilitarian lines: the Kantian regards that way of thinking as deeply misguided. He refuses to think in those terms about moral and political issues.

I think the barthian should feel free to think and argue as he believes he should. In doing so, he is exercising his natural right to religious freedom. Of course, nobody proposes that there be a law forbidding him from acting thus; everybody agrees that he should have the civil right to act thus. But beyond that, I fail to see that he is in any way violating the spirit, the ethos, the governing idea, of liberal democracy.

That's my view. But what does public reason liberalism of the Rawlsian variety say about the barthian? The answer to that question proves to be less obvious than one would have thought; in fact, the answer that I think the Rawlsian should give has an air of paradox about it.

Nowhere, that I know of, does Rawls consider the sort of religious citizen that I have invited the reader to imagine. So far as I can tell, he just assumes that no reasonable comprehensive doctrine – in his sense of

---

[65] In John Rawls, "The Idea of Public Reason Revisited," *University of Chicago Law Review* 64 (1997): 765–807. Rawls writes the following on pages 805–806: "Of course, fundamentalist religious doctrines and autocratic and dictatorial rulers will reject the idea of public reason and deliberative democracy. They will say that democracy leads to a culture contrary to their religion, or denies the values that only autocratic or dictatorial rule can secure. They assert that the religiously true, or the philosophically true, overrides the politically reasonable." The sort of person I have in mind is not Rawls's fundamentalist. He is in favor of liberal democracy, and he is opposed to autocracy and dictatorship. He realizes that liberal democracy may lead to a culture contrary to his religion. But he is willing to live with that fact.

[66] I call him a "barthian" on the grounds that it's likely the great twentieth-century theologian Karl Barth would have held such a position.

"reasonable" – would include the conviction that one should reason about political issues *only* in terms of one's own comprehensive doctrine. But suppose a Rawlsian were asked the question: what should a religious citizen of this sort do? What would the Rawlsian say? Would he say that if the barthian is unable or unwilling to renounce that troublesome component in his comprehensive doctrine, he should refrain from advocating in public for political positions and refrain from voting? Possibly some Rawlsians would say this. But given the Rawlsian position as a whole, I don't think that's what they should say.

The "should" in the imperative proposed by public reason liberals is a *prima facie* "should"; public reason liberals recognize that citizens may find themselves in situations in which they see themselves as having, and do in fact have, other *prima facie* obligations that conflict with and outweigh their obligation to conform to the public reason imperative. So I think what the public reason liberal *should* say to the barthian is that, since he regards himself as having an overriding duty to God to employ only the resources of his religion in thinking about political issues (plus whatever non-normative factual knowledge is relevant), and since he is entitled to that conviction, that's what he should do. He should not follow the public reason imperative. Perhaps others should. But he should not. Given his comprehensive doctrine, it is his *ultima facie* duty *not* to conform to the public reason imperative – unless his comprehensive doctrine has nothing to say on the matter at hand. Public reason liberalism leaves the barthian free to use religious reasons and only religious reasons in public debate on political issues and in deciding how to vote.

10

Religious Liberty, Human Dignity, and Human Goods

Christopher Tollefsen

An adequate account of the nature and value of religious liberty plausibly depends upon an adequate account of the nature and value of religion. As regards the question of the nature of religion, I understand religion as the attempt (a) to find out the truth about whatever transcendent source of meaning there might or might not be; and (b) to bring one's judgments, choices, and actions into harmony with that source. As I will discuss below, this may be done in various ways.

As regards the question of value, I hold that religion understood in the way just outlined is a *basic good*, a fundamental aspect of human flourishing. As such, it provides a basic reason for action for all human agents by offering them something of intrinsic benefit. Moreover, religion can provide a *common good* for the cooperative activities of groups of persons who act for its sake together. It is the individual and collective pursuit of this good that is, or should be, protected by the universal right to religious liberty. For religious liberty is at its core a right not to be coerced in that pursuit, but a right that also opens out onto wider horizons of freedom.

Because I frame my account of the value of religious liberty in terms of the *good* of religion, it might seem to differ from an analysis that rests upon claims about human dignity, such as that offered by Nicholas Wolterstorff in his contribution to this volume. Indeed, Wolterstorff believes not only that the two accounts differ, but that a goods-based account *cannot* explain and justify the right to religious liberty. By contrast, I think the two accounts are related, and that a dignity-based account absent a grounding in basic human goods is itself insufficient to ground a right to religious liberty in the right way.

In this paper, I sketch the goods-based account and its relationship to questions of human dignity. I then raise and respond to Wolterstorff's objections to what I argue is the priority of the good in this domain.

RELIGION AS BASIC HUMAN GOOD

Is religion as defined above a human good? Is that good basic? And is it a common good? It is a good if the pursuit of religion gives us intelligible reason for action by promising something desirable; it is a basic good if its desirability is neither instrumental nor reducible to the desirability of some other good; and it is a common good if its goodness provides shared reasons for multiple agents, who can thus, if they choose, cooperate in the pursuit of this good.

As regards the first question, it does seem that religion, understood as I have defined it, provides reasons for action for rational agents. Responding to a wide variety of prompts, some involving the grandeur and regularity of nature, some involving tragedy and the mysteriousness of death, and yet others involving the exceptional nature of human cognition and volition, human beings attempt to come to grips with their place in the larger cosmos and are led almost inevitably to the question of whether that place must be understood in relation to some greater-than-human source of meaning, value, and, ultimately, existence. And however that question is answered, human beings find it additionally desirable to make peace *with* that source, or to make their peace with their belief that there is no such source.

So religion really is a good: it is desirable, and provides reasons for action. Are those reasons basic? That question must first be answered by asking whether religion is merely instrumental in nature. Some human beings clearly do treat the good as instrumental, seeking peace with their deities in order to manipulate them and thus to control nature and human destiny for the sake, say, of some this-worldly interest, such as the material prosperity of their family or community. But the fact that this good can be pursued for instrumental reasons does not show that it is not basic, and indeed it does not seem unintelligible that an agent could pursue religious truth, and harmony with the object of that truth, simply for its own sake, because she recognizes that such awareness and harmony are good for their own sake. Put another way, the opportunity to achieve such harmony presents itself to reasonable agents as intrinsically desirable.

Nor does this good seem to be an intrinsic aspect of, or intrinsically reducible to, some other good. The good that religion offers clearly *involves* knowledge, but as Joseph Boyle points out, the devil knows a lot about God. So the good of religion cannot straightforwardly be identified with, or reduced to, the good of knowledge.[1]

The good of religion is similar to some other reflexive goods for it involves an attempt to achieve a form of harmony that depends upon an act of will on our own part.[2] Various forms of harmony for whose sake we can act are all apprehended practically as offering us benefit. We would prefer to be persons whose practical dimensions – reason, will, emotion – were not pulling in competing directions; and we would prefer to be persons whose relationships with others likewise did not pull us in competing directions.[3] A relationship of harmony with a possible transcendent source of goodness is similarly desirable. But it is not merely a form of personal integrity, though perhaps it requires and contributes to such integrity. Nor is it merely a form of friendship, for the equality characteristic of friendship does not seem possible here, though perhaps something like it is.

So religion seems to be a human good and a basic human good, not needing, for its intelligibility and desirability, to be pursued for the sake of some other good, and not reducible to any other good. But religion is also clearly a common good, shared and shareable among all beings with the common personal nature that human beings possess. Human persons who recognize this good as giving themselves basic reasons for action recognize that this very good likewise gives reasons for action for other agents *like* themselves. They recognize that other human persons will be benefitted by successful pursuit of this good. And they recognize that good as providing reasons for *shared* action and thus as providing a matrix for genuine cooperation.

Do atheists simply fail to pursue this good at all? I do not think that this follows straightforwardly. Some atheists may be understood to be pursuing this good if they have indeed carried out an honest search for the

---

[1] Joseph Boyle, "The Place of Religion in the Practical Reasoning of Individuals and Groups," *American Journal of Jurisprudence* 43 (1998): 1–24.

[2] Unlike, for example, the good of life, which can be realized and enjoyed even when we are, because of disability or disease, stage of development, or even sleep, incapable of actively willing anything.

[3] For an account of the goodness of various forms of harmony, including personal integrity and sociality, see chapter 5 of Christopher Tollefsen, *Lying and Christian Ethics* (New York: Cambridge University Press, 2014), 102–128.

transcendent source of meaning and goodness in the universe, if they have judged that such a source does not exist, and if they have existentially come to terms with this perceived absence. Nevertheless, it is a matter of public reason, and not private revelation, that even such atheists' pursuit of this good is deficient *if* it is a matter of public reason that there is, indeed, such a transcendent source of goodness, for their existential decisions are, in such a case, founded on a significant error. I'll assume the antecedent is the case, and refer to this transcendent source of meaning and goodness as "God."[4]

Similarly, while those who do recognize the existence of God, and who pursue harmony with that being, are so far forth better off as regards this good than those who deny the existence of God, here too there is surely room for qualitative discrimination. Some conceptions of God's nature, and of what is required to be in harmony with God, are incompatible with others; not all can be correct. Just as being in harmony with your friend requires correctly understanding her character, so does being in full harmony with the divine require correct understanding of *its* character. And just as being in harmony with your friend requires recognition and understanding of her attempts to communicate with you, so does being in harmony with the divine require recognition and understanding of *its* attempts to communicate; some putative revelations of this being are incompatible with others, and not all can be correct. Those who have rightly identified some alleged communication as true revelation of the divine are thus capacitated for a more adequate relationship with the divine.

Finally, the shared nature of this good, the importance of making correct judgments and choices as regards this good's object, God, and many instances of possible divine communication, suggest that the attempt to pursue such a harmony with God should be carried out in a cooperative way, by agents bound together (a) by shared beliefs about the existence, nature, and revelation of such a being and about the proper way to relate to that being; (b) by common traditions, for example, of worship; and (c) often by quasi-political structures of authority as well as (d) by more clearly nonpolitical forms of inspired authority. Moreover, such agents typically believe, rightly I think, that the demands made upon them by the need for harmony with God encompass large parts of their lives. Such agents thus

---

[4] I take this conclusion to be supported by evidence and argument, and more reasonable than its contrary. See, for one excellent example of argument leading to this conclusion: Germain Grisez, *God: Philosophical Preface to Faith* (South Bend: St. Augustine's Press, 2004).

typically work together not just to maintain belief and worship but also more broadly to structure their lives around activities, such as charitable endeavors, that put them in the right relationship with the divine.

So not just religion – comprising at a minimum, belief and worship, and also, typically, other activities – but *cooperative, collective, or communal* religion comprising the belief, worship, and action of believers *together* is essential to the well-being of human persons. As so essential, the state rightly takes *both a positive and negative interest* in this good.

That interest is *negative* insofar as a reasonable state recognizes that, to be authentic, religious belief, worship, etc., cannot be coerced – this is the essential core of the right. So the reasonable political community protects, by law, freedom of religious worship, and abstains from establishment of an in any way coercive form of state worship; from religious tests; and the like. Similarly, the reasonable political community prevents, to the degree possible, private coercion, protecting, for example, the right of exit from religious institutions and prohibiting more than disciplinary forms of punishment within religious institutions.

The interest is *positive* in that the reasonable political community would look benevolently on its citizens' reasonable attempts at piety and would aid them in ways that were fair and non-coercive. Here, the right to religious freedom goes beyond its core in ways that are nevertheless internal to that right's logic. One example may help. Policies favoring school choice for parents wishing to send their children to parochial schools, or even to educate them using a religious homeschooling curriculum, are not demanded by the principle of immunity from coercion that is at the core of the right to religious liberty. However, a reasonable political community should, I think, make an effort to support these forms of faith-friendly schooling.

DIGNITY AND RELIGIOUS FREEDOM

The preceding has been but the barest sketch of a justification for religious freedom. But the notion of human dignity has received not a word. Is the sketch compatible with a justification for a right to religious freedom that makes reference to human dignity? I believe it is.

Dignity is an excellence of some sort, and human dignity in the central sense is the excellence of being a person with the capacity for reasoned choice.[5] But the horizon of all such reasoned choice is the framework of

---

[5] For an elaboration of this account, see Christopher Tollefsen, "A Catholic Perspective on Human Dignity," in *Human Dignity in Bioethics: From Worldviews to the Public Square,*

the basic human goods that give persons their reasons for their actions. So dignity is intrinsically linked to the goods whose protection sets the parameters of our most fundamental rights; goods that include not just religion, but also life, work, friendship, and marriage, to name a few. Failures to acknowledge, or, worse, deliberate attempts to disrespect any one of those goods are thus additionally a failure to acknowledge and respect human dignity.

Indeed, the link between human dignity and human goods is essential to providing adequate content to the norm that human dignity should be protected. Human dignity is sometimes understood *merely* in terms of the human capacity to be self-determining, with no further account of the orientation of these capacities to what is genuinely fulfilling for agents with these capacities. What must be protected is simply the bare capacity, *however it is exercised*, so long as it does not coercively interfere with the exercise of that same capacity by others. Protection of human dignity might thus require, for example, protecting the right to *choose death*, in physician-assisted suicide or euthanasia. By recognizing that the horizon of authentic self-determination is in goods such as human life, however, a goods-based approach has within it resources to resist appeals to human dignity that fail to distinguish between what is life-affirming, and thus truly protective of human dignity, and what is life-denying and opposed to human dignity.

Because these basic human goods are, like the capacities of freedom and reason, also in a sense "excellent" we may likewise refer to the "dignity" of these goods: the dignity of human life, the dignity of marriage, the dignity of religion, and so forth. This extension of the language of dignity is helpful. Articulating the nature of and need for a right to religious liberty should work with the idea that there is dignity both in the person and in the good, for if there is no good to be found in religious belief and practice, then religious liberty will begin to look like a (perhaps unnecessary) concession to crazy, or at least seriously misguided, people whose capacity for self-determination has gone astray and is perhaps not being genuinely exercised at all. That attitude is not a promising one for the promotion of religious liberty.[6]

---

eds. Stephen Dilley and Nathan J. Palpant (New York: Routledge, 2013), 49–61. See also Patrick Lee and Robert P. George, "The Nature and Basis of Human Dignity," *Ratio Juris* 21 (2008): 173–193.

[6] One might wonder whether even the *toleration* of religion espoused by Brian Leiter is stable in face of the belief that religious believers are guilty of a "culpable failure of epistemic warrant." See Brian Leiter, *Why Tolerate Religion?* (Princeton: Princeton

The notion of dignity can also help us to articulate some important dimensions of the right to religious liberty. The dignity of persons, and of the goods of persons, grounds and generates certain ethical and political requirements and tasks.[7] The requirement aspect is captured in phrases such as "a violation of my dignity," or "an offense against the dignity of ..." In such cases, requirements imposed on others to protect or respect our human dignity have gone unfulfilled. That there should be robust respect for religious liberty in a society is a requirement – both ethical and political – that is entailed by the dignity of the person and by the dignity of religion.

The task aspect is captured in phrases such as "beneath my dignity," or "beneath us," to indicate that some person or group has failed to live up to the demands that their own dignity makes on them. Where religion is concerned, the ethical task of dignity includes the demand that agents pursuing that good not use their pursuit as a disguise for an agenda of political domination or manipulation of others, among other things. It includes the demand that they recognize and respect that which in other people also involves pursuit of the same good, even if in ways that may be perceived to be erroneous. And it includes the demand that they not be "blindly" faithful, so utterly unquestioning as to allow their faith to induce them toward violations and offenses against *other* basic goods. Such limits of religious liberty are internal to the dignity of religion when viewed in its task aspect.

The political task of dignity includes the creation and maintenance of a society in which this ethical standpoint is fostered, and in which grievous violations of it are checked for the sake of the common good, including the religious liberty of others. While the content of this task obviously overlaps to a considerable extent with the requirements of the dignity of the person and of religion, the task concept should be understood from the perspective of a society asking the practical question: what sort of a people should we *be*? The requirement concept can be understood in terms of that same society asking: what do we *owe* to others, including our own citizens?

University Press, 2012), 81; and, in response, Christopher O. Tollefsen, "Are We Guilty for Our Religious Beliefs?" *Public Discourse* (Witherspoon Institute), March 14, 2013, www.thepublicdiscourse.com/2013/03/8072/.

[7] I discuss this feature of dignity in Christopher Tollefsen, "The Dignity of Marriage," in *Understanding Human Dignity*, ed. Christopher McCrudden (Oxford: Oxford University Press, 2013), 483–499.

So the language of dignity is fundamentally tied, in my view, to the language of human goods. Each complements the other in the attempt to deliberate about the right to religious freedom and in the attempt to articulate the results of these deliberations. However, Wolterstorff offers an account of religious liberty that, while focusing on human dignity, lacks the complementary concern for human goods. In fact, Wolterstorff explicitly criticizes accounts of religious liberty that are based on attentiveness to the basic human good of religion. In the remainder of this paper, I will address Wolterstorff's account and respond to his challenges.

WOLTERSTORFF'S DIGNITY-BASED ACCOUNT

Wolterstorff's positive account of the right to religious freedom emerges from two claims of philosophical anthropology that he makes. The first is: "To be a full-fledged human person is to have *the capacity to interpret reality and one's place therein.*" The second is: "To be a full-fledged human person is to have *the capacity to form ... a valorized identity,*" which involves a prioritizing of the commitments that are constitutive of the agent's practical self.[8] Religion, for Wolterstorff, is a "remarkable exercise of these two capacities," along with a third, the capacity for "rational and normative agency." Accordingly, Wolterstorff concludes,

If one holds, as I do, that these two remarkable and precious capacities give to those creatures who possess them great worth, as do the capacities for rational and normative agency, then one will have a *prima facie* reason to refrain from stifling or restraining the exercise of these capacities and for resisting the attempts of others to do so.[9]

The account is dignity-based because, in a way similar to the claims I have made above, Wolterstorff sees dignity as the excellence of beings that possess these capacities. But unlike me, he does not link the actualization of these capacities to the goods to which they are oriented. Thus the success of "interpretation" on Wolterstorff's account does not seem strongly linked to its orientation to truth. And his use of capacities tied to religion does not seem specially oriented toward apprehension of the truth about whatever transcendent source of meaning there might be and the realization of genuine harmony with it.

---

[8] Nicholas Wolterstorff, "Why There Is a Natural Right to Religious Freedom," this volume, p. 219 (emphasis original).

[9] Ibid., 220.

Why is this failure important? Consider two contexts in which dignity is invoked, that of end of life care and that of religious liberty. Does an account of human dignity that orients the exercise of our special and "amazing" capacities toward genuine human goods make a difference? I suggested earlier that it does: when mere dignity is invoked, then there is little ground on which to challenge the choice to end one's life. But when dignity and autonomous self-constitution are linked to the good of human life as a real fulfillment of human persons, then it becomes possible to deny that a choice to end one's own life deserves the protection that life-affirming choices do.

The implications for religious liberty are also important. Consider Wolterstorff's extension of the right of religious liberty to the self-proclaimed "New Atheists" such as Daniel Dennett and Richard Dawkins. Wolterstorff's account requires, he argues, "the same protection in law as does the free exercise of religion."[10] We agree on this; it would be wrong, for example, for the New Atheists to be legally prohibited from holding their beliefs, publishing their books, or otherwise expressing their views. Yet my account justifies drawing a distinction between Dawkins's and Dennett's *deficient* exercise of their dignity-bearing capacities, and the fuller and more authentic exercise of those capacities by those who recognize a theistic creator who deserves public acknowledgement and respect. Accordingly, I can, as it seems to me that Wolterstorff cannot, hold that traditional forms of theistic worship should be accorded certain public forms of positive respect and promotion that atheism need not and should not be accorded. It is open to me to argue, for example, that the creator should be explicitly acknowledged by a nation, as, for example, in its Constitution or by means of its public holidays; or that religious worshippers should be provided accommodations from otherwise just laws that would inhibit their religious pursuits *even when it would be unreasonable to extend the same or equivalent accommodations to nonbelievers such as Dennett and Dawkins.*

So, there are differences between an account that rests only on dignity, and one that incorporates a concern for the genuine human goods to which our dignity-grounding capacities are intrinsically oriented. But it is not just that Wolterstorff fails to do justice to this orientation toward basic goods. Worse, he denies it any role whatsoever in his account of religious liberty. And so it is to his arguments *against* goods-based accounts of the right to religious freedom that I now turn.

---

[10] Ibid.

WOLTERSTORFF'S OBJECTIONS TO GOODS-BASED ACCOUNTS

Wolterstorff makes three objections against goods-based accounts. The first is that "if religion is just a great good in our lives, then it's possible that situations would arise in which a society would judge that the form religious exercise has taken in that society is so destructive of the common good that it should be severely restricted."[11] The objection here seems to rely on a deeper sense – perhaps akin to the view of Ronald Dworkin – that goods-based considerations must be weighed or proportioned relative to one another, while dignity-based and rights-based considerations function as trumps.[12]

Here, as elsewhere, it is necessary to distinguish between coercion that is intrinsically directed against the exercise of religion and coercion that is only incidentally so. I believe that the seeds of this distinction are present in the Second Vatican Council's Declaration on Religious Liberty, *Dignitatis Humanae*:

This Vatican Council declares that human persons have the right to religious freedom. This kind of freedom consists in this: that all human beings ought to be immune from coercion whether by individuals or social groups and by every kind of human power, so that in religious matters no-one is compelled to act against his conscience or impelled from acting according to his or her conscience, whether acting publicly or privately, alone or in association with others, within due limits.[13]

Here the Council acknowledges in its final clause what it seems that Wolterstorff denies, namely, that for the sake of the common good, religious exercise can indeed be coercively restricted. Does this denude the right of any absolute force it might claim? I do not think so, for the first part of the explication – "that in religious matters no-one is compelled to act against his conscience" – is I think absolute, and is violated whenever an attempt is made to coerce an agent into doing that which he believes *he ought never to do*: foreswear his faith, swear allegiance to false gods, commit acts he believes his faith condemns as intrinsically evil, etc. For one cannot so coerce contrary to conscience without intending that the

---

[11] Ibid., 215.

[12] See Ronald Dworkin, *Taking Rights Seriously* (Cambridge: Harvard University Press, 1978). Dworkin is extensively and helpfully criticized on these matters in Paul Yowell, "A Critical Examination of Dworkin's Theory of Rights," *American Journal of Jurisprudence* 93 (2007): 93–137.

[13] Second Vatican Council, Article 2, "Declaration on Religious Freedom," *Dignitatis Humanae* (1965).

agent act directly contrary to the basic goods of religion, truth, and personal integrity.

But restricting an agent from doing what he takes himself in conscience to have a positive, even a very stringently positive, obligation to do need not require the intention that he act contrary to his conscience. For positive obligations are never absolute, and a legal command that agents desist from, for example, stirring up religious hatred, or killing infidels, or ... can be followed precisely in consequence of a conscientious judgment that the law has now given one an authoritative and overriding reason to stop doing what one otherwise had – one thought – good reason to do.[14]

But if the command can be *followed* for this reason, then it need not be *given* with the intent that the agent violate her conscience. And if the agent persists contrary to the legal command, she may be coercively restrained, again with no intention that she violate her conscience. And this seems exactly right: the immunity from coercion that the good of religion demands is absolute only in one dimension, and though it is important and stringent in its other dimension, it can nevertheless indeed be overridden for the sake of the common good. So, this objection of Wolterstorff's does not work.

Wolterstorff's second objection is that:

> ... one cannot pull the rabbit of rights out of a hat that contains only life-goods. It would be a great good in my life if the Rijksmuseum in Amsterdam gave me Rembrandt's *The Jewish Bride* to hang on my living room wall, along with a round-the-clock security force to stand guard. But I don't have a right to their doing that; the Rijksmuseum is not wronging me by not doing that.[15]

But this argument is multiply flawed. *The Jewish Bride* is a single piece of property, and so the right that Wolterstorff proposes for our consideration would be a right of ownership or entitlement against the museum and all others to possess that piece of property and have authority over its treatment. But the right to religious freedom is nothing at all like that right. Religious freedom is not a bit of material property capable of being owned by anyone; and the right claimed to it is first and foremost an immunity from coercion, as I have noted, not a right of entitlement.

Third, Wolterstorff argues that there can be violations of right that involve little harm. But he claims that this would be odd were rights based

---

[14] For further discussion of this point, see Christopher Tollefsen, "Conscience, Religion and the State," *American Journal of Jurisprudence* 54 (2009): 93–116.
[15] Wolterstorff, this volume, p. 215.

in goods. Infringement of a right on such an account must be understood as a form of harm, and were the harm minor, it would seem there was no right (or at least no weighty right). Wolterstorff gives an example of what he has in mind: "the brusque reply to my inquiry, by the receptionist . . . is but a small harm in my life. Nonetheless, I have a right to her not answering me in that way."[16]

But the good at stake here is great, even if the harm to it is only minor and hence the violation of the right relatively insignificant. We should therefore distinguish between the *importance* of a good or right, and the *degree or significance of its violation*. Even important goods and rights may be violated to minor or insignificant degrees. In fact, the goods-based approach seems explanatory: because the good is basic, the right is such that it extends to cover even minor violations. But a violation can be real though minor precisely because the good is real and basic but susceptible to varying degrees of damage, from negligible all the way to very grave.

So I find Wolterstorff's objections unconvincing. A goods-based account of religious liberty is defensible and, as I have argued, essential. Nevertheless, it is worth stressing an ecumenical point about our two approaches. As I hope my remarks have communicated, I join Wolterstorff in seeing great value in an approach to religious liberty that stresses human dignity. Such an approach is genuinely complementary to my own and is of great philosophical, religious, and political value.

CONCLUSION

Those who, like myself, believe that religious liberty is currently under grave threat worldwide will likewise agree that the task of providing an adequate justification for religious freedom is only part of the solution to the problem of religious persecution and intolerance, and perhaps only a minor part. But intellectual error can have enormous consequences. In much of the world, error about the *implications* of religion's claims to truth has generated corresponding errors about the permissibility of coerced conversion and religious cleansing. In the West, a different set of errors predicated on the *denial* of religious truth is in part responsible for a growing belief that religion deserves no special favor or protections in a society. In both cultural contexts, clarity is needed about the nature of

---

[16] Ibid.

the good of religion and the moral implications of acknowledging that goodness. *Only* an approach that begins with a discourse on the goodness of religion will do; but such an approach leads naturally, and is not at all inconsistent with, a complementary discourse on the importance of human dignity. The timeliness of such discourses can hardly be overstated.[17]

[17] My thanks to Jack Friedman for extremely helpful comments on an earlier draft of this essay.

11

Human Rights, Public Reason, and American Democracy

A Response to Nicholas Wolterstorff

Stephen Macedo

In "Why There Is a Natural Right to Religious Freedom," Nicholas Wolterstorff provides an interesting account of the human capacities that underlie the religious temperament and on this basis he defends the idea of a "natural right to the free exercise of one's religion." His account is even broader, in fact, and speaks to the philosophical foundations of human rights more widely. He adds, for good measure, some criticisms of the idea (and practice) of "public reason" in democratic deliberation. The argument is subtle and revealing throughout, but I believe, and will argue here, that the practice of human rights does not rest on a particular philosophical foundation. In addition, and relatedly, I offer a friendlier view of public reason and argue, contra Wolterstorff, that it is well established in American political practice.

PHILOSOPHICAL FOUNDATIONS FOR HUMAN RIGHTS?

Wolterstorff argues that humans' special dignity is grounded in two capacities distinctive to normal persons. "To be a full-fledged human person is," first, "to have *the capacity to interpret reality and one's place therein.*" In addition, it is "to have *the capacity to form*" what he calls a "*valorized identity.*"[1] This is the capacity to assign special importance to some of one's own projects and commitments, and to some of the "states and events" in our lives. In religious experience, we manifest these capacities in forming a conception of the universe and our place in it.

---

[1] Nicholas Wolterstorff, "Why There Is a Natural Right to Religious Freedom," this volume, pp. 218–219 (emphasis original).

Wolterstorff rightly emphasizes that if we understand the religious temperament properly we will see that religious freedom extends equally to those whose worldviews do not include a God or a supreme being.

Wolterstorff distinguishes his account of the foundations of human dignity and natural rights from James Griffin's alternative view that human dignity is grounded in our capacity for "rational agency."[2] If I understand him correctly, Wolterstorff asserts, on the basis of his preferred account of universal human capacities, that there are certain natural rights that are held by all human beings as such. These include freedom of speech and the free exercise of one's religious beliefs.

Granting that Wolterstorff's abstract assertions concerning the foundations of human rights are of philosophical interest, we can nevertheless ask: how much work do such assertions do when it comes to human rights in practice? There, what is most important is getting governments to respect basic human rights, while acknowledging that people's religious and philosophical traditions differ very deeply. Offering a particular philosophical grounding that purports to universality could get in the way of securing a reasonable consensus based on a variety of grounds that can be invoked to justify basic human rights. This is something that those who framed the Universal Declaration on Human Rights recognized. The preamble of the Universal Declaration begins by affirming the "inherent dignity and the equal and inalienable rights of all members of the human family," but the Declaration does not elaborate upon the deeper foundations of that dignity. That is sensible, for it is unlikely that representatives of the world's peoples – including Confucians, Buddhists, Muslims, etc. – would ever come to an agreement on the philosophical account of Wolterstorff, Griffin, or someone else.[3]

In thinking about universal human rights, in the sense of the important global practice that has now been institutionalized, we must begin with the fact of great human diversity. Our aim is to justify the practice and secure basic standards in the face of this great diversity. Notwithstanding this challenge, many basic human rights claims are very widely affirmed: their violation is widely recognized as a matter of

---

[2] See James Griffin, *On Human Rights* (Oxford: Oxford University Press, 2008), as described in Wolterstorff, this volume, p. 217.

[3] This is an insight nicely articulated by Amy Gutmann in her introduction to Michael Ignatieff's *Human Rights as Politics and Idolatry* (Princeton: Princeton University Press, 2001), vii–xxviii. See also Mary Ann Glendon, *A World Made New: Eleanor Roosevelt and the Universal Declaration of Human Rights* (New York: Random House, 2002).

international concern.[4] The practice of human rights has been successful in shaping global discourse, and in generating a widely understood and accepted global language for calling attention to abuses by governments.[5] This success has occurred in part because the focus has been on generating widely acceptable, reasonable standards, in the absence of an agreed account of philosophical foundations. International human rights represent a central component of an emerging global public reason.[6]

Insofar as this is true, Wolterstorff's account of human nature, while of philosophical interest, may not be especially helpful when it comes to understanding human rights in practice.

Nevertheless, Wolterstorff adds an important consideration that nudges the discussion back in the direction of political practice. He correctly insists that the shape of our civil or constitutional rights to religious freedom, or speech, etc., varies from one country to another. The Europeans call this a "margin of discretion." Wolterstorff puts the point very nicely: "the various contours of the civil right to freedom of religion are all to be understood as *positivizings* ... of the natural right to freedom of religion. Each particular contour of the civil right to freedom of religion is the articulated inscription into law, the positivizing, of the natural right to freedom of religion."[7]

This is quite important. Our "natural rights" prior to the existence of government are vague: their content and contours open to disagreement and contestation. John Locke imagined, for example, that in a "state of nature" prior to government, individuals could acquire private property rights in particular tracts of unoccupied land by working that land and "mixing their labor" with it, subject to two "provisos." Locke's account appeals, implicitly at least, to a sense of fairness: so long as there is "enough and as good" land available to others in a state of nature, for them to also labor upon, then it seems reasonable enough for an individual to assert a right to the land whose productivity is improved by his labor.[8]

---

[4] See the very valuable account in Charles R. Beitz, *The Idea of Human Rights* (Princeton: Princeton University Press, 2009).

[5] See Beth Simmons, *Mobilizing for Human Rights: International Law in Domestic Politics* (Cambridge: Cambridge University Press, 2009).

[6] For valuable reflections, see Beitz, *The Idea of Human Rights*; and also Joshua Cohen, "Minimalism About Human Rights: The Most We Can Hope For?" *The Journal of Political Philosophy* 12 (2004): 190–213.

[7] Wolterstorff, this volume, p. 207 (emphasis original).

[8] See John Locke, *Second Treatise Concerning Civil Government*, ed. C. B. Macpherson (Indianapolis: Hackett, 1980 [1690]).

And yet, in practice, as Locke recognized, when some assert rights to particular tracts of land and others see their interests at stake, rights claims are bound to give rise to disagreements and conflicts that admit of more than one reasonable answer. In modern circumstances, in particular, in which so many of the claims we advance against one another depend upon complex institutions and practices that are created and sustained by collective action, conflicts frequently require the weighing of many values and judgments about likely consequences.

The vagueness of natural rights is among the things that make public authority necessary.[9] The capacity of shared legitimate political institutions to authoritatively specify the contours of our fundamental rights, subject to ongoing disputation, is one of the great achievements of legitimate governments. Legitimate governments are able to announce and secure assent to public understandings of fundamental rights and entitlements that become the common authoritative terms of citizens' interactions: their community's shared law. In democratic societies, debating and deliberating on the shape of our basic rights, laws, and policies, is a project that all citizens properly participate in. They ought to do so on the basis of "common sense" reasons and evidence that are accessible to all.

PUBLIC REASON AND ITS CRITICS

I want to focus in the remainder of these remarks on the last two sections of Wolterstorff's chapter. I want, specifically, to defend the idea of public reason associated with the writings of John Rawls and others (myself included[10]), and which Wolterstorff criticizes, for reasons I find puzzling and also misguided.

The idea of public reason has been elaborated philosophically, but it articulates a norm discernible in our political and constitutional practice in the United States and elsewhere. This is the idea that citizens in a diverse democracy have an obligation to one another when deciding important political questions – including the shape and contours of our basic rights – to cite reasons and evidence that can be shared by citizens with a variety of ultimate religious and philosophical commitments. Citizens should cite

---

[9] As the philosopher Immanuel Kant most clearly recognized.

[10] I elaborate this idea in "In Defense of Liberal Public Reason: Are Abortion and Slavery Hard Cases?" *American Journal of Jurisprudence* 42 (1997): 1–29; and also in *Liberal Virtues: Citizenship, Virtue, and Community in Liberal Constitutionalism* (Oxford: Clarendon Press, 1990).

reasons and evidence whose force does not depend on accepting one particular religious worldview or a particular philosophical account of human nature. Citizens deliberating on important political questions in advance of deciding should instead draw on the shared ideals of our common political and constitutional tradition, along with reasons, interests, and evidence that appeal to common sense. When seeking to help define our basic rights in one way or another, they should look for ground that we can share.

Let us note one further important concession to religious believers. Rawls says that citizens are free to present reasons that come from their religious perspectives in public political discussions. But, in explaining and justifying their vote to others, they should *also* be able, in due course, to cite justifying reasons that can be appreciated by those citizens who do not share their religious point of view.[11]

This all seems very commonsensical to me and, indeed, most Americans seem to agree not only as a general matter but with specific reference to, for example, the role of religious beliefs in shaping one's vote on gay marriage. I will come back to this below.

Wolterstorff disagrees, at least somewhat. He is concerned that there are people in our political community who do not share these principles, and he is concerned that "Rawlsian" liberals have inappropriate expectations that those people should "shape up" and conduct themselves in accordance with public reason when deliberating upon and deciding important questions in politics. Wolterstorff seems especially concerned to defend those who are not in the habit of debating and deciding political issues on the basis of public reasons but rather do so on the basis of reasons drawn from their own particular religious tradition alone. He seems to agree with Rawlsians when it comes to establishing factual claims; religious people ought to be guided by reliable sources and common methods. But when it comes to moral or ethical beliefs about right and wrong, Wolterstorff argues that citizens ought not to be criticized if they form and defend politically relevant moral convictions based entirely on their religious beliefs. When it comes to making and defending their moral judgments in politics, in other words, religious citizens have no important political obligations to think beyond the views that they formed in church.

---

[11] John Rawls, "The Idea of Public Reason Revisited," *University of Chicago Law Review* 67 (1997): 765–807.

I disagree with Wolterstorff. The citizens I have just described, and who he is concerned to defend, are violating one important norm of citizenship in a diverse community: that we should look for common ground when we are justifying the law that will be imposed on all. It is not enough to say, "I believe the Bible says such and such, and that's the end of it." Saying that when deliberating on the law that applies to all is a form of religious zealotry: it is uncivil and it violates an important norm of citizenship. We should care about whether the law can be justified to all, and that is possible to ascertain in practice only if we all agree to adopt a public point of view when engaged in shared deliberation on the law. That is the only practically feasible way of acting on the concern that the law should be justified to all reasonable fellow citizens.

Citizens who refuse to deliberate about law on the basis of common interests and reasons fail to exemplify one important virtue of citizenship, though they may nevertheless exemplify other political virtues. If these citizens are pursuing a liberal democratic agenda, such as fighting for civil rights or fighting for the rights of the poor, as Wolterstorff hypothesizes, then they are doing good work. If their political positions are, as in these instances, justified by public reasons and it simply turns out that they are not interested in talking about those reasons then there is no great objection and one might only worry what their sectarian reasons might lead them to support in other cases. The members of the political community have reasonable grounds for concern about people who operate from purely religious or other sectarian frameworks in politics, even when on some particular range of issues their religious agenda happens to coincide with a wider public agenda.

Happily, there are, it seems to me, very few sectarian zealots of this sort in our politics in the US, especially at the national level. Arguing for a political program based on a particular religious framework is unlikely to be effective because we disagree about religion. Religious diversity is the salient political fact that makes deliberation in the currency of public reasons practically advantageous as well as respectful. Religious pluralism, rather than irreligion, is the source of the problem to which public reason supplies the answer. Numerous studies show that Americans are overwhelmingly religious, and these religious Americans, including very religious Americans, support the norm of public reason. Wolterstorff seems to doubt this, but, as I note later in my chapter, the best empirical studies support my contention and not his.

*****

Wolterstorff mentions the views of several other scholars who think that religious people should "shape up" in ways that have nothing to do with the norms of public reasoning that I have defended. I agree with him in rejecting these other claims. Richard Rorty's view is, as Wolterstorff presents it, that religion is dangerous unless it is fully privatized. This is an eccentric and unreasonable view that few people espouse. There is the view that Wolterstorff associates with Derrida and Kant that religion should be emptied of determinate content. There is also the view of John Hick which, as described by Wolterstorff, seems to be that religion itself should be non-exclusive: from a religious point of view, we should regard various religions as different paths to the same ultimate truth. This seems to be the view that all religions are the same in the eyes of God, not just in the eyes of the state. That is not part of liberalism as a political doctrine, though it is a view that could well lead people to support a comprehensive liberalism.

The aforementioned academic views are all religious claims about religion, and in this they differ sharply from the idea of public reason, which is part of liberalism as a political doctrine. Political liberalism confines itself to insisting that citizens' differing religious views are equal in the eyes of the state, the law, and the political community. It is up to citizens to work out how they bring the political view into alignment with their own religious views. Liberal political principles do not prescribe to religious people how they should go about reconstructing their religion in the face of religious diversity.

Wolterstorff and I agree on the further important point that some religions do need to "shape up" for the sake of securing the equal right of all citizens of many different faiths to exercise their religious beliefs freely. Religions that are intolerant and that advocate using state power to disadvantage, harass, or persecute those who dissent from the officially favored religious view certainly need to "shape up" and endorse basic rights to equal liberty for all citizens.

There were religions in the past that needed to shape up, and there are religions now that need to shape up for the sake of liberal democracy, and it seems that we agree on this. When John Locke wrote his *Letter Concerning Toleration* anonymously, arguing that the first duty of Christians was to practice toleration toward those with whom they disagree in matters of religion, he was expressing a view widely and generally rejected by the Christians of his day. There were many who thought it was both a religious duty and politically prudent to impose religious conformity. The *Letter Concerning Toleration* is, therefore, a plea to Christians to "shape up" and acknowledge the equal rights of all religions that are compatible with civil peace.

The practical importance of this religious "shaping up" can hardly be overestimated. Samuel Huntington's important book, *The Third Wave*, argues that the spread of democracy to Spain and Portugal and many other Catholic countries in Latin America was a consequence in effect of the "shaping up" that took place within the Catholic Church at Vatican II.[12] As Catholic doctrine and the church hierarchy shifted to affirm the equal political rights of non-Catholics, Catholicism went from being associated with authoritarian political regimes to instead being associated with democracy. This was a hugely important historical shift.

The stability and civic health of liberal democratic political communities depends upon the general support of societies' major religious communities. It is a matter of concern insofar as some religious groups have yet to bring their convictions into line in support of the equal basic human rights of all persons.

PUBLIC REASON IN AMERICAN POLITICS

Wolterstorff and I squarely disagree on a narrow but important point. He wants to defend, and I would criticize, citizens who espouse what he calls an "integralist view" (he also calls them "barthians," and I have called them zealots). These are citizens who believe that they should comport themselves in the public realm on the basis of their religious convictions alone and when deciding important questions, including the shape and contours of our basic civil rights. I agree that such people are free in a liberal democratic society to exercise their political rights however they wish: the right to free speech protects religiously based advocacy for laws, and the right to vote may similarly be exercised on a purely religious basis. But these ways of exercising our rights should be subject to criticism as failing in a basic duty of citizenship in a diverse democracy: the duty to exercise power over one another on liberal and democratic grounds that we can all share.

Wolterstorff says that he sees no chance of citizens in general conforming to the Rawlsian norm, but I contend that they already do so by and large. Evidence suggests that many serious religious believers espouse norms of public reason in democratic deliberation. So argues Jon

---

[12] Samuel P. Huntington, *The Third Wave: Democratization in the Late Twentieth Century* (Norman: University of Oklahoma Press, 1991).

Shields' *The Democratic Virtues of the Christian Right*.[13] This empirical study of Christian-right activists argues "that the vast majority of Christian right leaders have long labored to inculcate deliberative norms in their rank-and-file activists, and especially the practice of civility and respect, the cultivation of real dialogue by listening and asking questions, the rejection of appeals to theology and the practice of careful moral reasoning."[14] Shields adds that,

> Christian apologetic organizations teach thousands of citizens every year to make philosophical arguments rather than scriptural ones because Paul instructs Christians to give reasons for their beliefs. From this perspective then, Jesus Christ was not a belligerent moralist – thus ignoring deliberative norms is not merely impolitic, it is also considered to be unfaithful.[15]

Nathaniel J. Klemp found similar evidence in his examination of the Christian political organization, Focus on the Family, in Colorado.[16] Leaders at Focus recognize that, in speaking to the wider public about policy issues, it is both prudent and respectful of others to cite widely accessible reasons and evidence. The Christian Right leaders interviewed by Klemp also cite religious values in support of norms of public reason.

To take another example, the debate in this country over gay rights – from privacy rights to the debate about marriage – has been deeply informed by norms of public reasoning. Everyone knows that claims about sin are in the background and that religious teachings have shaped people's attitudes toward sex and marriage. But very many, on both sides of the issue, have insisted that religious convictions are not an adequate basis for lawmaking. Conservatives themselves have been embarrassed by some of the arguments that had been put forward in some authoritative institutions to deny equal rights to gays.

This was strongly exhibited in the case of *Bowers v. Hardwick* in 1986 when the Supreme Court upheld Georgia's criminal sodomy statute as applied to gays. Justice Byron White, writing for the majority, simply declared that the freedom to engage in "homosexual sodomy" bore no resemblance to the Court's previous privacy cases. Gay sex had "no connection" with "family, marriage and procreation." "Proscriptions against that conduct have ancient roots." To claim otherwise was "at

---

[13] Jon Shields, *The Democratic Virtues of the Christian Right* (Princeton: Princeton University Press, 2009).

[14] Shields, *The Democratic Virtues of the Christian Right*, 2.   [15] Ibid.

[16] Nathaniel J. Klemp, *The Morality of Spin: Virtue and Vice on Political Rhetoric and the Christian Right* (Lanham: Rowman and Littlefield Publishers, 2012).

best facetious." Never mind that those earlier privacy rights cases included the right to have an abortion, the right of married and unmarried couples to use contraceptives, and the right to read pornography at home. White insisted that "The law ... is constantly based on notions of morality," and "majority sentiments about the morality of homosexuality" are a fully adequate basis for law.[17] Chief Justice Warren Burger wrote separately to underscore that state criminalization of gay sex was "firmly rooted in Judeo-Christian moral and ethical standards. Homosexual sodomy was a capital crime in Roman law."[18] Blackstone described it as an "'infamous crime against nature' as an offense of 'deeper malignity' than rape, a heinous act 'the very mention of which is a disgrace to human nature' and 'a crime not fit to be named.'"

Justice Harry Blackmun, dissenting, laid down a principle that became a challenge: "The legitimacy of secular legislation depends instead on whether the State can advance some justification for its laws beyond its conformity to religious doctrine."[19]

Some conservatives were also embarrassed by the weakness of the arguments advanced by the Court's majority in *Bowers*. John Finnis observes that "embarrassment" makes "most people more than usually inarticulate" with respect to homosexuality. Nevertheless, he insists, "public policies must be based on reasons, not mere emotions, prejudices, and biases."[20] So, Finnis, my colleague, Robert George, and others in the natural law tradition have advanced public arguments against extending marriage rights to gay and lesbian citizens. I think these arguments are weak, but at least their force may be assessed without reference to matters of faith or theology. This exhibits respect for norms of public reasoning.

Norms of public reasoning are widely accepted on both sides of very difficult political controversies. The need to offer good reasons and some evidence has been widely asserted: not just in the courts, of course, but in legislatures, and even on television talk shows. Over and over it has been asked: what is the harm in allowing gays to marry? What public interest is served? What common-sense reasons and evidence can be cited in support of excluding gays from marriage? On an episode of *The Factor* with Bill O'Reilly – not someone we would think of as a Rawlsian – he asked

---

[17] *Bowers v. Hardwick*, 478 U.S. 186 (1986), www.law.cornell.edu/supremecourt/text/478/186#writing-USSC_CR_0478_0186_ZO.

[18] Ibid.   [19] Ibid.

[20] John Finnis, "Natural Law and Limited Government," in *Natural Law, Liberalism, and Morality: Contemporary Essays*, ed. Robert P. George (New York: Oxford University Press, 1996).

a conservative opponent of same-sex marriage: "Sir, what's the harm in same-sex marriage?" This was answered with fumbling inarticulateness, and then, "Sir, what's the harm?" and, "You are going to have to do better than that." Trying to find reasons and evidence that are common in order to address these matters is critical.

When *Bowers* was overturned in 2003, Justice Kennedy observed that, "many people condemned same-sex relations based on religious and ethical ideals to which they aspire and which thus determine the course of their lives . . . The issue is whether the majority may use the power of the state to enforce these views on the whole society."[21] Justice Kennedy was correct. And if there are religious people who do not recognize the essentially public nature of that question, and do not recognize that they must do more than cite their particular religious convictions when shaping the rights of all, then my assertion is simply that they are violating a fundamental norm of citizenship. They may be very good citizens in other respects, but not in this one.

With respect to same-sex marriage, the debate has returned over and over to certain matters of obvious public interest, with the well-being of children being central to the debate.

The arguments of the New Natural Law are based on philosophical and ethical claims, not religious premises. They are part of a wider sexual morality in which marriage must involve one man and woman so that it can be consummated by intercourse. It is because the sexual act that "seals" or completes a marriage is apt to procreation that allows us to make sense of marital norms of "twoness" (or monogamy), fidelity, and permanence.[22] "Same-sex marriage" cannot be sealed or consummated by coitus or intercourse and, therefore, two men or two women cannot properly be married.

The New Natural Law position is not particularly hard to explain, but very many people find it arbitrary and unpersuasive. One part of the debate has focused on whether it is inconsistent to exclude same-sex couples from marriage while welcoming the marriages of sterile and elderly couples, whose intercourse cannot lead to procreation. Why can their marriages be inherently ordered to twoness, permanence, and

---

[21] *Lawrence v. Texas*, 539 U.S. 558 (2003), www.law.cornell.edu/supct/html/02-102.ZO .html.

[22] See Sherif Girgis, Ryan T. Anderson, and Robert George, "What Is Marriage?" *Harvard Journal of Law and Public Policy* 34 (2010), 245–287; and their book elaborating their natural-law account of marriage: *What Is Marriage? Man and Woman: A Defense* (New York: Encounter Books, 2012).

fidelity, while the relationships of loving gay and lesbian couples cannot? Why is intercourse the *sine qua non* of marriage rather than loving commitment?

There was a revealing moment during the litigation over Proposition 8 in California, which defined marriage as the relationship of one man and one woman. Charles Cooper, the attorney defending Proposition 8, was asked the very question Bill O'Reilly asked his conservative guest: what is the harm of gay marriage? Cooper's frank response was, "Your Honor, I don't know."[23] In the United States Supreme Court, attorney Cooper attempted to advance the argument that marriage is oriented to procreation. That led to an exchange with Justice Kagan. Kagan asked Cooper: if the state's interest is in keeping marriage focused on procreation, would it be permissible if the state said that people over the age of fifty-five can't marry? Well, Cooper said, both parties to the marriage may not be infertile. Laughter in the courtroom. Justice Kagan: "I can assure you, if both the man and the woman are over the age of fifty-five, there are not a lot of children coming out of that marriage." More laughter. And then Justice Antonin Scalia joined in, "Well, I suppose you could have a questionnaire at the marriage desk when people come in, are you fertile or are you not fertile?" More laughter. Attorney Cooper came back, "Well, one of the parties may be fertile." At which point Justice Scalia added, "Strom Thurmond was!" More laughter.[24]

Obviously, Attorney Cooper did not, in these or his other remarks, present the New Natural Law argument, but this is as close as he got to it. The view that marriage must involve two people who can have procreative-type sex is very rarely heard outside the academic writings of natural lawyers and also, of course, outside Catholic theology. The reason, I believe, is that most people find it implausible and irrelevant. Indeed, the sexual ethics of the New Natural Law is bound up with other practical judgments deeply at odds with the views and practices of the vast majority of Americans. Consider one example: the New Natural Law holds that contracepted sex by married couples is necessarily morally wrong and non-marital, indeed, anti-marital, and morally similar to gay sodomy.[25]

---

[23] See David Boies and Theodore Olson, *Redeeming the Dream: The Case for Marriage Equality* (New York: Viking, 2014), 84–85.

[24] *Hollingsworth v. Perry*, 570 U.S. __ (2013), www.supremecourt.gov/oral_arguments/ar gument_transcripts/12-144_5if6.pdf.

[25] See my discussion, *Just Married: Gay Couples, Monogamy, and the Future of Marriage* (Princeton: Princeton University Press, 2015), discussing Germaine Grisez, John Finnis, Robert George, and others.

Paul Griffiths, a Catholic theologian at Duke University, has argued that even those who affirm the truth of natural law should be able to recognize that reasonable people can reject it. His sensible remarks are worth quoting:

I think the orthodoxy is true. I think the arguments are valid and it would be better if everyone thought so. But there are not, as a matter of fact, arguments available that do or should convince those who do not hold that orthodox view, whether Catholic or non-Catholic, that they should. The lack of such arguments, I'll call them public arguments, is empirically obvious. The premises are rationally disputable. The truth about none of these things is obvious or self-evident, which is among the reasons that thoughtful, well-meaning people differ so profoundly about them.[26]

On the other hand, the arguments for including gays in marriage are very straightforward, and they have been articulated by philosophers like Alec Baldwin: "There are people who are married in the eyes of the state, enjoying all of the legal benefits who have no intention of having children. They seek only companionship and all of the entitlements that come with marriage: sex, joy, partnering, caring, and so on, all of that is theirs, even though they'll never bear children and willfully so. If the state says they are free to, why aren't gay couples as well?"[27]

The widely affirmed insistence on testing the arguments for and against gay marriage on the basis of public reasons and common-sense evidence has helped discipline and elevate our collective conversation on this important subject. David Moats won a Pulitzer Prize as editorial writer for *The Rutland Herald*, in Vermont, for his work on the debates over civil unions in Vermont in the 1990s. Looking back, he reports this: "I had not read John Rawls at the time. But the editorials I wrote on the question of private morality and public justice reflected a Rawlsian conception of democracy."[28] He uses a homespun and apt metaphor:

The village green of a typical Vermont town was emblematic of my view. The green might be surrounded by a Congregational church, an Episcopal church, a Unitarian church, a Catholic church, a public library, and a tavern.

---

[26] Paul J. Griffiths, "Legalize Same-Sex Marriage: Why Law and Morality Can Part Company," *Commonweal*, June 28, 2004, www.commonwealmagazine.org/legalize-same-sex-marriage-o.

[27] Alec Baldwin, "Why Childless Straight Couples Make the Case for Gay Marriage," *Huffington Post*, June 28, 2009, www.huffingtonpost.com/alec-baldwin/why-childless-straight-co_b_208457.html.

[28] David Moats, "Civil Unions in Vermont: Public Reason Improvised," *Perspectives on Politics* 1, no. 1 (2003): 133.

Citizens would enter each place for their own personal reasons and they would be free to fashion their own moral codes from what they learned inside. But when it came time to develop public policy, the citizens would have to emerge onto the village green and meet together to pass laws that a majority could support. No individual sect would have the authority to force its moral views on the others. Somehow the separate groups would have to find common ground on which to act .... What Rawls called a "comprehensive" view of morality – as embodied in religion, philosophy, or some other moral teaching – is not the business of government.[29]

CONCLUSION

A norm of public reasoning is widely affirmed in American democracy, and it plays a salutary role in shaping public debate. It helps citizens with diverse religious and philosophical perspectives take part in a process of common deliberation: seeking common ground in settling policy questions and in setting out the contours of our fundamental rights. This is how we go about the task of transforming different people's abstract moral conceptions into shared authoritative, civil, or constitutional rights. Public officials of all kinds, in legislatures, courts, and executive departments, generally recognize and frequently affirm that authoritative decisions need to be based on public interests, good reasons, and evidence. Citizenship is itself a public office, and it is altogether fitting that, in a democracy, citizens should view themselves as bound to deliberate and then decide based on considerations that are, or could be, common to all.

One vitally important aspect of the common ground shared by Americans is the conviction that our right to the free exercise of religion is part of a broader and more general scheme of equal basic rights for people of different religious faiths. Citizens need to look beyond their particular religious frameworks in order to recognize the profoundly important fact of religious diversity, and the importance of maintaining equality of respect and concern amidst that diversity. The common resolve to deliberate about our basic rights and important laws more broadly on the basis of common-sense considerations, reasons, and evidence is the best way of respecting our fellow citizens whose religious convictions are different from our own. I have a hard time understanding why Wolterstorff thinks these norms of public reasoning are unimportant.

[29] Ibid.

None of this is going to help us much with difficult issues that face us nowadays concerning religious freedom and public policy. Is it, for example, legitimate for the state or federal laws in the US to mandate that the healthcare insurance plans of large for-profit firms must include certain contraceptive services (religious institutions and faith-based not-for-profits having been exempted)? The Supreme Court has held that, under the Religious Freedom Restoration Act, the owners of large "closely held" for-profit firms have the right to be exempted from the mandate if they object on religious grounds.[30] Claims about natural rights do not help much with specific practical questions of this sort, which are bound up with complicated institutional and legal structures and long constitutional and political traditions.

Given the size and diversity of the United States, our politics is bound to be fractious and arriving at a working consensus on fraught questions is bound to be difficult. The widely recognized requirement that participants in public deliberation should cite common-sense reasons and evidence rather than straightforward religious claim exerts a mild but useful discipline. Dispensing with the norm of public reasoning would make our politics even more chaotic and frustrating than it already is.

[30] *Burwell v. Hobby Lobby Stores*, 573 U.S. __ (2014), www.supremecourt.gov/opinions /13pdf/13-354_olp1.pdf.

Index